What they said about
Steve and Ruth Bennett's previous book,

*365 TV-Free Activities
You Can Do With Your Child*

"I suspect that many parents will appreciate the
creative ideas in your book."   — BARBARA BUSH

"A little wonder!"   — JOAN LUNDEN

"The chunky paperback is a rich source to ward off
boredom."   — *USA TODAY*

"Best TV alternative."   — *McCALL'S*

"One of the best books out there today for any adult
who wants to break tube dependency in children."
                — *THE SAN DIEGO UNION*

"A fat little book, full of fun stuff for families to do
that costs little or no money."— *THE ORLANDO SENTINEL*

"Refreshing!"   — *THE DAYTON DAILY NEWS*

365 OUTDOOR ACTIVITIES

YOU CAN DO
WITH YOUR CHILD

365 OUTDOOR ACTIVITIES

ACTIVITIES

YOU CAN DO
WITH YOUR CHILD

Steve & Ruth Bennett

BOB ADAMS, INC.
PUBLISHERS
Holbrook, Massachusetts

Published by Bob Adams, Inc.
260 Center Street, Holbrook, MA 02343

ISBN: 1-55850-260-2

Printed in the United States of America.

J I H G F E D C B

This book is available at quantity discounts for bulk purchases. For information, call 1-800-872-5627.

Cover photo credit: Superstock Four by Five

DEDICATION

*Once again to
Noah and Audrey,
who continue to teach us
about the wonders
in our own backyard.*

CONTENTS

Atlas Shrugged 13

Autumn Canvas 14

Backyard Diving 15

Barking up the Right Tree 16

Baseless Baseball 17

Beach Cleanup 18

Beach Finery 19

Beach Sculpture 20

Beach "Spot It" 21

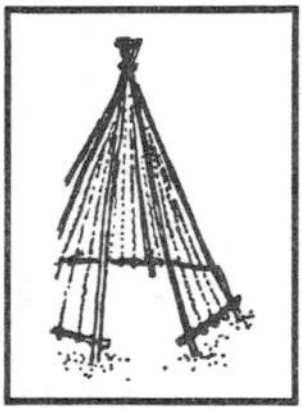
Beanstalk House 22

Bicycle Decorations 23

The Big Picture 24

Big-Time Composter 25

Bird Calls 26

Blades of Grass 27

Blind Man's Buff 28

Botany—Fruits 29

Botany—Leaves 30

Bottle Flip Cap 31

Brick/Concrete Rubbings 32

Broom Ball 33

Bucket Brigade 34

Budding Scientist 35

Building Name Game 36

Bulb Planting 37

Bumper Sticker 38

Butterfly Net 39

Camouflage It 40

Camping Stories 41

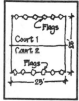

Capture the Flag 42

Car Wash 43

Cast in Sand 44

Catalog the Leaves 45

Catch Ball 46

Chalk Games 47

**Charitable
Donations 48**

Charlotte's Web 49

Chart the Rain 50

Check out the Slope 51

Cheerleaders 52

Christmas Ornaments 53

City Find It 54

Clothespin Jug Game 55

Cloud Identification 56

Cloudy with a Chance of Cucumbers 57

Code of Nature 58

Cold-Weather Bird Bath 59

Color Counts 60

Comb the Grass 61

Community Service 62

Comparing Weights 63

Construct a Nest 64

Container Garden 65

Cookie-Cutter Art 66

Corn Husk Doll 67

Corsages/ Boutonnieres 68

Country Store 69

Critter Tracking 70

Dandelion Jewelry 71

Date a Tree 72

Detective Work 73

Dino Soap Box Derby 74

Dirt City 75

Dodge Ball 76

Do-It-Yourself Cuneiform 77

Downtown Fossil Hunt 78

Drum Talk 79

Duck Duck Goose 80

Earth Puppets 81

Easy Bird Bath 82

Enchanted Houses 83

Evaporation Experiment 84

Family Totem Pole 85

Feed the Squirrels 86

Find a Path 87

Find It! 88

Finger Sports 89

Firefly Lamp 90

Fireless Fireworks 91

Fitness Stations 92

Five Dollars 93

Floaters and
Sinkers 94

Flower Anatomy 95

Flutter Ball 96

Flying Rings 97

Follow the Leader 98

Food Daring 99

Foot Measures 100

Footprint Scramble 101

Fossil Fun 102

Four-Leaf Clover Hunt 103

Four Seasons Cafe 104

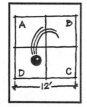

Four Square 105

Frisbee Games 106

Garage Ball 107

Garden Hose Phone 108

Gas Savers 109

Gem Museum 110

Geological Sculpture 111

Geometry Walk 112

Giant Writing 113

Going Places 114

Going-to-Canton Football Game 115

Gold Glove 116

Golf Ball Billiards 117

Gone Fishin' 118

Grass Words and Pictures 119

Grow A Butterfly 120

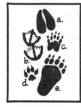

**Guess the
Footprint 121**

**Harvest Moon
Watch 122**

Heike Hike 123

**Herb and Fruit
Vinegars 124**

Hidden Faces 125

Hide and Sleuth 126

High Fly 127

Hobby Horse 128

Holiday Wreath 129

Hoola Hoop 130

Horse 131

Hot Potato 132

Hot-Weather
Fans 133

House Painting 134

How Old Is It? 135

Hummingbird
Feeder 136

Ice Brick
Architecture 137

Ice Cube
Sculpture 138

Icicle Art 139

Insect Home
Hunt 140

Instant Sandbox 141

Invent a
Constellation 142

Invisible Dog 143

Ironkids 144

King of the
Mountain 157

Landmark Catalog 158

Landscape
Calendar 159

Large-Scale Tic Tac
Toe 160

Lawn Helpers 161

Leaf It on the
Plate 162

Leaf Pile
Olympics 163

License Plate
Math 164

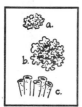

Lichens 165

Life Form Count 166

Litter-Free Zone 167

Living
Thermometers 168

Local History 169

Low-Tech Weather
Kids 170

Lynn & Richard's
Walking Game 171

Magic Acts 172

Mailbox
Decorations 173

Make a Rainbow 174

May Day 175

Measuring
Snowfall 176

Megaphones 177

Microworld 178

Middle of the
Pack 179

Midsummer Tree
Decorations 180

Migrating Bird
Watch 181

Milk-Jug Crosses 182

Milk-Jug Crosse
Games 183

Milkweed Games 184

Mime Sports 185

Miniature Golf
Course 186

Mini Obstacle
Course 187

Mirror Games 188

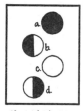

Moon Watch 189

Mostest and
Leastest 190

Mother, May I 191

Moths or
Butterflies? 192

Mud Flats (Basic) 193

Mud Flats (Advanced) 194

Mud Medallions 195

Musical Water Buckets 196

Naming the Flowers 197

Natural Memory Game 198

Nature's Art Forms 199

Neighborhood Fair 200

Neighborhood Walk Find It 201

New Orleans Experiment 202

Night Skies 203

Noisemakers 204

No-Net Tennis 205

No-Snow Men 206

Old-Fashioned Broom 207

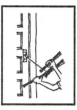

One-Way Timer 208

On the Road 209

Open-Air Theater 210

Orchestra of the Outdoors 211

Outdoor Checkers 212

Paper Weight 213

Pavement Art 214

Pavement Journeys 215

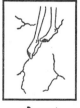

Pebble Art 216

Pendulum Art:
Model A 217

Pendulum Art:
Model B 218

People Watching 219

Pet "Beauty"
Contests 220

Pick-Up Twigs 221

Piece de
Resistance 222

Piñata 223

Pinball by the
Sea 224

Pitch Your Tent 225

Plant a Tree 226

Plant Cuttings 227

Plastic
Recyclers 228

Plates in Space 229

Pom Pom Pull Away 230

"Poohsticks" #1: (The Real Thing) 231

"Poohsticks" #2: (Urban Version) 232

Potato Planting 233

Potpourris and Sachet 234

Powers of Observation 235

Punch Ball 236

Putting the Garden to Bed 237

Quick Quicksand 238

Rain Dancing & More 239

Reading Tree 240

Recycled Boats 241

Red Light Green Light 242

Red Rover 243

Relay Races 244

Resident Expert 245

Retake-Out 246

Ricochet Ball 247

Ring Glider 248

Rites of Spring 249

Road Games 250

Rock Gardens 251

Rolling Stones 252

Rorschach Frost 253

Running Bases 254

Sand Castle Tools 255

Scarecrow 256

Scenic Landscapes 257

Scoop 'n Dodge 258

Search for Animal Homes 259

Seashore Wind Chimes 260

Seaside Obstacle Course 261

The Secret Lives of Animals 262

Shadow Games 263

Shell Faces 264

Shipwrecked Smarts 265

Sidewalk Game Boards 266

Sidewalk Globe Trotters 267

Signal Flags 268

Simon Says 269

Simple Croquet 270

Siphon 271

Skipping Stones 272

Skylines 273

Slopes and Angles 274

Small-Time Composter 275

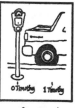

Smoots and More 276

Snowball Targets 277

Snow Bouquet 278

Snowdrift Patterns 279

Snowflake ID 280

Snowflake Observation 281

Snow Forts and Castles 282

Snow Maze 283

Snow Pies 284

Snow Shoveling Fun 285

Snow Topiary 286

Soda Can Bowling 287

Soil Sifter 288

Solar Lab 289

Sounds of
Silence 290

Souped-Up
Engines 291

Spaghetti
Garden 292

Spider Web
Detectives 293

Spot That
State #1 294

Spot That
State #2 295

Spring Garden
Clean Out 296

Sprinkler Games 297

Stacking Game 298

State Knowledge 299

Stationary
Volleyball 300

Statue Stories 301

Stick Letters (Easy) 302

Stick Letters (Advanced) 303

Street Math (Easy) 304

Street Math (Advanced) 305

Street Name Tales 306

Street Sign Word Game 307

Summer Forts 308

Summer Sled 309

Sum the Points 310

Sun Cards 311

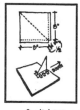

Sundial 312

Sunset Watching 313

Sun Tea 314

Surprise Map Games 315

Tadpoles to Frogs 316

Tag Games 317

Tail Games 318

Talking Heads 319

Target Throw 320

Teepees 321

Terrarium 322

Theories of the Universe 323

Thermometer Kids 324

Thirst Busters 325

Tiddlywinks 326

Tightrope Feats 327

Time Capsule 328

Tools of the Trade 329

Tour Guide 330

Town Planners 331

Trash Can Basketball 332

Trash Swap 333

Travelin' Games 334

Treasure Map 335

Tree Seed Art 336

Tree Swing 337

Tug of War 338

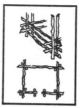

Twig Architecture 339

Urban Naturalist 340

Vegetable Garden Signs 341

Vicky and David's Game 342

Wagon Games 343

Watch a Fly 344

Water Slide 345

Water Tunnels 346

Water Waste Detective 347

Water Witching 348

Water Writing 349

Weather Vane 350

Weave a Basket 351

Weird Yoga 352

What's in the Bag 353

Wheelbarrow 354

Where's Bigfoot 355

Which Way? 356

Wind Sock 357

Winter Olympics 358

Words on the Go 359

World under a Rock 360

Worm Condo 361

Yard Signs 362

Yard-Waste Bag
Statues 363

Year-Round Easter
Egg Hunt 364

Zany
Television II 365

Acknowledgments

This book could not have come about without help from many people. First and foremost, we'd like to thank our families for contributing many great ideas. Arch Loetterle, who grew up in rural Nebraska, came up with many timeless ideas. He also turned his basement into an "adobe laboratory"—thanks for putting up with the mess! Lynn Loetterle and Susan Lozinyak contributed a wealth of ideas and botanical knowledge, and we are indebted to them for their help. Albert and Marilyn Bennett also had some great ideas from their own childhoods.

Murray and Yvette Rothstein taught us a lot about urban sidewalk sports games. David and Emily Hawkins also relayed great ideas, as did Gail Norcross. Mike Snell contributed many terrific ideas and Brian Tarcy, sports fan *par excellence*, devised all sorts of ingenious games for the book.

Hats off to our editor, Brandon Toropov, for brainstorming and helping us shape ideas, and to our publisher Bob Adams for supporting the project. We're deeply indebted to everyone at Bob Adams, Inc. for helping to make our TV-free books a success. In addition, we'd like to thank our copy editor, Kate Layzer, for doing a great job and contributing some wonderful activity ideas.

Finally, two very special people in our lives deserve the utmost thanks—our children, Noah and Audrey. Their willingness to test our ideas is unbounded. And they came up with quite a few variations and refinements of their own. Thanks kids—can't wait till you're old enough to write the next one!

Introduction

When our first activities book (*365 TV-Free Activities You Can Do With Your Child*) hit the stands, we were astonished at its success. We were also surprised that the national interest in our book was fueled less by television "bashing" than by a desire to have more quality family time. We discovered this by talking on hundreds of radio shows, with callers from Miami to Walla Walla.

While few people had anything good to say in defense of commercial television, many offered suggestions for future editions of our book and asked us to revive some of the games they played when they were children. They also asked us for more outdoor activities to help them through the long summer months. So in this book, we've focused exclusively on outdoor activities, and not just for summer but for every season of the year.

We asked people how they entertained themselves when they were children, before the advent of television. They told us of traditional games (many of which we played ourselves but had forgotten), as well as unique variations of their own. In the following pages you'll find instructions for "golden oldies" interspersed among the many novel ideas we and our friends developed and kid-tested in the "field."

As in our first book, we've tried to include activities that foster a love of learning and a sense of family, neighborhood, and community. We've also included a balance of educational, artistic, and sports activities, so there should be something for every child in the following pages.

Safety First

Safety Reminder

Safety is a prime concern of ours—especially with outside activities. We've included a safety reminder for any activity that involves small materials or cutting, or that requires special supervision. For the most part, the best advice is to exercise common sense, but it's easy to get absorbed in a project or game, so we recommend keeping the following in mind as you do the activities in the book.

- Do any serious cutting of materials yourself, and put the cutting implement out of reach while working on the project. Supply safety scissors when it's appropriate for your child to help.

- Use non-toxic, water-based markers, paints, and glues. They're healthier for your child and the environment. Never use rubber cement.

- Make sure any pieces of wood (garden stakes, etc.) are smooth before your child handles them. Keep sandpaper handy.

- Be street-conscious. Keep your eyes open for cars, especially when doing activities with groups of kids.

- Check out your yard or the playing field. Many of the activities involve running, jumping, hiding, and other physical activities. Make sure your yard doesn't contain any "booby traps" or potential hazards before playing.

- When engrossed in a project, make sure younger siblings aren't making a meal out of small parts.

Again, just use your innate common sense as a parent, and you'll be on the way to relaxed and fun play.

Tips for Outdoor Play

Playing should be the easiest thing in the world. But as adults, we sometimes forget how to do it; we're so often caught up in doing it right, doing it the best, or doing it efficiently. Here are some things we've learned.

- There is no "right" when it comes to young children's activities. As long as no one is getting hurt, let your child invent the rules—it will give him or her a sense of ownership. (Besides, following kid-invented rules is half the fun!)

- Make sure the activities are appropriate for your child's age and skill level. We've tried to present guidelines for making the activities challenging for kids of different ages. Since you're the best expert on your own child, you should be able to select and adapt activities to his or her capabilities and interests.

- Foster team spirit. Many of the activities are great opportunities for your child to learn how to play as a team member, in the spirit of cooperation.

- Tailor the competition to your child. For young children, competition can be problematic, so we've provided options in which kids compete against themselves rather than each other. For older kids involved in the sports activities, adjust the competitive level to whatever you feel is appropriate.

Using Outdoor Activities to Reduce Indoor TV Watching

In our original edition, we advised parents to wean their children off the tube gradually, warning that simply unplugging the set and forcing a "cold turkey" approach could be interpreted as a form of punishment. Our research since then confirms that gradually cutting back viewing hours is the best way to get your child off the couch and into the great outdoors.

First, determine how much television your child is watching, then reduce that amount by half-hour or hour intervals. Make sure you substitute activities that you know will capture your child's imagination. Eventually, you'll reach a level of watching that you find acceptable. It may be zero, it may be an hour a day—whatever you decide, be assured that you have control and that by doing the activities in this book you'll make headway toward your goal.

*   *   *

One final point before launching into the activities. We were asked by numerous reporters and radio talk-show hosts whether our activities can really compete with Saturday morning "high velocity" cartoons. We always answered the same way: "Yes. This might sound old-fashioned, but the one thing that your child wants more than anything else in the world is to spend focused time with YOU."

We hope you'll find that an empowering response to a tough problem. Here's to a year of loving, outdoor fun in which you strengthen your ties to your child.

Steve Bennett
Ruth Loetterle Bennett

Acorn Toss

Acorns, walnuts, and pine cones make for wonderful natural sports games. Here are some easy tossing games that you can play any time even in a postage stamp-sized backyard, a driveway, or the front walk.

Perhaps the simplest game involves gathering a handful of acorns or other nuts. One person tosses his or her acorn from an official throwing point, marked by a line in the ground or a stick. The other players then toss their acorns, trying to come as close as possible without touching the first acorn.

Another game entails drawing a series of lines in the ground or laying down a series of sticks. Each round, one person selects a line or stick, and the players then try to toss their acorn as close as possible to the designated line. Alternatively, draw targets on the ground or make a target from sticks and branches.

Finally, you can dig holes in the ground or arrange buckets or pails on the tossing field. The players can decide which holes and buckets are worth the most points, then let the tossing begin!

Required:
- Acorn, walnuts, pine cones, etc.
- Sticks

Optional:
- Buckets or pails

2 Alphabet Signs

Safety Reminder

Adult Supervision

Required:
• Your time only

Cities are brimming with signs that can be put to other good uses besides informing people of the names of stores and streets. This activity is great for wandering around a city or just observing on a street corner.

The basic idea is to be able to find the alphabet letters, in sequence, by looking at signs on stores, streets, cars, and trucks. In its simplest form, just bop around the city looking for words that begin with the desired letter ("X" ought to keep everyone busy).

Your child can also play "specialty" games. Perhaps only passing trucks can be used for one round; in another, only store signs. Yet another variation is to find all the alphabet letters in the license plates of cars parked on the street.

Finally, while young children learning their letters will certainly enjoy the game as just described, you might have to spice it up a bit to interest older children. One way to do so is to announce that vowels can only be obtained from the letters on passing trucks, and consonants from street signs. Or vice versa.

How about this as a stumper—vowels must come from names that contain the letter "q!"

Amazing Mazes

Does your child love to squirm through small spaces? If so, this activity should be a major hit.

Use lawn and other outdoor furniture to create a maze. The object is to crawl underneath the furniture and reach the end of the maze within an allotted amount of time. You can increase the difficulty by placing various obstacles along the way. For example, tie a string between the legs of the chair—your child must pass over or beneath the string without touching it. Or you might place a flower pot or bucket under one of the pieces of furniture. Your child's mission: get around the object without disturbing it.

Should your child find it too easy to pass through the maze, you can increase the difficulty by seeing if he or she can do it while holding a plastic cup of water and not spilling anything. Another way to make things more difficult is to have your child hold a baseball in each hand—a real challenge for a cramped maze.

Finally, on a hot day you can always add a surprise element at the end of the maze—an oscillating sprinkler!

Required:
- Lawn furniture

Optional:
- String
- Flower pot or bucket
- Plastic cup
- Baseballs
- Oscillating sprinkler

Animal Antics

Can you cluck like a chicken, meow like a cat, bark like a dog, or howl like a wolf? If so, your younger kids are in luck!

You'll need four or more children to play this game, which is a variant of Mother May I (#191). Make a sound, say, a cat's meow. The children then begin acting like cats—arching their backs, stretching, pouncing, and so on. When everybody seems content to lie in the sun, start clucking. The players then start doing chicken antics—walking with their arms folded like wings, bobbing their heads as if they're pecking for food, and anything else they imagine a chicken might do.

If you call out an animal sound and someone forgets to change their behavior, they're out of the game until the next round. Continue this until only one player is left, at which point that child becomes the caller and you join the other kids.

So what will *you* do when your child makes the inaudible howl of a crayfish?

Required:
• Your time only

BWACK! BWACK!

Animal Footprint Casts

Your child would probably enjoy having a permanent record of critters in the area. This activity shows you how to do just that.

First, find footprints. Check your garden or flower beds. A walk through the park or woods will undoubtedly yield some interesting signs of life. Dig up the prints with a small shovel, maintaining enough dirt on all sides to keep it from falling apart. Carefully place the footprint in a cardboard box or plastic container.

When you return home, mix up a batch of plaster (buy it at the hardware store and follow the directions). Pour the plaster into the footprint and let it harden. (If the soil containing the print is dry, moisten it with a spray bottle first so you'll have a smooth cast). Even the top of the plaster with a piece of cardboard, wood, or trowel.

Once the plaster has dried, after fifteen minutes or so, brush off the dirt, turn over the cast, and you should have an excellent replica of the bottom of the animal's foot. Allow the cast to dry completely overnight and then paint it, if you like. Let your child's friends and relatives guess its origins.

Now, just what *is* that creature that's been prowling around the back yard?

Required:
- Animal foot print
- Small shovel
- Cardboard or plastic containers
- Plaster
- Piece of cardboard, wood, or trowel

Optional:
- Paint

Anywhere Baseball

Here's a fun variation on traditional baseball that can be played with less than a full team. In fact, you just need a batter and a few people to field the ball. You also don't need a set of bases. (Select the kind of ball based on the players' ages or abilities.)

The batter tosses the ball in the air and hits it to the outfield. Instead of running for the bases, though, the batter tosses the bat on the ground. Whoever catches the ball rolls it toward the bat. If the ball touches the bat, the person who rolled it steps up to the plate. If the ball doesn't touch the bat, the present batter continues.

To make things a bit more challenging for the batter, you can draw a circle in the ground around the plate. When the batter tosses the bat to the ground, it must land within the circle; otherwise, whoever catches the ball is automatically up.

Encourage your child to invent his or her own rules—remember, the main object is to have fun!

Required:
• Baseball gear

Archie's Bricks

People have been building mud houses for thousands of years. Your kids can continue this tradition right in your own backyard.

Clay soil is ideal, but if yours is sandy, try adding one part flour per four parts of soil (a formula discovered by Arch Loetterle who, for the purpose of this book, selflessly converted his basement into a mud brick laboratory).

Add water to the soil until the texture is like bread dough. Shape it into a rectangle or place it into a baking pan. Allow the mixture to set, then use a wet table knife to cut various-sized bricks. Make the bricks as small as you can for the kind of buildings you envision making— the smaller the stronger. To make very large bricks, add straw, hay, or grass clippings for additional strength. (But omit the flour unless you own a flour mill. You might also need a wood or milk-carton form.)

When the bricks have dried, let the construction begin (see Mud Flats—Basic #193, and Advanced #194, for building ideas).

Required:
- Soil
- Water
- Table knife

Optional:
- Baking pan
- Sand
- Straw, hay, or grass clippings
- Flour
- Milk cartons or wood form

Archimedes Redux

Remember the Greek mathematician Archimedes, who ran naked through the streets of Athens shrieking "Eureka!" after discovering the principle of displacement? Well, your child doesn't have to run naked through the backyard to appreciate the thrill of understanding the principle.

Archimedes, the story goes, demonstrated to King Hiero that his crown was not pure gold because it displaced more water than a chunk of pure gold identical to the crown in weight. He knew that the amount of water displaced by an object equaled the volume of the object; the crown had some lighter-weight silver in it, making it bigger in volume.

Your child can use water displacement to compare other hard-to-measure objects—say rocks. First collect pairs of rocks of similar size—a minimum of two inches in diameter. Then have your child make guesses as to which is larger. Test your child's guesses using a transparent container as close in diameter to the rocks as possible. Fill the container one third full, and mark the level. Then put the first rock in and mark the new level. Remove the rock and replace the water, then add the second rock and note the water level.

Which one's bigger?

Required:
- Rocks
- Transparent plastic container

Arm's Length

Here's a tracing activity in which you draw the outline of your child with chalk—then take some vital measurements.

Your child lies face up on a driveway or sidewalk, while you trace the outline of his or her body. Once the tracing is done, your child gets up and guesses various measurements—arm length, finger length, and so on. (Of course, the measurements won't be exact, since you're doing a chalk tracing. Even so, it's fun). With a group, the children guess each other's vital measurements. When the guesses are in, players use a yardstick or tape measure to get the actual measurements.

Among the measurements children can guess and take are the length of the forearm, distance from elbow to ear, the diameter of the head, the length of the bottom of the foot, the distance all the way around the body, and the distance from the knee to the toe.

After measuring, children can embellish their outlines—with designer chalk clothing and accessories.

Required:
- Chalk
- Yardstick or tape measure

Optional:
- Notebook to keep track of measurements
- Pencil

Around the World

Here's a variation on traditional basketball that develops court awareness and shooting skills as players make their way "around the world."

Before the game, players agree on and mark seven stations on the floor of the basketball court (the kids can name them). Small twigs (if it isn't windy) make fine station markers. On windy days, use small stones.

Once the stations are marked, the first player starts at the first station and shoots. If that player sinks the ball, he or she moves to the next station. Every time a shot is made, the player advances. If the shot is missed, the player stays at the same station and the next player takes a turn.

For a more advanced version, allow players who missed once to "risk it" by shooting again. If the second shot is made, the player can continue to the next station. But if it is missed, the player passes the shot and goes back to the first station.

Who will be the first in your family to go around the world?

Required:

- Basketball
- Station markers (twigs, stones)
- Basketball court

Art from the Sea

Does your child enjoy collecting shells and driftwood from the beach? With this activity he or she can make decorative shell posters that bring back warm memories of days on the beach.

During various visits to the beach, have your child collect small shells with interesting colors, shapes, and textures. While you're at it, look for small pieces of driftwood. Spread your collection on a picnic table, driveway, or porch floor. Your child might want to organize the shells by size and type, so he or she will know what's on hand. Same with the driftwood.

Show your child how to attach the shells to the posterboard with non-toxic glue. The shells and driftwood can be arranged in random patterns, or in the shape of familiar animals or objects. An array of small purple-colored shells makes a lovely peacock tail or a sunset (use driftwood to make the outline of a house). Suggest making trees with the driftwood as the trunk and the sea shells as the leaves.

When complete, find a deserving wall in your house so everyone can enjoy the beach art.

Required:
- Sea shells
- Small pieces of driftwood
- Non-toxic glue
- Posterboard

Arts and Crafts Show

If you have kids in your area who paint, draw, or make crafts objects, why not sponsor a kids' arts and crafts show?

First make some "exhibitor" invitations regarding the time and place for the show. Let your children help write or decorate. Take the invitations to a copy shop (a potential outing), then hand-deliver them to your children's friends in the area. (A mailing and trip to the post office can also make for a good outing.) Finally, you'll need a set of announcements for the neighborhood to attract viewers.

When you've made arrangements with all parents involved and the day arrives, set up a table or boxes in your backyard or driveway. The children should display their wares in whatever way they choose.

You might want to charge a minor admission fee (25¢), the proceeds to go to a local charity. In that case, let the children make up tickets and manage the cash box, too.

Whatever you do, it's sure to be a major cultural hit in the neighborhood. And who knows—maybe you and your kids will start a community tradition.

Required:
- Pencil and paper
- Outdoor tables or boxes
- Children's arts and crafts

Atlas Shrugged

Here's the ultimate test of balancing skills!

The idea is for children to use their bodies to balance common objects while racing to the finish line. For instance, they could each hold a feather in one hand and a heavy book in the other while balancing a shoebox on their head and walking backward to a finish line.

They can vary this activity many ways. How about hopping, skipping, jumping on one foot, or running toward the finish line? They can put things inside the box on their head, or they can carry cups of water. The cups can be filled with varying amounts of water to increase or decrease the difficulty.

Children could also lie on their backs with their feet in the air and then balance items such as shoeboxes or baseball gloves on the bottoms of their feet. For another challenge, they can try and move their feet in a bicycling motion while balancing the items on their soles.

Try it. The possibilities for feet and feats are endless!

Required:
- Your time only

Optional:
- Feather
- Heavy book
- Shoebox or boxes
- Cups for water
- Two baseball gloves or other soft objects

Autumn Canvas

If you live in an area with vividly colored autumn foliage, here's a way to put nature's artwork to good use.

First conduct a leaf expedition in your backyard, around your neighborhood, or in the park. Try to collect as many different varieties as you can (look for leaves that have recently fallen and aren't completely dried out yet). When you get home, place the leaves between two pieces of wax paper, then insert the wax paper into a heavy dictionary or encyclopedia.

Once the leaves are dried (a few days to a week), affix them to a piece of posterboard with glue. Overlap the leaves so that the entire board is covered. You can stretch plastic wrap or a used plastic bag (keep out of young hands) around the front to keep the leaves from breaking, or simply hang the canvas in the family gallery.

Alternatively, make small leaf canvases and use them as greeting cards. You'll definitely want to cover the fronts with plastic wrap, or your recipients may find themselves with a pile of leaves to rake . . . indoors as well as out!

Required:

- Leaves
- Posterboard
- Glue
- Plastic wrap

Backyard Diving

No, this isn't about building a swimming pool in your backyard. In fact, you don't need water at all.

This activity involves making a pretend deep-sea diving helmet from a paper bag. Explain to your child that in the olden days, people wore deep sea diving suits that included a gigantic ball-like helmet (you might want to visit the library and find a picture of one).

You can easily make a deep sea helmet by cutting a round hole in the front of a paper shopping bag. Attach a segmented cardboard tube for an air hose (see illustration), and your child is all set to walk around the "bottom of the ocean" (your backyard). For added fun, you can fashion an "aqualung" from an oatmeal container or two.

To make the ocean floor more interesting, arrange your yard chairs so they form an undersea "grotto" or cave system. Remind your child that the water makes it hard to walk, so he or she must move slowly.

When to come up? Snack and meal times!

Required:

- Paper shopping bag
- Crayons and markers
- Tape
- Cardboard tube
- Scissors

Optional:

- Oatmeal containers

Barking up the Right Tree

Required:
- Paper
- Crayon

We look at tree bark everyday, but rarely, if ever, stop to notice its intricate patterns. With this activity, you and your child can stop and smell the roses, and feel the bark while you're at it.

Gather some sheets of white paper and crayons (with the sleeves removed), then find yourself a tree with an interesting texture. Show your child how to rub a crayon gently on the paper to create an impression of the bark without piercing the paper. Also, by rubbing several different colors on the same sheet, you'll create an interesting "rainbow" effect.

If you know the name of the tree, all the better. When your child has done enough rubbings, put them into a scrapbook dedicated to your backyard, neighborhood, or local park. In the fall, if the tree is deciduous, you can add to the entries in the scrapbook by affixing a pressed leaf or two.

Finally, you can use the bark rubbings to make a local tree identification book. (Proving that you can, after all, judge a tree by its cover.)

Baseless Baseball

This is a game played much like pin-ball. Players throw a rubber ball or tennis ball at targets and award hits (singles, doubles, triples and home runs) for striking each one.

First, players need to decide upon a throwing line and targets. Rocks can be targets. So can boxes, toy cars, piles of leaves, and old sweatshirts. Make the scoring system equal to the task. Each target is worth a certain kind of hit. Easy targets are singles, harder ones are doubles, and so on.

Players take turns throwing at the targets. If the target is hit, the player's team gets the corresponding award. If the target is missed, that player's team is given one out. When the thrower has three outs, the next thrower comes to "bat." Play as many innings as you like, keeping score. The player who wins gets to pick the next targets.

All right, batter up!

Required:
- Rubber ball or tennis ball

Beach Cleanup

Required:
- Paper bags
- Watch or timer

This is a great activity for a group of kids, and one that performs a needed public service. All you'll need is a box of paper bags and a watch, kitchen timer, or egg timer.

First designate bags for different kinds of beach litter—returnable soft drink and beer cans, recyclable plastic bottles, Styrofoam and plastic cups and containers, six-pack rings, etc. Then set your kids loose to see who can collect the most litter in a set period of time. Alternately, you might make each child a "specialist," assigning him or her a particular kind of litter.

Dump all nonrecyclables/returnables in the nearest trash can. If there aren't any trash cans nearby, take the beach refuse home with you and dispose of it as you would your regular trash. If your state has a bottle bill, cash in the cans. And at the end of the summer make a donation to your favorite environmental cause. For more beach ideas, see activities #19, 20, and 21.

Beach Finery

The beach is a treasure chest of supplies for the budding jewelry maker. All you need is some string and an assortment of natural items. If you want to get fancy, purchase a batch of fishing snap swivels so your finery can be easily taken off and put on. (You can find them at any sporting goods or bait and tackle shop. Better yet, find discarded ones on the beach. Discarded plastic rope and netting can also be recycled for jewelry.)

Next, look for sea shells and pieces of driftwood that have holes in them and can be easily hung on a length of fishing line, twine, lanyard, shoelace, or string. Small shells can be used as "spacers" for larger objects. In any case, let your child decide the most pleasing arrangements for necklaces, bracelets, and pendants. The shells can also be decorated with paint, markers, glue and sequins, or stickers.

The finished products can be worn during beach cleanups (to get everyone in the spirit), displayed during family bazaars, or used for special costume pageants.

Seems to us that the green driftwood pendant would look simply smashing with your new sun visor!

Required:
- String, fishing line, lanyard materials, shoelaces
- Snap swivels
- Shells, driftwood, beach objects

Optional:
- Paints, markers
- Sequins and glue
- Stickers

Beach Sculpture

W ho says sand sculpture has to be restricted to castles? Why not turn your beach outings into opportunities to create animals, cars, and all kinds of things?

Suggest a theme, then see how inventive your children can be. Encourage them to use shells and other natural elements to add fine details to their works of art. For animal beach sculptures, shells can be used as eyes, ears, and other facial features. Driftwood makes fine whiskers, antlers, tusks, etc. Use seaweed for fur, manes, tails, and so on.

For objects such as cars, use the shells as headlights, hood ornaments, and door handles. Pieces of driftwood make great bumpers, radio antennae, and other car parts.

A group of kids can form a zoo squad that creates an entire sand jungle of animals, or a classroom brigade that creates a true "student body." Your sand artists might even create a Museum of Modern Sand Art, with avant garde sculptures of common objects.

Ah, what a lovely Venus of Seaweed at the base of that sand dune!

Required:

- Shovels, buckets, and other sand-digging tools

Beach "Spot It"

This is a good beach game that will keep you and your children occupied while you get that golden tan you've been promising yourself.

The idea is to start with a list of five or more items devised by one of the players. The list might include a plain seashell, a colorful seashell, a flying seagull, a standing seagull, pilings, driftwood, a beach umbrella, beach grass, a bottle of suntan lotion, a portable radio, someone reading a book, a person making a sandcastle, a child playing with shovels and buckets, a white rock, a colorful rock, seaweed, a big wave, or a puffy cloud.

Once a player finds all the items on the list, he or she gets to make up a new list. Children with reading skills might want to carry around a small pad and pen.

For variety, go for a walk down the beach with your children rather than staying in the same spot—you're bound to find interesting things to add to your list. For more beach activities, see activites #18, 19, and 20.

Required:
• Your time only

Optional:
• Pencil and paper

Beanstalk House

Beans are fun to grow, not only because they generally do well, but because they require a climbing structure. This activity describes how to make a Beanstalk House that will be a unique addition to your garden.

Required:

- Five 5-foot stakes
- Four 2-3 foot stakes
- String
- Pole bean seeds

First, make a teepee-like frame out of six to eight five-foot-long bamboo or wood stakes. Draw a circle about four feet in diameter in the dirt. Evenly space the stakes around the circle and push the bottoms into the ground. Then tie the stakes together at the top. Lash seven two-to-three-foot cross-stakes to the stakes near the ground, leaving a door (see illustration). Tie three to four strings between each of the stakes from the top to each of the cross stakes (illustration).

Next purchase pole bean seeds, such as "Kentucky Wonder," and plant three seeds below each string and stake. As the seedlings grow, gently help them get over to the nearest string. Eventually, the beans will "learn" to grow on the strings by themselves. In about a month (depending on the seed variety and your growing season), the entire bean house will be covered with green stems, flowers, and eventually . . . beans.

By the way, the reason you left one side open is to allow your child the pleasure of enjoying a fresh garden snack—while sitting in his or her very own bean house.

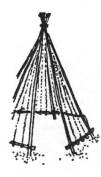

Bicycle Decorations

Just as it is sometimes fun for children to get all gussied up in their best clothes, it is also fun to decorate their bicycle, tricycle, or stroller as if it were the lead vehicle in an important parade. In fact, why not sponsor a bicycle parade for your block?

There are many materials children can use to decorate their bicycles. They can tape streamers to the handlebars that fly behind the bike when it is ridden. They can also tape colored paper around the crossbar, put ribbons on handle grips, or attach flowers to the handlebars. They can draw small pictures resembling license plates and attach them to the back of the seat. And if you have any pinwheels handy, affix them with twistems to the frame. (Make sure your child doesn't fasten anything to the bike that makes it top-heavy.)

Of course, there's the old stand-by—use a clothes pin to hold a playing card so the card projects into the spokes. This makes for a great bike "engine" (see "Souped-up Engines" #291).

Or put a city emblem on the side of the bike, strap on a flashlight, and you have . . . the new volunteer fire department!

Required

- Bicycles/trikes
- Colored paper ribbons
- Streamers
- Flowers
- Cardboard
- Pinwheels
- Twistems

The Big Picture

Safety
Reminder

Adult Supervision

Required:
• Magnifying glass

The magnifying glass opens an incredible world to your child. If you have one around the house, here are some ways to put it to good use; if you don't have one, now's the time to make a minor investment.

Before taking a closeup look at your backyard, explain to your child that the magnifying glass is a tool to unlock hidden views of nature. But it can also start fires or burn holes in skin and clothes when used improperly—monitor closely! With that understanding in place, have your child train the lens on:

Plants. Use the glass to reveal the wonderfully rich network of veins in leaves . . . the texture of bark and stalks . . . the features of flowers.

Building material. Note the pores in brick . . . the grain of wood . . . the surface and details of granite.

Critters. Observe the rings on worms . . . the antennae of ants . . . the incredible leg architecture of grasshoppers (if you have any handy).

Finally, look at the tires of bicycles and cars—note the wear. Then examine the surfaces of grates, fire hydrants, and other everyday objects. Everything tells a visual story when it's under the lens!

Big-Time Composter

Composting is an age-old method of putting back what you take out of the land. Your child will enjoy making dirt, then tilling the results back into a garden plot.

To make a compost bin, you'll need to make a frame of some kind. The simplest frame consists of a box lined on the inside and covered on the outside with dark trash bags. Cut holes in the sides to ensure proper air flow. You can also use a plastic milk crate (don't buy one just for this occasion). If you're up for some carpentry, make a frame out of wood slats, or four garden stakes and a length of chicken wire (make sure no sharp ends protrude).

Place the compost frame where it will get plenty of sun. Have your child add kitchen scraps (no animal protein), plant matter, and a bit of dirt (which contains the micro-organisms necessary for the composting action).

Have your child help turn the compost pile every few days with a shovel, and if the temperature is right, he or she should have "nature's gold" in a couple of weeks, ready to enrich a garden plot or flower bed.

Required:
- Box and trash bags or plastic milk crate
- Plant matter, dirt, and vegetable scraps
- Small shovel

Optional:
- Wood slats or garden stakes
- Chicken wire

Bird Calls

Your child will probably be surprised to learn that different birds have their own unique song (except for the mockingbird and relatives, which can copy most anybody's call). Here are some common ones to listen for; use them as a starting point. Your child may want to go to your library and find a tape or record to learn more.

Required:
• Your time only

Black-capped Chickadee: *Chick-a-dee-dee-dee*

Bobwhite: *Bob White!*

Cardinal: *What-cheer-cheer-cheer*

Chestnut-sided warbler: *I wish to see miss beecher*

Greater yellowlegs: *Dear! Dear! Dear!*

Ovenbird: *Teacher-Teacher-Teacher*

Rufus-sided towhee: *Drink Your TEEEEEEEA*

Whippoorwill: *Whip poor will*

Be sure to take your child for a walk at a time when the neighborhood or park is fairly quiet. Recognize anybody?

What cheer cheer cheer!

Blades of Grass

This is a set of games that can be played just about anywhere. The basic idea is simple—guess the number of natural objects in a certain space, then count and see how close each person comes.

For example, how many blades of grass does a square inch of lawn contain? How about three square inches? A square foot? And so on. If you want to get precise, you can either measure off the area to be counted with a ruler, or make some paper templates—cut out square holes the desired size, place them over the grass, then start counting.

A variation on the game involves looking at a plant, bush, or low-lying tree branch, then guessing the number of leaves. Count them and find out.

You can do the same thing with small pebbles in a garden or small rocks on a crushed-stone pathway. Try it with twigs. Or in the fall, guess the number of leaves or acorns that have fallen in a square foot. At the beach, guess how many shells occupy a square foot.

And for real wizards? How many grains of sand fit on your fingertip?

Required:
- Your time only

Optional:
- Ruler
- Pieces of paper
- Scissors

Blind Man's Buff

Safety Reminder

Adult Supervision

Required:
• Blindfold

This is a traditional children's game in which a blindfolded player gropes around to find other players in the yard.

Play this game in an easy-to-monitor area and be sure to clear away any toys or other objects the blindfolded player could trip on. (Supervise carefully.)

The player who is "it" wears the blindfold. While he or she spins in place five times, all the other players run around the yard looking for a good spot to hide. When "it" finishes the fifth spin, he or she yells, "Stop," and all the other players must freeze in place.

"It" then begins to search for the other players by yelling "blind man's . . ." All other players must yell "buff," although they can disguise their voices. The searcher uses the vocal clues to track down the other players.

A variation of this game is to play without the verbal clues—the person who is "it" walks around the yard feeling for the players. The hiders must keep their feet in the same spot, but they can move the rest of their bodies in an effort to avoid getting tagged. The biggest challenge for the hiders? Don't giggle!

Botany—Fruits

Most plants you can see have a fruit that disperses seeds. The dispersal gets the young plant far enough away from the parent plant so that it doesn't have to compete for sunlight and nutrients. Some fruits, like apples, are eaten by animals—the seeds are then eliminated far from the parent plant. Other fruits, such as the burdock, have hooks on them and hitch a ride on passing animals. Others have tufts or wings, allowing them to fly with the wind; maples are a good example. Still others, like the touch-me-not, project their seeds from their fruits like catapults. Finally, some fruits just float in the water (coconuts).

The illustration below shows some common fruits. Have your child study it, then try to identify the seed dispersal systems that the plants and trees in your area use. See activity #30 for another botany exercise.

Required:
• Your time only

Botany—Leaves

To the naked eye, it's hard to appreciate what's going on inside a leaf. A leaf is a growing thing and must get food, water, and nutrients necessary for life. This is done by means of an intricate system of tubes, called "veins." The veins in leaves appear in three main patterns, which you can see more closely with a magnifying glass. Have your child look for the following kinds of simple vein systems (refer to the illustration below): a) *Palmate* (e.g., maple leaf)—looks like fingers on a hand. Several veins branch and diverge at the base of the leaf. b) *Parallel* (e.g., lily leaf or blade of grass)— veins branch at the base but lie next to each other. c) *Pinnate* (e.g., oak leaf)—one main vein runs through the center of the leaf. Smaller veins branch off of it.

Required:
• Your time only

Optional:
• Magnifying glass

Now that you've explained the major vein types, which ones can your child identify on his or her own? For another botany exercise, see activity #45.

Bottle Flip Cap

Just about anything can be turned into an entertaining game, and this activity proves it. All you need is a handful of bottle caps and a small rubber ball. You simply place the bottle caps upside down on the ground, then try to flip them over by hitting them with the ball. Here are some games you can play with your child based on this idea.

The easiest game entails randomly placing the bottle caps on the sidewalk or your driveway. Establish a throwing line that players must stand behind when they try to toss the ball at the bottle caps. You can use a chalkline, a crack in the pavement or concrete, or the expansion line between two sidewalk slabs. Take turns trying to flip the bottle caps. A variation involves having one player continue to toss the ball as long as he or she is successful.

To make things more difficult, introduce a rule that the ball has to bounce one or more times before flipping a bottle cap. And for a real challenge, designate a certain sequence in which the caps must flip over.

Keep practicing and you'll be ready for the major leagues in no time flat!

Required:
- Twist-off bottle caps
- Small rubber ball

Brick/Concrete Rubbings

Required:
- Large pad of paper
- Crayons

Optional:
- Scissors
- Scrapbook

If you live in a city, you and your child can probably find many different kinds of building materials, especially brick and concrete. This activity is fun from an art standpoint and will sharpen your child's powers of observation.

The idea is to travel about the neighborhood or downtown area with a large pad of drawing paper. You'll also need a good supply of crayons with the paper sleeves removed. Wherever you and your child spot an interesting brick or concrete pattern, place the paper against it and then lightly rub the paper with a crayon. Look at buildings, walls, sidewalks, steps, and anything else that might make an unusual rubbing (observing privacy rights and trespassing laws, of course). On the corner of the paper, note the date and place where your child made the rubbing.

When you get home, your child can cut out portions of the rubbings and tape them in a scrapbook, or he or she might want to make a giant collage. Later, you might see if your child can remember the rubbings' sources.

Ah yes, that weird crack did come from the park wall, didn't it?

Broom Ball

If you think brooms are just for sweeping, you obviously haven't played broom ball!

For this sports activity of the future, you'll need a broom for each player (kids should use child-sized or light plastic brooms), a large rubber ball, and an assortment of boxes or buckets.

In its simplest form, the game entails sweeping the ball into a single bucket or box on a driveway or walkway. Players take turns sweeping the ball until it goes where they want it to go.

For a variation, the players have their own buckets or boxes. One player sweeps the ball; if he or she doesn't get a "hole in one," the next player has the chance to sweep the ball toward his or her own bucket or box. (Keep it orderly, one "sweep" at a time—you don't need any backyard broom brawls!)

Finally, designate certain areas of the "court" as "sand pits." (Draw chalk circles.) If the ball rolls in one of the "pits," the play starts over again.

By the way, there is a fringe benefit—you will probably get a clean driveway by the end of this activity.

Required:

- Brooms (adult and child sized)
- Large rubber balls
- Boxes or buckets

Bucket Brigade

Here's an activity that's sure to keep a group of kids occupied on a hot summer day—it's a re-enactment of the old-fashioned bucket brigade. But instead of using the water to put out a fire, the brigade will water a tree or garden or fill a wading pool.

The brigade works like this. The children line up at a spiggot, and the person at the end of the line begins filling buckets and passing them on to the next in line, who passes the buckets ahead to the next child, and so on, until the person at the front of the line gets a bucket and dumps it in the spot you designate. That person then goes to the end of the line and becomes the bucket-filling person. In this way, each child gets a turn to fill buckets and empty the water.

On a dog day, the first child can step out of the brigade and into a wading pool. The next person in line can then dump a cool bucket of water on his or her head. That child then moves to the bucket-filling position, refreshed and ready for action.

Buckets up!

Required:
- Water
- Buckets/pails

Optional:
- Wading pool

Budding Scientist

If you and your children look around your neighborhood, you'll probably find many plants that grow and change as the seasons and years pass. Rather than passively observing this phenomenon, encourage your child to design a plant journal that notes characteristics of particular plants relative to the time of year.

For this activity you'll need a notebook and paper. Your child records the sizes of plants and the dates that they bloom and, in the case of trees, notes when the leaves turn color. Your child could also adopt a tree in the neighborhood and periodically bring it water while keeping a careful journal of its growth and changes. You could also add pressed leaves to the journal (cover them with wax paper) and sketches of plants.

A plant journal can be especially interesting if you have a vegetable garden. Children can watch as plants sprout from seeds and reach fruition, recording the times involved. They can also write down details such as how many leaves the plant has, how many vegetables it produces, and so on. You might just find the journal invaluable in planting next year's garden.

Required:
• Notebook and paper

Optional:
• Wax paper

Building Name Game

If you lived in New York, you could walk by the Empire State Building and ask your children which name they liked better: the real name or the "Giraffe Building." Chances are, the Giraffe Building would win.

In this game of urban exploration, you and your children walk through town and make up names for all the interesting buildings you see. The names can be anything, but one easy way to name buildings is after the animals they resemble.

A giraffe building could be the tallest. An elephant building could be the widest. A turtle building could have a domed roof.

Your kids could also name a building after friends or relatives ("Uncle Dave Tower"—a glistening dome) or stuffed animals (the "Pooh Bear Building").

A variation of this activity entails finding out the real names of the buildings and then discussing where the names came from. If the building is named after a person, your children could make up a biography. (You might also want to go to the library or town hall and find out information about the real person.)

See those twin towers over there—how about the "Mom and Dad" buildings?

Required:
• Your time only

Bulb Planting

Would you like to spruce up your yard in the spring with some early flowers? Plant bulbs in the fall—and delight your child at the same time.

Bulbs are self-contained seeds and food storage containers. As the temperature warms up, the bulbs begin growing and burst through the ground, eventually blooming. (By the way, when the flowers finish blooming, don't cut the stems—that will stop the food production and weaken the bulb. Let the stems wither naturally.)

First decide where you would like to see flowers in the spring. You can do a random "surprise" pattern, or something more formal (in which case you might want to draw a bulb map).

Next, purchase bulbs from your local garden store or nursery. Each bulb type has its own optimal depth. As a rule of thumb, dig the hole to a depth two and a half times the diameter of the bulb. (Ask your garden supplier for any special instructions or recommendations for your area.) Have your child help dig the holes, fertilize as necessary, place the bulb root side down in the hole, then fill the hole and water the area.

In the spring, your yard will be an explosion of color.

Required:

- Flower bulbs
- Trowel or small shovel

Bumper Sticker

Tired of seeing run-of-the-mill political bumper stickers and bumper stickers with trite sayings? If so, here's a chance to improve the scenery on the roads.

You and your child can make bumper stickers out of pieces of construction paper, then tape them to your bumper with wide clear tape. You can also cover the paper with plastic wrap, then tape it to the bumper with regular-width tape.

Here are a few suggestions from our neck of the woods:

"Later Bedtimes"

"Have a Nice Sleep."

"Beep if You Like Fig Newtons"

"I'd Rather Be Finger Painting"

"I'd Rather Be in the Sandbox"

"Have You Brushed Your Teeth Today?"

"Have You Hugged Your Brontosaurus Today?"

What important messages does your child want to share with the world on wheels?

Required:
- Paper
- Crayons or markers
- Clear tape (regular or wide)

Optional:
- Plastic wrap

Butterfly Net

Every junior naturalist needs a good net to capture specimens. You can easily make one out of an onion or plastic mesh bag and a yogurt container (or lengths of pipe cleaners).

Cut the clamp off one end of a mesh onion bag (your job). Also cut the rim off the top of a large yogurt container (also your job). Thread one end of the yogurt container rim in and out of the top edge of the bag, then join the ends of the rim with a piece of tape. For a wider net, make a rim of pipe cleaners attached end to end.

For a handle you'll need a very stiff cardboard tube, like the kind found in a roll of wrapping paper. Cut two slits on opposite sides of a large cardboard tube, then insert and tape the rim. Or, sandwich the rim edge between two small tubes (like those from coat hangers) and tape the assembly together.

Once you've made your child a net, catch some local critters, put them in a "bug motel" (an oatmeal container with screened windows and a good supply of leaves inside), and observe them. Finally, impress upon your child the importance of letting them go—fair is fair.

Required:

- Large yogurt container or pipe cleaners
- Onion or plastic mesh bag
- Long cardboard tube(s)
- Scissors
- Tape

Optional:

- Oatmeal container
- Screen/nylon stocking

Camouflage It

Safety Reminder

Adult Supervision

Required:
• Your time only

Here's a variation of the old "hide-and-find it" game. It uses natural coloration and texture to make the hidden objects harder to find.

To play the game, have your child collect various small household items—a wooden spoon, a green plastic utensil, a red napkin, etc. The idea is for the "hider" to place the items where they will be camouflaged by plants, rocks, leaves, etc. You might, for example, place the wooden spoon next to a stick of similar color. The green plastic utensil might be nestled among the branches of a living plant. And the red napkin could be placed by a red flower. (Of course, make sure that your child won't have to go picking through thorns or nasty plants.)

If you're playing with one child, see if he or she can find all of the items, then become the hider (again monitoring for safety). You can also have a group of players try to see how fast they can detect all of the items, then take turns doing the hiding.

Now then, is that really a rock, or is it your son's toy turtle?

Camping Stories

If you've set up a quick tent in the back-yard (#225), you'll definitely want to get into some storytelling—an essential part of any backyard camping experience. Here are some suggestions for spinning a good yarn.

Think up a plot ahead of time—even if you're a good ad libber, it's hard to make a plot work when all eyes are staring at you and the pressure is on. Stories can be designed to inform, impart a moral lesson or family value, or just plain entertain. Pick a topic.

Try to use your children's or family's experiences as a basis for your stories—kids delight in listening to stories related to their own adventures. A trip to the store, a backyard nature walk, or a cloud-watching session are all grist for great stories.

Don't try to develop more than a few characters—the complexity may get out of hand very quickly.

Keep it short! Unless you're trying to put them to sleep, you'll probably do a better job with several short stories then with one epic tale.

So, what *did* actually happen on that dark and stormy night?

Required:
• Your time only

Capture the Flag

Here's a traditional game you can play with a group of kids (at least six).

First, designate a playing field—about twenty-five feet square. Draw a divider line in the middle, creating two "courts" (see illustration). Pair off the two teams and give each player a "flag" (a paper towel). The players place their flags on their back or "home" line. (Variation: use one flag per team).

Starting from the home line, the players dash into the opposite court and try to pick up a flag. If a person is tagged in the opposing team's court, he or she is "out" and must stand behind the opposing team's line of flags. If a player succeeds in snatching a flag, however, he or she is safe from getting tagged and can return it to his or her court. The object is to capture all of the opposing team's flags first.

A wrinkle: players can either try to collect a flag and make it to home court, or they can "rescue" a tagged teammate instead. What do you think—is your child going to go for the flag or get you back in the game?

Required:
- Paper towels or rags

Flags

Court 1

Court 2

Flags

25'

25'

Car Wash

There's nothing like an eager troop of kids to keep your car clean. Just provide them with buckets, water, appropriate soap, sponges, and a hose. You can also turn the washing process into a game that's fun for everyone.

Try "Car Wash Olympics" for starts. Assign each child a specific task—wheels, hood, trunk, etc. Try to make the tasks appropriate for the age range. Start the timer and see who can finish their job within the allotted time (which is somewhat less competitive than seeing who can finish first). If only one child is involved, see if he or she can finish each task before you call out, "move on."

In the process of cleaning, the kids might want to write their names with a soapy sponge. They can also create soap pictures and see if their fellow car washers can guess what they've drawn.

Of course, you'll have to do a little quality control to ensure that your car looks better after being washed than before. And you'll want to keep the hose spraying at a minimum to save water. But as an occasional activity, it's bound to be a hit.

Required:
- Hose
- Sponges
- Buckets
- Dish soap

Cast in Sand

Safety Reminder

Adult Supervision

Required:

- Sand
- Common objects
- Cardboard or plastic containers
- Plaster
- Piece of cardboard, wood, or trowel

Optional:

- Paint
- Rod or straw

You and your child can use sand and plaster to make fascinating casts in the backyard or at the beach.

To make a cast, you'll need a mold, which can be made from a cardboard box or plastic container filled with sand. Moisten the sand, then make an imprint with one of your hands or feet, or a common object, such as a toy boat, car, animal, etc. You can also make an unusual footprint with talons or claws (Bigfoot, perhaps).

Once you've made the imprint, mix up a batch of plaster, which you can find at any hardware store. Follow the directions regarding proportions. Fill up the print with the plaster, then smooth out the top with a trowel or piece of cardboard. Let the plaster set (about 15 minutes), brush away the sand, and you'll have a fine casting. Allow the casting to dry fully (overnight). Finally, have your child paint the casting, then use it as decorative art or a paper weight.

You can make smaller casts of shells or other interesting small objects and use them as medallions. Use a rod or straw to poke a hole through the plaster once it sets (but before it hardens). Have your kids paint the medallions, and they'll be the talk of the neighborhood!

Catalog the Leaves

You don't have to be a botanical wizard to enjoy the different species of plants in your area—you and your child can simply appreciate the wonderful variety of leaf shapes.

Begin with your backyard. Have your child collect samples of leaves, then see if he or she can identify like characteristics. For example, leaves that are pointed, pear-shaped, or long and skinny; have "fingers" or lobes (like a maple or an oak leaf); are thick and shiny or thin and dull; are fuzzy underneath, or just have small bits of fuzz on the veins; have long or short stems.

Once you determine how many different leaf types you have in your backyard, take a neighborhood walk—any new candidates? What about the local park? How about in your city?

Of course, knowing the names of the leaves will add another dimension to the activity, so you might take a trip to your local library or bookstore for a plant identification book.

Either way, one leaf you should definitely become familiar with comes in clusters of three and grows in wooded areas and fields—poison ivy!

Required:
• Your time only

Optional:
• Plant identification book

Catch Ball

Safety Reminder

Adult Supervision

Required:

- Milk jug, yogurt container, or milk carton
- Scissors
- Rubber bands
- Ping-Pong ball

Here's how to make a homemade paddle ball game that's sure to delight and challenge your child.

To make a catch ball, you'll need a milk jug, a small yogurt container, or a quart-size milk carton. (The following cutting/hole punching activities are for adults.) Slice the bottom four inches off the milk jug and punch a small hole at the cut edge opposite the handle. If you're using a yogurt container, punch a hole near the top edge. Finally, for a quart milk container, cut off the bottom three inches and punch a hole near the cut edge.

Next, tie a handful of rubber bands together to create an elastic cord about two feet long (keep out of the hands of very young children). Tie a knot at the end and punch a small hole in a Ping-Pong ball. Force the knot into the hole in the ball and then tie the other end of the cord to the hole in the container. You're now ready to play. (You can also tie the end of the rubber-band cord to a whiffle ball.)

Your child simply tosses the ball and then tries to catch it with the milk jug, yogurt container, or milk container (which is why we recommend this activity outdoors).

How many times can your child toss and catch the ball? Be sure to enter the results in your family book of outdoor records.

Chalk Games

A box of chalk can be your key to many hours of fair-weather fun for kids of all ages.

Young children will enjoy "riding the rails." Draw a network of railroad tracks on your driveway or sidewalk. Your child can pretend that he or she is the "little engine that could" or any other kind of train. Perhaps one area is the roundhouse. You might also want to set up two brooms as a gate crossing.

For older kids, make a chalk maze that twists and turns tortuously. The idea is to walk on the line without stepping off.

Alternately, draw a series of lines, then see if your kids can jump from line to line, or jump over the lines without touching them.

Other chalk activities include hopping on one foot along a trail of X's, and playing chalk toss (draw a set of circles, say five, then see if your child can toss a pebble into each one).

One nice thing about chalk games is that you don't have to worry about the mess—nature will take care of it for you.

Required:
• Chalk

Optional:
• Brooms

Charitable Donations

Children are generally moved by the plight of those in need. Here's an activity that will enable them to participate in a neighborhood drive for food or clothing.

Required:
• Paper and pencil

First, do some telephone research and find out what your area needs. Perhaps there's a food distribution program or a home for the homeless that needs clothing.

Next, as an example, gather things from your own house that can be taken to a shelter or food program—ask your kids to part with a toy or two. Make up a flyer asking people who wish to make a donation to call your number and arrange a time for you and your child to come by with a wagon or a box. Your kids can help write or decorate the announcement. Make an expedition to the local copy center, then go on a neighborhood walk with your kids to distribute the announcement to households in your area.

Your child will feel a sense of satisfaction that could lead to a lifelong interest in making charitable contributions.

Charlotte's Web

Kids don't seem to have the same fear of spiders that haunts many adults. One way to help them avoid arachnophobia later in life is to introduce them to spiders early on.

First, talk about spiders as helpers who eat bugs that otherwise might harm plants in our gardens. (Of course, if there are poisonous spiders in your area, encourage due respect.)

Next, find a web—not too hard if you look in your garage or near the foundation of your building. Then wait for its inhabitant to return, if it's not already present. Notice how the spider moves about the web. And what of the web itself? (See #293 for web patterns.) Is it regular, like that of an "orb weaver," or irregular? Count the cross pieces, and perhaps sketch the pattern (keep young fingers out of the spider's way).

Gently tap the spider with a leaf or blade of grass—how does it respond? Does it have a hiding place, or does it seek a certain place in the web?

Finally, if you find a dead insect, push it onto a leaf and offer it to the spider—perhaps someday she'll return the favor and save your lettuce plant or rose bush from a pest.

Safety Reminder

Adult Supervision

Required:
- Your time only

Optional:
- Paper and pencil

Chart the Rain

How much rainfall does your area receive in an average week or month? Your junior meteorologist will be able to tell you after doing this activity.

Get a wide-mouthed plastic container with STRAIGHT sides (you won't get an accurate reading if the sides are angled. Either your child can hold up a ruler next to the container when it's filled with rain water, or you can use an indelible marker to draw tic marks for each inch and the fractions in between. (This is also a great way to teach the concepts of fractions, if you keep it simple.)

Have your child maintain a log book showing rainfall per week and per month (another opportunity for kids to practice addition.) You might also want to provide a calendar and let your child write in daily entries. If you want to get real fancy, buy some graph paper and plot a simple line chart—even kids who don't understand the concept of graphing will intuitively appreciate the up-and-down "blips," the fact that some days have lots of rainfall and others have none. Maybe that's how Mark Twain came to his famous conclusion about New England—if you don't like the weather, just wait a minute!

Required:
• Plastic container
• Ruler
• Paper and pencil

Optional:
• Indelible marker
• Calendar

Check out the Slope

Does your lawn slope slightly? How about your walk or driveway? Your child will be able to tell you after evaluating it with a hose level.

For this activity you'll need a length of garden hose, two identical funnels, and a waterproof marker. Draw a line on the funnels about midway down and parallel with the top. Then insert the funnels into both ends of a length of hose. Have your child pour enough water into the hose to fill both funnels up to the line when the hose is stretched level. You now have a giant leveling device. Explain to your child that water is always level in its container, and in this case, the hose is a container, albeit it a funny-shaped one.

Take the two ends of the hose to the points you wish to compare, making sure that as you walk the water stays at the mark on the funnel. When you get to your destination, take a measurement from the line on the funnel to the ground at each point. The shorter measurement is the higher point.

Now set about finding out what really slopes in your yard. Check out the driveway, the lawn, flower beds, walkways, or the sidewalk in front of your house.

Does this work? Absolutely—we're on the level.

Required:
- Garden hose
- Two identical plastic funnels
- Indelible marker

Cheerleaders

Two bits, four bits, six bits, a dollar, all for [our family] stand up and holler!

Remember chants like that at high school football games? Well, you can do them at your own family sporting events (or during any of the group games and sporting activities listed in this book).

Required:
• Your time only

Boys should be encouraged to do cheerleading too—it's time to break the stereotypes regarding this important and fun activity. For added effect, try making pom poms out of newspaper strips.

Dig back into your bag of memories from your own youth and you'll probably remember numbers like, "We're from [name of city] and couldn't be prouder, if you can't hear us now we'll yell a little louder!"

Of course, your kids can make up their own cheers, emphasizing the rhythm with body motions (pointing, arm waving, jumping, kicking, etc.). Perhaps something like, "We're the [family name] and we come from the Moon, and if you don't believe us, we'll dance like a loon." At which point the cheerleaders waddle across the yard like loons, cheering on the players as they slug it out in a game of Stationary Volleyball (#300) or Soda Can Bowling (#287).

Christmas Ornaments

Making Christmas ornaments is not only economical, it's a way for your child to feel very special about your Christmas tree.

You can find all kinds of natural ornaments in the world about you. Take a hike through the woods, the park, or just walk about the neighborhood. You're bound to find things you can use. Pine cones can be decorated with glitter and glue—just add a paperclip hook or attach a piece of fishing line. Sweet gum balls can be suspended by fine wires from boughs; small twigs can be connected with yarn and woven into a star pattern; acorn caps can be strung across a piece of fishing line to make a garland (punch holes in the caps to thread the line through—an adult job).

But don't stop with these—anything that looks interesting can potentially become a fine ornament with a personal touch.

Required:
- Yard materials
- Fishing line
- Glitter
- Glue
- Paper clips
- Wire
- Yarn

City Find It

In this game, children try to be the first to find a list of pre-determined items common to the city. This is a fun way for children to observe their surroundings and get some exercise as well.

The idea is to start by having one of the players make up a list of five items. The list can include things such as a clock, a taxi, a pigeon, a penny on the ground, a gargoyle, tinted glass, a sign with the word "be," a restaurant that serves hamburgers, a traffic light, a hotel, a light pole with public notices, an iron gate, a parking lot, a convenience store, a police car, or a construction work site.

As soon as someone finds all the items on the first list, that player gets to choose the items for the next game.

This game is challenging for the players who are trying to find the items as well as for the player making up the list.

Now, how about finding a statue with a pigeon on its head?

Required:

• Your time only

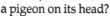

Clothespin Jug Game

This is a fun activity for two or more children—it's kind of a variation on pin the tail on the donkey.

In this game the children try to drop clothespins into a gallon plastic milk jug—with their eyes closed. Supervise to make sure no one wanders off into a flower bed or trafficked area. For young children, you might want to cut off the top of the jug so it's easier to insert the clothespins. You might also want to fill the jug with a layer of rocks to keep it from tipping.

A variation of this game is for the children to line up and take turns putting the clothespins in the jug. As the children queue up to try their skill, spin them around several times, then aim them in the right direction.

Yet another way to play is for one child to try and direct another to the jug. This can be hilarious as one child says, "This way" and the child trying to find the jug asks, "Which way?" The children take turns acting as guides and as clothespin droppers. When the jug is filled, the game starts again.

Safety Reminder

Adult Supervision

Required
- Gallon milk jug
- Clothespins

Optional:
- Scissors
- Rocks

Cloud Identification

Most of us look up at the clouds and think "rain/no rain," then go about our merry ways. You can get your child to stop and admire the clouds by teaching him or her the different types. While a good weather book from the library will give you detailed pictures, here's a starter vocabulary you can use right now.

Required:
• Your time only

Optional:
• Weather book

Cumulus (Fig. A) are puffy white fair-weather clouds.

Cumulonimbus (B) are tall dark puffy clouds that indicate rain or snow is on the way.

Cirrus clouds (C) are composed of ice, and are high up and wispy (they also indicate foul weather)

Stratus clouds (D) are a grey layer, associated with drizzle.

If your child can't remember or doesn't like these names, he or she can invent his or her own (see next activity)— what's today's forecast according to your kids?

Cloudy with a Chance of Cucumbers*

In the previous activity, we listed four basic kinds of clouds. In this activity, your child can invent some names that might make more sense within the context of his or her own world. Here are some examples:

Required:
• Your time only

Alligator clouds: *Patches of cumulus clouds in rows*

Camels-in-desert clouds: *Cumulus by another name*

Cat-whisker clouds: *High wispy cirrus clouds*

Cotton-ball clouds: *Cumulus clouds, of course*

Cucumber clouds: *Elongated cumulus clouds*

Floating-hippo clouds: *Cumulus by another name*

Mouse-tail clouds: *Thinner alligator clouds*

Skeleton clouds: *Cirrus clouds that look like ribs*

Next time you turn on the news and the weatherman shows an aerial shot, you might want to call in a correction: "Sir, that's really *not* a cumulonimbus—it's a large eggplant cloud."

---

* With high regards to Judi and Ron Barrett, whose *Cloudy with a Chance of Meatballs* is a favorite in our household.

Code of Nature

Required:
- Common yard or beach objects

What does "acorn, acorn, acorn, pebble, maple seed mean?" To a squirrel, probably lunch. To your kids, it might mean something like, "Jump three times, run through the sprinkler, then have a glass of lemonade." Here's a natural sign language that can be used with children of all ages.

First, have your child gather objects abundantly available in the backyard or at the beach—seeds, leaves, rocks, shells, driftwood, etc. Next, show how to assign an action or a word to each object. Then let the fun begin!

For younger children, keep things simple. If red leaves mean "hop," and twigs mean "clap your hands," then hold up a red leaf in one hand followed by the twig in the other. Once your child gets the hang of it, increase the complexity.

Older kids will enjoy deciphering more complex natural "sentences" laid out on the ground and acting out the silliest messages (see if you can get your child flapping his or her arms around the backyard while yodeling!)

Reverse the process and have your child compose a message for you. Quick—rock, leaf, pine cone, leaf, rock. Well, get going!

Cold-Weather Bird Bath

It's natural to think of bird baths in the summer (see #82), when the local winged creatures in your yard enjoy a refreshing dip. But birds need water in the winter, too. Here's how you can help out.

Take a plastic dish, like the basin from a plastic flowerpot or a dishpan. Find a place outdoors where a bird will enjoy drinking—it will feel safer if the pan is elevated rather than on the ground. Place a rock in the pan to keep it from blowing over. Each morning, pour hot water into the pan (a job for you; on a mild day if there's no chance of freezing, use room-temperature water, in which case your child can do the transporting and pouring). The birds will enjoy a nice thirst-quenching drink!

Your child can keep track of the birds that take advantage of the local fountain. As the birds drink, your family will be able to get a good look at their plumage and features. Encourage your kids to keep a log of the visitors who come by to wet their whistles.

Required:

- Catch pan from flowerpot
- Brick or rock

Color Counts

The world about us is a rich source for color counting games that can occupy kids of any age. And they'll sharpen everyone's powers of observation at the same time.

While walking down the street, one person calls out a color, and the others try to find as many examples as possible. (Obviously, "green" would apply to all leaves and foliage, rather than to specific plants).

If you and your child keep your eyes open to the unexpected, you're bound to find all kinds of subtle examples. Look carefully at signs displayed on buildings and trucks; goods displayed in windows; road signs; uniforms; passing vehicles (including bicycles); people's clothing; birds, dogs, cats, and insects; newspaper vending machines; trash cans—just about everything in your immediate environment has color.

Variations of this activity entail looking for combinations of colors, or multiple shades of the same color. You might also stipulate certain sizes—like all green things smaller than your finger or bigger than your head.

Finally, don't forget to look right under your own nose—without looking, what colors are you wearing today?

Required:
• Your time only

Comb the Grass

A nice lawn or grassy area in the park isn't just for sitting, it makes a wonderful game board. Here's a game you can play with a small patch of lawn and some common household items. It was a summertime favorite in our households.

First, take some green construction paper and cut it into very fine strips about the length of your lawn grass (an adult job). Alternately, you can take a sheet of white paper and color it with the side of a green crayon (a kid's job), then cut the paper into strips.

Count the number of strips, then dump them into a designated area. Gently work them into the lawn with your hands. Set a timer or check your watch, then see if you and your child can find all the paper strips within a set period of time.

For groups of kids, give each a designated area and see who can beat the clock. You can also hide the strips, then give hints as to the whereabouts of the area that contains them.

By the way, if your lawn looks like ours, you'll make the game harder by making light *brown* strips of paper!

Required:
- Paper and crayons or green paper
- Timer or watch
- Scissors

Community Service

The idea of this activity is to get children to understand that there are people in their own community (the elderly, sick, or physically challenged) who may not be able to do household chores for themselves.

Explain that these neighbors would probably appreciate help from strong young bodies, and that by doing such acts they'll feel the special sense of personal satisfaction that comes from helping others. Among chores you and your children can offer are:

Required:
• Your time only

Shoveling snow in the winter
Pulling weeds in the spring
Cutting grass (older children only) in the summer
Raking leaves in the fall
Washing cars
Carrying groceries
Running errands
Sweeping walks and porches
Watering plants and flowers

Call or visit your neighbors to find out who's interested in your troupe of little helpers. Supervise all helping activities, and set an example yourself by pitching in. Better yet, make the activity one that the whole family does together. Family helping family—that's the real spirit of any community.

Comparing Weights

Ask your child which weighs more—a small rock or a pine cone?

To find out (and compare other things as well), set up a simple balance. You can use a ruler and a stick about an inch in diameter (the fulcrum), a ruler and a plastic container with straight walls, or many other combinations of indoor and outdoor objects (just make sure that the center of the ruler is directly over the fulcrum.)

Have your child compare various objects from around the yard, first guessing which would be the heaviest. Suggest weighing things like twigs, clumps of dirt, and different vegetables.

You might also ask why one object weighs more than the next. Young children will probably go solely on the basis of size; older kids will be able to give some intuitive sense of density. You can prod this line of thinking by demonstrating that a small rock is heavier than a long plant stem.

How about having your child compare a piece of wet and dry sponge? That should stimulate some interesting speculation.

Safety Reminder

Adult Supervision

Required:

- Ruler
- Stick (about 1 inch in diameter)
- Yard objects

Construct a Nest

64

Birds' nests are more than just straw baskets—they're great engineering works.

The weaver bird of Africa builds a spiraling, hanging nest with a special trap door. The albatross makes mud chimneys in which to lay its eggs. Storks make huge six-foot nests on the roofs of houses in Europe, where they're considered good luck.

Required:
- String
- Dried grass
- Twigs
- Scraps of paper
- Cloth

Your local birds may not make such exotic nests, but they're no less wondrous. When the leaves have fallen from the trees in your area, take a walk and see how many nests you can find. (Don't confuse them with the ill-engineered nests of squirrels, which tend to be in the high forks of trees). Perhaps you'll find a nest that has fallen to the ground, or one that's low enough to study.

To appreciate the engineering feat, have your child try building a nest of his or her own, with twigs, string, dried grasses, scraps of paper, and cloth.

Difficult, isn't it? Just imagine trying to do it with your mouth!

Container Garden

If you have a patio or terrace, a driveway or parking lot, but no garden space, you can still grow a summer's worth of vegetables. You just need to start a container garden.

As the name suggests, a container garden consists of various crops grown in flower pots. (You can also use window boxes or buckets—just make sure you have adequate drainage. If not, be sure to put a couple of inches of rocks in the bottom, and be careful not to overwater.)

Here are some plants that do well in container gardens: Cherry tomatoes (they're quite manageable); herbs (also quite manageable); strawberries in hanging baskets (require little care); peppers (ditto); lettuce (just keep it well watered); carrots (they like sandy soil); potatoes (easy—see #233); and radishes (fast-growing for eager gardeners). Follow the directions on the seed packages or starter plants from your local garden shop.

Plants to avoid include squash, cucumbers, melons, and pumpkins—these can take over by the end of the summer.

Finally, consider planting a little grass—just think of how easy it will be to mow the lawn.

Suggested:

- Large flower pots or window boxes or buckets
- Potting soil
- Vegetable seeds or starter plants
- Grass seed
- Rocks for drainage

Cookie-Cutter Art

Who says that cookie cutters are just for making edibles? They make scrumptious play cookies, too.

Backyard mud cookies. Whip up a batch of mudpies—add water to a bucket of dirt until the mixture is stiff, like bread dough. Flatten the mud into a sheet and apply the cookie cutters, trimming excess mud from the sides. You'll be left with delicious-looking mud cookies that your child can "serve" at the Four Seasons Cafe (#104).

Snow cookies. You'll need some sticky snow, the kind suitable for making good snowballs. Have your child make a rectangle of snow about a half-inch high and apply the cookie cutters. Remove the snow around the cutters and presto! Instant snow delicacies. Decorate your driveway or porch with the snow cookies. You can also make a snow cookie mountain by building up a large mound of snow, then applying the cookie cutters and trimming the excess.

Sand cookies. At the beach, mix sand and water until the mixture is thick enough to shape into clumps; then flatten it and use the cookie cutters to make sand "cookies." Make a pattern up and down the beach—that'll keep the gulls guessing!

Required:
- Cookie cutters
- Mud, sand, or snow

Corn Husk Doll

This summer, as you prepare corn on the cob, save some of the husks. Soak them in warm water for five minutes, or until they're pliable. Tie three of them together in the middle with a piece of string or a sliver of husk. Then position the knot on top of an acorn or other nut. Pull the husks down so they cover the nut. Tie at the bottom of the nut to make the head.

Next, make the arms by rolling two husks together. (Roll them around a pipe cleaner or twistem if you want the arms in a certain position.) Tie at the "wrists." Place the arms between the husks under the neck, and tie all the husks together again to form a waist (stuff a piece of tissue under the husks to make a torso).

Finally, take six to ten corn husks and lay them around the doll, covering up the body. Tie them securely again, and then fold them down. This makes a skirt or, if you tie the husks into two bundles, pants.

Bend the arms, arrange the skirt, and allow to dry for a day or two. Then glue on the corn silk for hair and draw or paint facial features. Voilà! A perfect doll.

Required:
- Corn husks
- Corn silk
- String
- Pens, crayons, markers, or paints
- Glue

Corsages/Boutonnieres

A re you and your spouse going to a special event like an anniversary dinner? The Grand Ball? Then you'll want to wear a fine corsage or boutonniere. Your child can help provide you with the best-looking flowers in town.

Have your child collect an assortment of flowers—put in a request for your favorite colors—as well as buds, interesting leaves, and ferns. Use a twistem to hold the bundle together. Cut a hole in a doily and pass the stems through the hole. Mom can pin the corsage to her dress or blouse. Store the corsage in a covered container and a few drops of water to keep it fresh. Add a doily when putting it on.

Now for the dads. Have your child pick a flower that matches your jacket or shirt. Push the stem through a button hole and you'll be the best dressed man at the event,

Of course, you don't have to wait for a special event—corsages or boutonnieres can liven up anyone's day, any time of the year—and they're not just for adults. Kids can wear corsages and boutonnieres just to feel good, too.

Required:
- Flowers
- Buds
- Ferns
- Leaves

Optional:
- Doily
- Scissors

Country Store

Every backyard needs a country store—and your child is the ideal proprietor.

Make-believe country stores can be as simple as a box for a counter and a few buckets of goodies. On a more complex scale, you and your child can set up a board on bricks or cinder blocks, or make a complete set of shelves.

What should you be able to find at your backyard country store? Any store worth its salt will have a good variety of tea bags and cinnamon sticks (leaves and twigs); various kinds of flour (dirt in plastic jars); candies (pebbles and acorns); firewood (sticks or driftwood); and common tools (sticks, stones, etc).

Of course, you can substitute the real thing if you want to get fancy. In any case, your child is sure to delight in doing business with local family members and friends.

Older children might want to create labels and list the prices. They can also keep tabs on the cash box. Speaking of which, in keeping with the traditional lifestyle, no plastic accepted here. Just the real green stuff—leaves!

Required:

- Box or board on cinderblocks
- Buckets or clear plastic containers
- Yard matter (dirt, leaves, twigs, etc)

Critter Tracking

Safety Reminder

Adult Supervision

Required:

• Your time only

Many children play with stuffed animals, pretending to know all about the lives the critters lead. But what do they know about real animals?

How about spending some time learning about the life of a squirrel or bird? Follow a squirrel in your neighborhood to see where it goes. (Parents should never let children get close enough to pet or hand-feed squirrels.) Can you find its nest? How does it behave around other squirrels? What are its favorite haunts? What does it do for fun?

Alternatively, try to track a bird in your yard as it jumps from branch to branch. Does it have a nearby nest? Is there a purpose to its movements, or does it seem to move randomly from place to place? What does it eat? Toss out some bread crumbs and see whether the bird forages on the ground or takes the meal back to its nest or a safe spot.

You can do this with grasshoppers, spiders, or just about any other creature in your immediate environment. But there's another question to ask: are any animals watching you?

Dandelion Jewelry

What's our first impulse when we see a dandelion growing in our yard? Pull it! Here's a way to put those pesky "weeds" to good use.

If your yard is "blessed" with dandelion weeds, just walk about with your kids and collect the best specimens. Otherwise you might need to find a field with a heavy dandelion population.

Once you've collected a couple dozen or so (you might want to make a basket for the occasion, as described in #351), you're ready to make some dandelion jewelry. The easiest way to connect the dandelions is to wrap one stem carefully around another and tie a knot.

Another technique is to carefully slit the stem of one specimen close to the flower, then feed the stem of another through it. You'll need to collect dandelions with thick stems for this technique to work.

Tailor the "jewelry" pieces to your child's head or wrist, then deck them out for a dandelion appreciation day!

Required:
• Dandelions

Optional:
• Homemade basket (#351)

Date a Tree

This activity teaches your child how to determine the age of a tree by counting its "annual rings."

Explain to your child that each year the tree grows, it adds a new ring of cells just under the bark. These cells form channels that bring water from the roots and sugars from the leaves to all other parts. They also form a ring, which you can see at the end of a log or tree stump. Actually, you'll see alternating light and dark rings—each light and dark ring together represents one year's growth. The light part is formed in the spring, when growth is rapid and the cells are large, and the dark part forms during the summer, when water is scarce and growth is slower (the summer cells are smaller and denser; hence the ring looks darker.)

The width of the ring tells how favorable the year was to the tree. A wide light ring tells you that one spring was conducive to tree growth; a narrow ring bespeaks a hard spring.

As you and your child walk about the neighborhood or the woods, look for tree stumps or logs. How old are the trees? And how were their growing seasons? Your child should have some interesting answers.

Required:
• Your time only

Detective Work

What has a blue body, four legs, a bald head, and a gaping mouth? Answer, a mailbox.

No, this activity isn't about making jokes; rather, it's a guessing game in which you try to provide as few clues as possible about an object you see. Your child continues to ask questions until he or she gets the answer. Then it's his or her turn to select an object. You can play the game in your backyard, on a neighborhood or urban walk, at the beach, at the park—anywhere. It's also great for groups of kids—the first child to get the answer selects the object to be "discovered."

For younger children, keep the activity simple. You might, for example, give clues for a yellow house with a cat in the window by saying, "I'm thinking of something big and yellow where a kitty lives."

For older children try more subtle clues, like the ones described for the mail box. The more unusual the descriptions, the more fun the game.

Just keep your eyes open and you'll find a world of clues right at your doorstep. From street signs and cars to inchworms and birds—it's all fair game for this game.

Required:
• Your time only

Dino Soap Box Derby

Safety Reminder

Adult Supervision

Required:

- Small cardboard box
- Four yogurt container tops
- Four brads
- Crayons or markers
- Tape

Optional:

- String

Our son Noah once had a small plastic dinosaur he called "Bobby." Here's how we gave Bob his own set of wheels—you can do the same for Mickey or Barbie or anyone else in your child's toy chest.

Start with a small box and punch four small holes (your job) on the sides, about half an inch from the bottom at each corner. Then take four plastic yogurt tops and punch a small hole in the center of each (also your job). Affix each yogurt top to the box with a brad and you instantly have four wheels (cover the sharp ends of the brad with tape for safety). Attach a string and handle, if you like. The rest is artwork, as you and your child decide whether Bobby (or whomever) wants a school bus, racing car, or pickup truck to cruise around in.

When it's finished, let Bobby take it out for a spin. But be forewarned—someday Bobby may want to trade it in for a new model.

Dirt City

A patch of garden or a vacant end of a flower bed can be the site of a great metropolis. Well, maybe a nice village. Just supply your child with some tools—spoons, small pieces of sanded lumber, a blunt trowel, or other safe digging tools—and you're all set for some small-scale construction.

Every dirt city needs a good roadway system. Roads can be created with any digging implements. Have your child use twigs along the side as lamplights or telephone poles. For additional detail, use strings between the telephone poles. Popsicle sticks make excellent road signs and traffic lights (your child can add red, yellow, and green circles to the sticks with markers).

Once the road system is in place, your child can create some buildings (see Twig Architecture #339 for suggestions, or Mudflats, Basic and Advanced #193 and #194).

Finally, your child can do some landscape architecture. Plant various weeds as shrubbery, with taller ones as trees. Add some toy cars to the roadway (or use imaginary cars consisting of pine cones, thick sticks, etc.), and Dirt City will be ready for occupancy.

Suggested materials:

- Digging implements
- Twigs
- String
- Popsicle sticks
- Mud building materials (#193 & 194)
- Toy cars

Dodge Ball

Required:
- Open field
- Soft rubber balls

This is a team game played with one or more soft rubber balls and a group of kids.

Divide the field in half and divide the group into two teams. The game begins with the balls evenly distributed between teams. If there is only one ball, or an odd number, flip a coin to see who starts with the ball or with the extra ball.

The idea is for players to aim the ball at those on the other team. If the thrower touches a player on the other side of the dividing line, the player who got hit is out. If the player being thrown at catches the ball, the thrower is out. If neither one of these things happens, the ball is retrieved and play continues.

Players cannot cross the middle line at any time and must stay within marked-off boundaries, except to chase a ball. Once players start to get eliminated, they can chase the balls. Whichever team has players left in the game wins.

Dodge 'em!

Do-It-Yourself Cuneiform

Y ou don't have to be an ancient
Sumerian or Egyptian to have fun
writing on the walls—your child can do
some mud inscribing right in your backyard.

First, make slabs of mud. For soil with
a high clay content, just add water. Otherwise, mix one part flour with four parts
of soil. Mix soil or the soil/flour combination with enough water so you can
knead it, then spread it out in a baking
tin. Now let your child get to work with
a twig, chopstick, or popsicle stick to do
some good old ancient writing.

Younger children will enjoy doing simple picture writing. Older children might
enjoy making up their own cuneiform
(wedge-shaped character) language. For
example, a left wedge might represent
the letter "a" while a right-pointing
wedge is the letter "e." Two left pointing
wedges might represent "i" and so on.

When the slabs dry, your child can display them as artistic renderings. Or you
can use them for markers in a treasure
hunt.

Required:

- Soil
- Water
- Flour (for low-clay content soil)
- Baking tin or pan
- Sticks, twigs, chopsticks, or popsicle sticks

Downtown Fossil Hunt

Did you know that fossils can some-times be found in the materials used to construct buildings? It's true. So next time you're downtown, try a little local palaeontology with your child.

Fossils are most often found in lime-stone, a greyish material commonly used in older buildings (it's more uniform in appearance than granite, and often looks like concrete). The fossils were water dwellers that often predate dinosaurs—ancient clams, corals, snails, sea lilies (which look like soda straws composed of small sections), and "brachiopods" (which look like clamshells).

You can search for fossils on the out-side of large old buildings like libraries, museums, and municipal offices. Look carefully, because each fossil will prob-ably be smaller than a penny.

"Collect" the fossils by making a list in a notebook and writing down their lo-cation. Your child might want to sketch them, too.

How's that for ancient history right in your own town?

Required:
• Your time only

Drum Talk

Since the beginning of civilization, people have used drums to communicate messages cosmic and mundane. You and your children can continue this ancient tradition right in your own backyard.

Now, the neighbors probably won't appreciate the sounds of spoons banging on trash cans or pots, so you'll probably want to use something a bit more delicate—like sticks or wooden spoons and large yogurt containers with lids. Coffee cans and oatmeal containers with lids also make pleasant-sounding drums.

Once you've chosen your instrument, invent a drum language. For example, one beat might mean, "Hello to anyone in the galaxy." Two slow beats could be: "Hello to you, too," while two rapid beats might signify, "Tyrannosaurus rex approaching from the driveway—take cover in lawn furniture fort!"

A variation is to incorporate the drums in "mobile" hide and seek games. The "hiders" might use drums to give the seeker hints about their whereabouts, then move on. Conversely, the seeker might thump on a drum to indicate his or her presence, so the "hiders" can find new spots and keep the game going.

Thump . . . Thump, Thumpity Thumpity Thump! (Live long and prosper!)

Required:
- Wooden spoons or sticks
- Yogurt, oatmeal, or coffee containers (with lids)

Duck Duck Goose

This traditional game for five or more players can be played in a backyard, at the park, or on a beach.

All of the children except one sit in a circle facing each other. The remaining person goes around the circle, tapping each child gently on the head and saying "duck." When the "tapper" says "goose," the child whose head was just touched jumps up and chases the tapper around the circle. The tapper in turn tries to get all the way back to the goose's spot without getting tagged by the goose. If the tapper succeeds, the goose becomes the new tapper and the game continues. But if the goose catches the tapper, the tapper continues his or her walk around the circle..

A variation is called "Drop the Hanky." Instead of sitting down, the players stand in a circle facing each other. Another person walks outside the circle, and drops a "handkerchief" (or piece of cloth) at the heels of one of the players. That player then picks it up and chases the hanky dropper, who races around the circle and tries to capture the other person's space without getting tagged.

Fun is guaranteed for all—ducks and geese alike.

Required:

• Minimal or no props

DUCK

Earth Puppets

Your backyard, the park, or the beach offers a wealth of puppet-making supplies.

The easiest kind of puppets can be made from a twig. Select a twig with a fork—you now have a handle and two arms. Find a fallen flower and tape the stem to the handle, and you have an instant head. You can also tape a small branch with a single leaf to the handle, and use the leaf as the head. For clothing, wrap a leaf around the handle, and your puppet will be decked out in the latest in nature wear.

For a more complicated puppet, use a pine cone. You'll need some white glue to affix the various features. Dried grass makes terrific hair, beards, and moustaches. Use seeds to make a nose and pair of eyes. Make clothing out of leaves (acorn tops make snazzy caps) and you're all set for a pine cone puppet show.

Driftwood from the beach also makes good puppet materials. Glue on popsicle sticks for arms, paint faces, and use shells for hats.

Finally, set up a large box that your child can sit behind, and get set for the greatest puppet show on earth.

Suggested:
- Yard/beach materials
- Tape
- Glue

Easy Bird Bath

O ne way to attract birds to your yard is to offer them a free dip in your homemade bird bath.

First, you'll need a pedestal base. This can be made out of a gallon milk jug. Slice off the top (an adult job only). Then cut curves in the top so that an inverted garbage can lid or an old shallow plastic bowl will sit securely on the milk jug.

Required:

- Plastic milk jug
- Scissors
- Trash can lid or shallow plastic bowl
- Sand or brick

To set up the bird bath, first select a site. The birds won't be comfortable if the bath is too near foot or car traffic. Also, if you have any noisemakers (#204), a scarecrow (#256), or animal sculptures in your yard, they're likely to be scared off.

Once you've found a site, put enough sand or a brick in the milk jug to keep it from toppling over. Place the upside-down trash can lid or bowl on the jug-pedestal, and fill it with water and a layer of small rocks.

Finally, don't expect the birds to flock in for a bath instantly. Let them discover it, and your child will be in for a great show as local residents come to cool their feet.

Enchanted Houses

An island off New England's coast has a magical tradition; passersby through a state forest create elf houses out of pine cones, twigs, and other ground floor materials, nestle them amidst the tree roots, then leave them for other walkers to find. You and your child can continue this activity in the woods in your own area, creating houses for leprechauns and other beings to enjoy.

Required:
- Ground materials in woods or forest

First pick a site. You'll want a place that's not obvious (like the middle of the trail), but not so remote that someone would have to go stomping through the brush to find it. A crook between large tree roots is a good spot, as is an open area under a branch of a small bush.

Once you have your site, you'll need to put up some walls. Pine cones make good corners, and so do twigs and sticks. For the sides, lay down leaves or pile up twigs. Roofs can be made out of leaves and small twigs, or pieces of long dry grass. A covering of pine needles will give the enchanted house an air of authenticity. Make a pebble path leading to the door. (See "Twig Architecture," #339 for more ideas.)

Check back in a few days—you might find some surprising signs of life!

Evaporation Experiment

Required:
- Plate
- Containers with various-sized mouths

Children are often intrigued by the concept of materials changing state. With this experiment, you can demonstrate the concept of evaporation.

Water evaporates when exposed to air because the molecules in the water are constantly in motion and are "looking" for somewhere to go to; the air is simply a convenient place. To show how evaporation works and how you can affect it, gather plastic containers of various shapes and widths, from a plate to a baby bottle. Fill them with equal amounts of water (say, a quarter of a cup—the less water, the less time the experiment will take). Let the containers sit in the open air.

The water in the containers with the widest mouths (the plate, in this case) will evaporate first, because the greatest surface of the water is exposed to the air. Conversely, the container with the narrowest opening will evaporate last.

Allow plenty of time—remember, a watched container never evaporates.

Family Totem Pole

Every house or apartment needs a good totem pole, and no one is better at helping to create such a piece of symbolic art than your child.

An easy way to make a totem pole is to cut off the tops of milk cartons, then cut two-inch slits in the corners so the bottom of one container can be wedged inside the top of the container beneath it. (Of course, cutting is an adult job.) Experiment to see how high you can stack the cartons without creating an engineering disaster. Also, you might need to put a rock or weight in the bottom carton for stability.

Once you've experimented with the height, unstack the containers and cover them with paper bags. Have your child decorate the covered containers with designs and faces, or pictures from magazines or junk mail catalogs. (Our daughter Audrey decided that a bunch of bananas from a grocery store circular captured our family spirit!) Older children may want to inscribe the containers with ancient writings.

When your child is finished, assemble the totem pole and watch the neighbors gaze with envy.

Required:
- Milk cartons
- Scissors
- Kraft paper
- Crayons, markers, or tempera paint

Optional:
- Magazine catalogs

Feed the Squirrels

Safety Reminder

Adult Supervision

Required:

• Acorns, walnuts, etc.

Squirrels are pretty skilled at finding food for the winter, but they'll surely appreciate anything you can do to help.

As the fall progresses, collect acorns and various kinds of nuts that have fallen from trees. Select several feeding sites, then place a few goodies on the ground so the squirrels can forage. While you want to pick a spot that will allow you and your child to observe your dinner guests (stress that squirrels are not to be petted, no matter how friendly), bear in mind that most animals in the wild prefer not to collect food or eat in open spaces, where they are vulnerable.

Have your child keep a log of the following kinds of information: Do the squirrels visit the feeding area at a regular time? Do they prefer a certain kind of offering to other kinds? Do they eat some of the food and collect the rest?

By the end of the activity, your child will have become the world's foremost expert on your own backyard squirrel population.

Find a Path

Have you ever been on a trail where the path is marked by ribbons or signs on the tree trunks? It's reassuring and fun to know you're going in the right direction. Here's a way to make your own path markers in a wooded trail of your choice.

Safety Reminder

Adult Supervision

Required:
• Rocks and pebbles

First decide on a convention. For example, three rocks stacked with a fourth rock to the right might indicate that the person on the path is to turn right. Three rocks and one to the left could mean turn left. Two rocks stacked could mean go straight ahead to the next marker. You can also indicate how many paces or steps are between markers by leaving the corresponding number of pebbles (make each pebble represent five or ten steps).

You can go out yourself and set up the markers, then have your child decide which way to go. Or, you can do the activity with another adult, giving yourself a head start. Keep making markers as the other adult and your child try to find you.

See you back at camp.

Find It!

Here's a game that will improve everyone's detective skills—and provide a lot of fun to boot. We call the game Find It, and play it year-round.

One person collects a group of items (flower petals, leaves, etc), while the others close their eyes and turn their backs. When the person who gathered the item calls out "Find It!," the players turn around or open their eyes, then set out to locate the source of each item.

Flower petals are excellent Find It! items (make sure no one's flower garden becomes part of the game). Seeds are also good candidates, if they've fallen near the plant that produced them. In the spring, buds can make interesting Find It! items.

An icicle makes a good Find It! subject in the winter—the players will have to look for the patch where it originated. In the fall, leaves of a particular color and shape can be traced to a particular tree (a good way to recognize tree types). Same with acorns and other nuts.

All right, feet up—what's the source of that piece of bubblegum?

Required:
• Backyard materials

Finger Sports

E ven if you only have a single slab of
sidewalk or a few square feet of
driveway, your child can still play big-
time sports. Here's how.

Micro Hockey. Use two cardboard boxes
as the goals. Supply chopsticks and a
checker for a puck. Encourage civility!

Micro Soccer. Use the same boxes as for
micro hockey. The players use their
fingers to kick a Ping-Pong ball
along the "field."

Micro Basketball. Take two milk cartons
and slice off the tops (your job).
Next, cut a hole in two six-inch-long
pieces of corrugated cardboard
(same width as the carton). The hole
in each piece should be just small
enough to catch the rim of a paper
cup. Bend the cardboard at ninety
degrees, remove the bottom from a
paper cup, and drop the cup into the
hole. Staple the cardboard to the
milk carton (see illustration).

Suggested:

- Chopsticks
- Ping-Pong or
  small rubber balls
- Two small
  cardboard boxes
- Two milk cartons
- Corrugated
  cardboard
- Paper cups
- Sand or rocks
- Stapler
- Scissors

You now have two backstops and
hoops. Fill the milk cartons with sand or
rocks, place at either end of the "court,"
provide a Ping-Pong or small rubber ball,
demonstrate how to "dribble," and the
kids' fingers will be just a few steps away
from the NBA!

Firefly Lamp

Do you have fireflies in your area? If so, you have nature's lighting at your fingertips.

Fireflies are easy to catch with a large plastic jar or net (you can purchase an insect net or make one yourself (see #39). Place them in a transparent plastic container, using a piece of stocking and a rubber band for a top. Be sure to explain to your child that the insects are fragile (supervise their capture and transfer), and that you're going to let them go when it's time to turn in.

Once your child has collected a dozen or so fireflies, place the jar where its inhabitants can be easily observed. See if your child can time the intervals between flashes. Is it always the same? What is the greatest number of fireflies lighting up at the same time? Do some fireflies seem to light up more than others?

Another game involves anticipating when the lights are actually going to flash on.

Camera, action . . . lights!

Required:
- Plastic jar
- Piece of stocking
- Rubber band

Optional:
- Homemade insect net (#39)

Fireless Fireworks

Here's a way you can create your own fireworks display without the teeth-rattling booms—and without fire. And you don't have to worry about keeping young kids up late to enjoy the festivities.

All you need is a sunny day and a colander. Hold the colander above the sidewalk so that it casts a shadow. Each hole in the colander will let through a dot of light. These are the "fireworks." Now, shake the colander and move it up and down and around to make your fireworks dance around. If you do want sound effects, put a few small pebbles in the colander, and rattle them around while you make the fireworks flicker.

Alternatively, take a sheet of heavy paper and cut small designs into it (safety scissors for kids). Move the paper around to make the fireworks come to life. See how many other common objects you can use—a strainer, a slotted spoon, etc.

For added fun, get several people going with colanders or sheets of paper—the crisscrossing lights will create dazzling displays that bring "oohs" and "ahs" from any onlookers.

Hey, with a little imagination, you can make believe that it's the Fourth of July anytime—without the kaboom!

Required:
- Colander
- Kraft paper

Fitness Stations

A well-regimented fitness program fights the dreaded "Couchus Potatoitis Syndrome," which is caused by TV viewing.

Set up a race with four fitness stations. Mark off the stations with sticks, toys, or other objects. Contestants run from the starting line to the first station, where they must do ten pushups. Then they run to the second station for ten situps. At the third station, they do ten jumping jacks, and at the fourth there are lightweight dumbbells (toilet paper tubes filled with rocks and taped at the ends; they do ten curls in each arm.

The winner gets to decide on the stations for the next race. The winner could choose leg lifts, knee bends, running in place, pushup/situp combinations, or toe touching. Or, the winner could choose hop, skip, walk, crawl, run backward while singing, and run forward. The winner also decides how contestants travel between stations in the next game.

For variety, add more stations or more repetitions of each activity. And remember the slogan of those who do fitness stations: "No couch potatoes here."

Required:
- Sticks or old rags
- Homemade dumbbells

Five Dollars

This is an old baseball activity that adds an interesting twist to the traditional game and helps with math skills at the same time.

You'll need a bat, a ball, and mitts. You can play with a hardball, softball, or even a whiffle ball—whatever your kids are accustomed to using. You won't, however, need a full complement of in- and outfielders. Everyone except the batter takes a position in the outfield.

The batter tosses the ball and hits it to the other players who collect various *imaginary* rewards: One dollar for whomever catches the ball on the fly. Seventy-five cents for anyone who picks up the ball on one bounce. Twenty-five cents for anyone who picks up a grounder.

The first person to rack up five dollars gets to bat next, and continues until someone else earns five dollars through his or her brilliant fielding efforts.

You can scale the game up or down by assigning different amounts to various fielding actions. You can also invent categories of your own, such as a double bounce. Or you might wish to substitute points instead of money. Whatever—the idea is to keep everybody's eyes on the ball.

Safety Reminder

Adult Supervision

Required:
- Baseball
- Bat
- Mitts

Floaters and Sinkers

Safety Reminder

Adult Supervision

Required:

- Bucket
- Yard materials
- Plastic toys
- Misc. objects

A rock will sink in water, but a clothes-pin will float. Why?

It all has to do with weight and density. Which is what this activity is all about.

Fill a bucket or wading pool with water and then let the experiment begin. Have your children gather up a number of items that can be safely immersed, and then guess which objects will float or sink when dropped one at a time into the water. Once they have tested a number of items, they can discuss the similarities and differences.

Later they can hold contests, guessing what an object will do. The winner gets to pick the next object to drop into the water. Among items children could test are: toy cars, plastic dolls, rocks, toothpicks, sticks, plastic yogurt lids, leaves, dandelions, acorns, and wooden blocks.

What would your favorite toy boat do in a sink-or-swim situation?

Flower Anatomy

Flowers aren't just for our benefit—they perform an important job for the plant that grows it. When pollen from one flower reaches another of the same species, the plant can produce seeds.

As different as flowers look on the outside, they generally all have the same functioning parts (see illustration). Your child will enjoy learning about them:

a) petal—attracts insects.
b) sepal—green petals that enclose and protect the bud.
c) pistil—female part of the flower, consisting of three parts: the stigma, or sticky top part that traps pollen from other plants; the style, or stalk that holds the stigma; and the ovary, which contains the eggs that will develop into seeds once fertilized.
d) stamen—the male part of the flower, composed of the anther, which produces pollen, and the filament, which holds up the anther. Some plants have separate male female flowers.

A magnifying glass will be helpful in examining the flower parts and introducing your child to the intricacies of the plant world. Set up your picnic table as an outdoor lab, and your child might embark at an early age on a distinguished career in botany.

Required:
• Your time only

Optional:
• Magnifying glass

Flutter Ball

Here's a great way to make a ball do wacky and unpredictable things.

Take a small foam ball and tape a quarter onto one side of it. Have your children play catch and watch as the added weight makes the ball turn in a bizarre fashion. Encourage them to toss the ball high into the air, since the funniest movements occur as the ball descends.

For a variation, tape a different-size coin to the ball. Try a penny. A nickel. Two coins. See if the heavier coins make the ball behave differently than it did with the lighter ones. If you get a really wacky ball, use it to play volleyball or "tennis"—it will truly challenge the players.

Another variation is to use a different kind of ball. Ping-Pong balls, because they're so light, are very much affected by the added weight—try throwing the weighted Ping-Pong ball in the air to see how it flutters.

When you're done experimenting, take the most unpredictable ball and sponsor a Whacky World Series.

Required:
- Foam ball
- Coins
- Tape

Optional:
- Ping-Pong ball

Flying Rings

What flies like a banshee but is easy to catch? Answer: Flying Rings!

You can purchase a flying ring at a toy store, or spend nothing by making one from a piece of corrugated cardboard. Find a round object approximately twelve inches in diameter, like a plate. Trace it onto a piece of heavy corrugated cardboard, then cut it out (your job). Now find another object about an inch and a half to two inches smaller. Place it in the center of the twelve-inch cardboard disk, then trace it. Cut out that disk, too, leaving a ring.

Now fling the ring with a little wrist action, and it should fly across your yard. You can play catch with your kids or use it for target practice—see who can get it to land on a branch or inside a box.

Oh, sure, the cardboard flying ring won't be as durable as a store-bought version, nor will it glow in the dark. But at that price you can afford to keep making new ones when they break. Besides, when it gets dark, your kids should be in bed!

Required:
- Piece of cardboard
- Round objects to trace
- Scissors

Follow the Leader

OK, everybody line up and do whatever your fearless leader at the head of the line does. Here are some leadership ideas for the TV-free nineties.

Required:
• Your time only

Mild days: hopping, skipping, "tightrope walking" on a piece of string placed on the ground; somersaults and other acrobatics; animal impersonations (kangaroo jump, frog calls, etc.).

Rainy Days: singing in the rain; using arms as windshield wipers: umbrella twirling; puddle splashing; puddle hopping/straddling.

Hot weather: walking a figure eight around a sprinkler; sitting down in a wading pool; pouring sprinkling can of water on head.

Autumn: kicking up a pile of leaves (don't worry—#163 shows you how to turn leaf raking into a fun activity); balancing a leaf on your shoulder; sliding in leaf piles, playing leaf jack-in-the-box.

Winter: hopping through the snow and making footprints; kicking up a snow bank; juggling two snowballs; rolling a giant snowball.

On the beach: making footprints in sand; burying feet in sand; juggling shells; flinging a seaweed bouquet.

The leader takes a time-out for a treat. Is there anybody in line who doesn't want to follow this one?

Food Daring

Remember the old-fashioned country pie-eating contest? This activity duplicates the fun right in your own backyard. You can do it anytime, but it's also well-suited for parties or whenever a small group of kids gets together.

Safety Reminder

Adult Supervision

You'll need a table and some food treats, such as donuts. Line up the donuts on the table, with each child standing in front of a donut, hands behind his or her back. When you say "go," the children try eating the donut—with no hands!

Required:
- Table
- Donuts, cookies, whole fruit, or other food treats

For silly fun, try using powdered, jelly, or cream-filled donuts, cookies, or cupcakes. In fact, just about any food will do—the messier the better! For a more nutritious alternative try: pieces of peeled, seedless fruit; whole ripe fruit such as nectarines, pears, or bananas; whole-wheat muffins; or sugarless cookies.

For a small group of kids, try lining up a row of small treats, such as halved-grapes, the length of each side of the table. Watch what happens as they eat their way around! (Caution—only use foods that do not present choking hazards!)

Finally, if your kids get too good at this activity, have them try it with their eyes closed—this is not only a true test of skill, but it's hilarious to watch. As long as you don't come too close.

Foot Measures

How long is your backyard? Your car? Your front walk? When you finish this activity, your child will give you a pretty close estimate.

First measure your child's normal stride (the distance between two right steps). Using a yardstick or ruler, take the measurement several times and average the results. You might also want to measure your stride as an accuracy check.

Required:

- Ruler, tape measure, or yardstick
- Paper and pencil

Now get down to the act of taking measurements. Try measuring things around your house or apartment—driveways, walkways, front walks, etc. If your child's stride doesn't fall exactly on the nearest foot, keep the measurement in inches, multiply by the number of strides, then divide by twelve—a good exercise for youngsters learning multiplication and division.

You and your walking yardstick might also measure cars parked on the street, the length between telephone poles, or the number of feet to the bus stop or nearest store.

In addition to satisfying everyone's curiosity about such matters as the length of the front porch, you can play a game in which everyone guesses the distance between various points before the measuring begins.

Remember, in this game everybody has to give an inch!

Footprint Scramble

Here's an activity that's sure to challenge and delight kids of all ages. And unless you have a back problem, you'll probably get a few chuckles yourself.

First you'll need to make a "playing field." In a garden area that hasn't been planted yet, or on the beach, smooth an area ten feet by ten feet and then make a variety of footprints oriented in all directions. You can also do the same with a fresh snowfall. On a driveway or pavement, draw footprints with a piece of chalk.

The players assemble on the field, placing one foot in one of the "footprint" holes or chalk circles. Each player then takes turns telling the player to his or her right which footprints to step in or put some body part in next, without getting out of the current set of footprints (players may pivot on their hands and feet). This is great for plenty of laughs and is also a good way to find out who can do the splits, who can squeeze between another's legs, who can do the fourth ballet position . . . and who has two left feet.

Required:
• Your time only

Optional:
• Chalk

Fossil Fun

Who has the time or money to go on a paleological dig? Well, you can save on both by making fossils right in your backyard.

If your soil has a low clay content, mix in one part flour for every four parts of soil. Add enough water to make a bread-dough-like texture, then smooth the mixture into a tin or pan. Now you're ready to make fossil imprints with toy dinosaurs or animals. You can also make impressions with sticks, stones, shells, leaves, and interesting yard objects. Cut the "fossils" into irregular shapes and let them air dry.

Your child can also create bone impressions of ancient creatures by pressing twigs into the mud mixture to make a skeleton, then removing them before the mud dries (or how about popsiclestick-osaurus?)

Finally, try making "prehistoric" footprints. Have your child step or press his or her hand lightly into the mud pan. Then, use a twig or stones to embellish the hand or footprint—add claws, talons, or an extra digit or two. When the mixture dries, you'll have evidence of the most outlandish creature that ever walked the planet!

Required:

- Soil
- Water
- Flour (for low-clay-content soil)
- Baking tin or pan
- Toy animals
- Sticks, twigs, small rocks

Optional:

- Popsicle sticks

Four-Leaf Clover Hunt

Since ancient times, clovers have been held in high esteem. For the Druids they were sacred plants. The Greeks used them as garlands and for ritual decoration. And of course, there's the old Irish shamrock, derived from the clover and considered to be a sign of good luck.

Required:
- Wax paper
- Colored paper or card stock

Just how much good luck will a four-leaf clover bring? Find out with your child. They're hard to find, but the good news is that once you find a four-leaf clover, you're apt to find more in the same place later on. (A neighbor of ours made the mistake of rewarding an energetic neighborhood child $5.00 for each four-leaf clover he could find—in his *own* yard; over time, the child could count on a handsome regular income!)

Once you or your child finds a four-leaf clover, try extending his or her luck by making a good-luck charm. Press the clover between pieces of wax paper and place in a heavy book. Once the plant is dried out, paste it to a piece of colored paper or cardstock. Cover the paper with wax paper to protect the clover, and good fortune will be just around the corner. Well, maybe . . . .

Four Seasons Cafe

Children love to pretend that they're serving up delicacies to their parents and older brothers and sisters. With the Four Seasons Cafe, your kids can serve up a storm regardless of the weather. Provide pots and pans or plastic plates, and you're in for a treat that your mental palate will never forget!

Required:
- Yard materials
- Pots and pans
- Plastic plates

Spring. Imagine main courses such as sumptuous buds and freshly sprouted grass, rolled in dirt and garnished with leftover autumn leaves.

Summer. Here we have a selection of mud pie hors d'oeuvres and entrees. Menu also features cold green leaf vichyssoise with fresh twigs and grass clippings. Mud pie pate available at slight extra charge.

Fall. Definitely the time for a multicolored leaf souffle. Arrange the leaves in a recycled aluminum pie tin, alternating with fresh mud. Garnish with brown grass and twigs. A winner on a crisp fall day.

Winter. This is the season for a full-course meal. Start off with slush soup, followed by a snow loaf. Serve with icicle spears. And for dessert? Why ice cream, of course!

Mmmm...

Four Square

Here's an old-fashioned game that's still a lot of fun for big and small kids alike.

The game requires a flat, hard surface and a large rubber ball or basketball. The first thing to do is draw a twelve-by-twelve-foot square with a piece of chalk. Inside, draw four equal-sized squares labelled "A," "B," "C," and "D" as shown in the illustration.

Players stand in each of the squares (four total). The player in square "A" serves, bouncing the ball first into his or her own square, then batting it with an open hand into any of the other three squares. The receiving player must then bat the ball with an open hand into one of the squares other than his or her own. The idea is to keep bouncing the ball until one player misses or the ball is hit but does not land completely in a square.

When a player misses or does not make a good shot, he or she moves to square "D," and the players in the squares following him or her advance one square towards "A." (The nice thing about this arrangement is that no one is ever a loser.)

Keep your eye on the bouncing ball!

Required:
- Rubber ball
- Chalk

Optional:
- Basketball

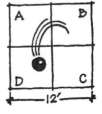

Frisbee Games

Your children can use a Frisbee for much more than just playing catch.

But in fact, even playing catch with a Frisbee can be fun with a little imagination. Instead of just the routine toss, have the players invent new ways to catch, such as on one finger, behind the back, between the legs, bounced off the top of a toe and then caught, or with their arms bent over their heads.

Required:
• Frisbee

Optional:
• Box

Another way to play is to do target throws. Set up boxes, pick out trees, or, an old favorite, throw it to a running dog. Still another variation, good for a group of kids, is to play a game similar to touch football in which the "quarterback" throws the Frisbee to a running teammate who is guarded by an opponent. If the teammate catches it, the play resumes with a new line of scrimmage at the point of the catch. If the opponent catches it, it is an interception and the other team gets the "ball" at that spot. There is no running allowed after the catch. Score this game with seven points for a touchdown.

Heads up!

Garage Ball

This is played exactly like volleyball, except you have to hit the ball onto a garage wall or slanted roof (for that matter, any high wall will do).

You can play it with two, four, or six players. All you need is a wall (without windows) and a volleyball or any other large rubber ball. Split into teams and then have everyone line up alongside the wall. One team serves against the wall, and the other must bat the ball back to the wall without catching or dropping it.

The back-and-forth volleying continues until one team misses. If the serving team drops the ball, it loses the serve. If the receiving team misses, the serving team gets a point. Play to see which team gets to fifteen points first, then start again.

For variety, change teams, up the number of points that need to be earned to win, or change walls.

In a neighborhood with a large group of kids, you could create a garage ball league. Declare an official garage ball season, and sponsor a playoff. Perhaps even a world series.

Required:

• Volleyball or rubber ball.

Garden Hose Phone

Here's a variation on the old tin can telephone system. Instead of using a piece of string and tin cans (or yogurt containers) for "transmitters" and "receivers," simply insert a funnel at each end of the hose and let your kids carry on a conversation. One person speaks while the other uses the funnel as an earpiece. For best results, the hose should be taut and the funnels snugly in place.

Your kids will enjoy pretending that they're carrying on long-distance conversations with each other. You, too, can pretend that you're reaching out and touching someone you haven't seen in years: "Yes, son, it's *so* good to hear your voice. Have you grown much? Is your hair still blond? Do you still like cookies? Well, we're having some after dinner, so why don't you head back cross-country for a home-cooked meal . . . ."

We found that our hose phone works so well that we're donating a model system to the major telecommunication companies in the hopes that they'll study it. Perhaps we'll all have better phone service in the near future.

Required:

- Hose
- Two clean funnels that will fit snugly in hose ends

Gas Savers

M ost of us only think about checking the air in our tires when the car looks to be riding low. Well, there's good reason to be more conscientious—under-inflated tires can reduce your mileage by 5 percent!

Safety Reminder

Adult Supervision

Required:
• Tire gauge

Your child can assist by prompting you to check your tire pressure regularly. If you don't have a tire gauge, this is a good excuse to get one (they only cost a few dollars; a bit more for a meter type).

Always check pressure when the tires are cold. Show your child how to remove the valve cap, fit the gauge over the valve, and press (not to be done without your supervision). If your child has counting skills, let him or her read off the number (go by the line closest to the edge for "stick"-type tire gauges, or read off the number with dial-type gauges). Now compare the tire inflation with the recommended pressure—check your manual—and head down to the service station if necessary.

With a little reminder from your kids you might save gas and some wear and tear on your tires, and do the planet a favor, too.

Gem Museum

When you were growing up, did you ever discover diamonds, emeralds, or other precious gems in your backyard? We did, and reveled in the idea of having such "valuable" resources right in our backyard.

Encourage your child to explore the rocks and minerals in your neighborhood. (If you aren't familiar with the geology of your area, you might want to go to the library first and find a rock and mineral identification book.)

You might take a field trip and collect samples in a canvas bag. Older kids can describe their findings in a notebook—shape, size, color, and location ("in front of Mr. Smith's house"). Once you've brought the rocks back to your house, have your child wash them. The water will make the colors vivid—something sure to excite your junior geologist.

In addition to cataloging neighborhood rocks, your child might enjoy displaying his or her finds in a shoe box. Assemble enough shoe boxes and your child can open the neighborhood gem museum. Who knows—it just might fund his or her college education.

Required:
- Minimal or no props

Optional:
- Shoe boxes
- Rock and mineral identification book

Geological Sculpture

Whether or not you're an aficionado of southwestern art, this activity is sure to generate something your child will be proud to display on your living room mantle or in the family art gallery.

First, round up a clear plastic container with a lid. Then head for the backyard, the park, the woods or whatever, and have your child collect handfuls of soil, pebbles, and other plentiful items and place them layer by layer in the jar.

Required:
- Plastic jar
- Yard materials

For example, the jar might contain: a layer of black topsoil, a layer of tan sand, a layer of pebbles, a layer of reddish clay, a layer of hemlock needles, a layer of pine needles, and so on. The result will look like a geological exhibit showing different layers of the earth.

On the beach, your child can create an interesting variation by laying different kinds of sand, shells, small rocks, beach glass, and small pieces of driftwood. As long as the layers are distinctive, the jar will have a striking appearance when your child is finished.

And if your child gets bored with the sculpture piece? Just empty the contents and start again.

Geometry Walk

This activity, invented by our friend Gail and her daughter Anna, involves looking for different shapes in the world about your child. It's also great when you're walking someplace and your child gets bored.

Required:
• Your time only

To play, ask your child to identify all of the circles, rectangles, squares, and triangles in the immediate environment. Look at tree leaves and shrubs, utility covers in the sidewalk and street, and fences. Be sure to observe signs in windows and on buildings, trucks, buses, and cars. (Just standing on a street corner and looking for shapes on moving signs can make for a fascinating time.)

Road signs are a natural source of geometrical shapes, as are cars (look at the tires, hub-cap designs, windows, fenders, hood ornaments, manufacturer insignias, etc). Bicycles are rich sources of common shapes. So are people—look at T-shirt designs, pockets, purses, briefcases, knapsacks, etc.

Finally, look up at the sky; telephone, power, and trolley lines might intersect and create regular geometrical shapes.

For variety, look for shapes of a specific color—that'll keep your child's eyes open for the return trip.

Giant Writing

Wouldn't it be neat if beings from another planet just happened to be passing by the beach and saw your child's message? (In Kurt Vonnegut's *Sirens of Titan*, the Great Wall of China was merely an interplanetary road sign).

The trick with giant writing is first to rough out the message in smaller letters so everyone understands the game plan. If only one child is playing, he or she can write the entire message; for a group of kids, assign each one a letter or word. Sand scribes can use shovels, buckets, or their feet to shape letters.

But what about the message itself? Consider these: "Greetings and salutations from Earth." "Be sure to visit the Grand Canyon." "No spaceship parking before 8:00 p.m." or "Beam me up, Scotty." For fancier sand writing, use seaweed to dot "i's" and cross "t's," or to underline key letters or words.

A variation on this activity is for you to write a giant message in the sand and see if your children can decipher it—from Earth. Or whatever planet they happen to be on.

Required:
- Your time only

Option:
- Buckets, shovels, etc.

Going Places

I n this urban observation game, a street corner or a park bench on a well-trafficked road is all you need.

The idea is to assign different points to different kinds of vehicles, then have the players find examples and reach a hundred (or some other agreed-upon number within their counting range).

Required:
• Your time only

Optional:
• Pad and pencil

For instance, you could make a fire engine worth fifteen points, a bus worth ten, a tow truck worth five, a taxi worth three, and a bicycle worth one. Before assigning values, think of the many different kinds of vehicles to which you could assign values—construction vehicles (cranes, dump trucks, backhoes, etc); police cars, motorcycles, taxis, vans, convertibles, delivery and courier trucks, etc.

The first person to spot an assigned vehicle calls it out and receives the designated points. If two or more people call out the vehicle simultaneously, they split the points (each would be guaranteed at least one point per call-out).

You might have to decide on the spot how much an undesignated vehicle is worth. Like that pogo stick making its way down Main Street.

50 POINTS

Going-to-Canton Football Game

The National Football League Hall of Fame is in Canton, Ohio.

In this game your children show why they are headed for Canton with some of the most spectacular plays they or you could ever imagine. All you need is a football and a flat field of soft grass.

Starting with a kickoff, the children all play on the same team against an invisible opponent who always seems to be playing defense. As you can see, this is a pretend game. But the children take it most seriously, because they're the stars of the day making spectacular runs, catches, and throws. (Suggestion: A videotape of your children playing like superstars would make a great momento.)

The kids make up plays, with the quarterback pretending to barely avoid a sack while running backs or wide receivers run patterns or block. Sometimes the players should just wing it and see where their feet will take them. Other times they'll have specific assignments for such "famous" strategies as The statue-of-liberty double-reverse end-around flea-flicker bomb-followed-by-a-lateral-play.

Hope to see your kid in Canton.

Required:
- Football
- Flat field of soft grass

Gold Glove

This game lends itself very well to record breaking—and it's great material for a family score book that notes each family member's sporting achievements.

Two players line up about thirty feet away from each other, then play catch with a baseball. One or both players count each catch. When the ball is dropped, the pair starts counting again, this time back at one. The game can also be played with a football, frisbee, or badminton racquets and a birdie (count the hits).

In one variation, played with a football, a player (the receiver) runs while the other (the quarterback) attempts to fire off a pass that the receiver can complete. This works especially well if the receiver runs a pattern. Your child can count how many touchdown passes/receptions they get in a row.

Have a ball!

Required:
- Baseball
- Two gloves

Optional:
- Football
- Frisbee
- Badminton racquets and birdie

Golf Ball Billiards

This is a variation of an old marble game.

Draw a circle about three feet in diameter in the dirt, or draw one with chalk on the sidewalk or driveway. Put nine white golf balls (or other small balls) inside the circle. Each player gets a colored golf ball (you can mark white golf balls if colored ones aren't available) and a "pool stick." Players can use a stick from a tree, a chopstick, a wrapping-paper tube, etc. Use any of these implements like a real pool stick, sliding it along one stationary hand and then pushing the colored ball with the end of the stick.

The object is to knock one or more white golf balls out of the circle. If the player succeeds, he or she gets another shot, always starting with the colored ball outside the circle. The player continues shooting until he or she fails to knock a white ball out of the circle, at which point it becomes the next player's turn. Whoever gets five balls first wins.

A variation would be to alternate shots whether or not they are successful. This would be for more skilled players. Another game for skilled players would be to see how many shots (or full "tables" of nine balls, for those who are really good) they could get in a row. *Rack 'em up!*

Required:

- Golf balls or other small balls
- Wrapping-paper tube, chopstick, or short tree branch

Gone Fishin'

E ven if you live in an apartment building far from a stream or lake, your
children can have a great time "fishing"
in their very own backyard.

You'll need a few sheets of paper, a
pencil, some Styrofoam packing material, a bucket or wading pool, a strainer,
and a yardstick or wooden dowel.

First, have your child draw fish
shapes on the paper (make sure they're
no longer than the diameter of your
strainer). Then cut the fish out (safety
scissors for kids). Next, have your kids
trace the fish onto a sheet of Styrofoam.
Finally, cut out the Styrofoam fish (your
job). You can also have your kids decorate the fish with markers, but you'll
have to use waterproof ink—take appropriate precautions.

To make a "fishing pole," attach the
handle of the strainer to the yardstick or
dowel with masking tape.

Fill the bucket or wading pool with
water and let the fish loose in their native
habitat. Issue some fishing permits (supervise closely around wading pools),
and your kids are ready for a day at the
fishing hole.

Prepare yourself for some stories
about the ones that got away.

Required:

- Pencil and paper
- Strainer
- Styrofoam
- Yardstick or dowel
- Masking tape
- Bucket or
  wading pool

Optional:

- Waterproof
  markers
- Scissors

Grass Words and Pictures

Would your child like to make "living" alphabet letters? If so, this activity will fit the bill.

You'll need a small patch of garden or flower bed space. Or, if you live in an apartment, some aluminum pie pans will do—just punch holes in the bottom for drainage, then fill them with potting soil.

Have your child write something or draw pictures using a twig, popsicle stick, or utensil (a finger works well, too). Pre-readers might want to write individual letters or draw shapes. Older kids might want to write their names or draw simple scenes. Your child should make indentations about half an inch deep.

When the words or pictures are complete, give your child grass seed and demonstrate how to place the seeds an eighth of an inch or so apart. Fill up all the indentations, cover with a fine layer of top soil, water, and in ten days your child should begin to see grass words and pictures.

Try this one: "Please Keep off the Grass."

Required:
- Garden or flower bed space, or aluminum pie pans
- Grass seed
- Twig, popsicle stick, or plastic utensil

Grow a Butterfly

There's something magical about the transformation of a caterpillar into a butterfly.

This summer, when caterpillars are traipsing about, make a trip to an open field where milkweed grows. Milkweed, the sole food of the monarch butterfly caterpillar, is a plant about three feet high. It has a stiff vertical stem, large paired five-inch leaves that produce a milky substance when broken off the stem—hence the name—and four-inch-long bumpy green pods that split open in the fall to reveal hundreds of seeds, each with its own silken parachute.

Collect milkweed plants with Monarch caterpillars on them, then gather several extra plants and take them home (the caterpillars have black stripes on them). Put the stems of the plants into a container of water as if they were a bouquet, to keep them alive. The caterpillars will munch on the leaves and will be happy to stay there—no need for a cage (although you may need to provide fresh leaves, and a stick to hang out on).

Toward the end of August, each caterpillar will form a chrysalis. About two weeks later, a monarch butterfly will emerge—watch it as it breaks free of its cocoon and a day or two later takes to the sky. What could be more magical?

Required:

- Milkweed
- Monarch caterpillars
- Container of water

Guess the Footprint

This activity will challenge your child's imagination and stimulate your creativity, too. You can play it on the beach, in a garden plot that hasn't been planted yet, or on a driveway, sidewalk, or lawn or on a driveway, sidewalk, or lawn after a snowfall.

The idea is to create footprints of various animals, real and imaginary, and see whether your child can guess them. Use a stick or spoon to dig the footprints. For starters, try making the ones shown below: a—deer; b—sea gull; c—raccoon; d—gray fox; e—black bear. Or make up some of your own, using beach or gardening tools—do you know the footprint of the wild beach bucket bearcat?

Required:

• Trowel or spoon

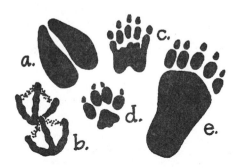

Harvest Moon Watch

Ever see a moon that's so big it seems like you can reach out and touch it? That's the harvest moon (actually the September full moon), so named because it sheds enough light for the farmers to harvest their crops at night. (What's actually happening is that instead of moving quickly to its high point in the sky, the September full moon travels along a much more graceful angle as it rises. It's therefore closer to your reference points on earth, and appears to be much bigger.)

Just as the farmers prepared for the harvest moon, you and your children can prepare your own harvest moon rituals. Think about hosting a Harvest Moon pageant—your kids can pretend they're harvesting the fields; a Harvest Moon picnic or snack—enjoy an evening of burgers, chips, dessert, and (legal) moonshine; or a Harvest Moon sports night—catch, frisbee, or any other sport. After what might be a later-than-usual evening, you're sure to reap an additional benefit—an easy bedtime ritual.

Required:
• Your time only

Optional:
• Picnic fixings
• Sports gear

Heike Hike

We thank our baby-sitter friend, Heike, for suggesting this activity—it's a winner on long walks with the kids.

The idea of a Heike Hike is to use whatever you encounter as an opportunity for gymnastics. For instance, let's say you take a walk in the park. First you encounter a low wall. Have your kids walk along the top (no high-wire acts, please). Then you come up a set of steps—have the kids hop down. Now perhaps you meet some trees. The kids can run around individual trunks, or race between two or three trees.

After the kids have rested a moment, you continue along the sidewalk and notice some cracks. See who can walk along or jump over the cracks, or take the fewest number of steps between two points. Finally you come upon a manhole cover—have each child do a broad jump over the cover, then head for home.

This should not only make for a fun walk, it might also tire 'em out for the rest of the afternoon. Thanks, Heike!

Safety Reminder

Adult Supervision

Required:
• Your time only

Herb and Fruit Vinegars

Required:

- Freshly harvested herbs and berries
- White wine vinegar
- Sugar (for berry vinegars only)
- Plastic containers

Here's a good reason for growing herbs and berries in your garden—you and your child can make vinegars to use in your own kitchen or as gifts.

For homemade herb vinegars, basil, tarragon, rosemary, and thyme all work well. All are also easy to grow in a garden; purchase seeds or starter plants at your nursery and let your child help with the planting. Garlic can also be used and is easy to grow.

In the fruit department, raspberries, blackberries, and strawberries make for tasty vinaigrettes. They're also fun to grow.

Once you and your child have harvested the herbs or fruits, head for the kitchen. Mix the herbs with four cups of white wine vinegar. For the berries, mix a quarter of a cup of sugar with the vinegar and heat until the sugar dissolves (your job). Pour the heated vinegar over the berries (also your job) and mash the berries slightly.

Place the herb and the berry mixtures in plastic containers and allow them to sit for three weeks in the dark. Filter the vinegar when you're done and add a few fresh berries or herbs. The final product is ready for use or for bottling as a gift.

Hidden Faces

We've all heard about the man in the moon. How about the bear in the bark? Or the cat in the clouds?

We're talking about finding hidden faces in everyday objects. Here are some suggestions for discovering faces during walks in your backyard, park, neighborhood, or city. Don't just look for human faces—think of animals, fish, dinosaurs, etc.

Required:
• Your time only

Backyard or park. Examine tree bark, mounds of dirt, arrangements of rocks, flowers, patterns of grass or leaves, etc.

Residential Neighborhoods. Look for faces in houses. You'll find them made up of windows, doors, architectural features, surrounding shrubs, trees, etc.

Urban Areas. Look at doorways, rooftops, windows, patterns in brick or granite, etc.

Our son Noah once reported seeing a grinning gorilla on the face of a building. Now that's imagination.

Hide & Sleuth

Safety Reminder
Adult Supervision

Required:
• Yard materials

This variation of Hide & Seek challenges your children to use their imaginations as well as their detective skills.

It starts the same as always—the seeker closes his or her eyes and counts. The hiders do more than hide, though—they leave clues. A clue can be anything from a chalk-drawn arrow on the driveway or twig arrow on the grass to the hider's name spelled out with small branches (make sure the seeker gives the hiders plenty of time to construct their clues).

Hiders can invent their own trademark or insignia (such as a leaf or twig arrangement, a dandelion, three pebbles, etc), and then use it as a clue to their hiding place. For a more complex game, encourage hiders to use multiple or linked clues (like an arrow pointing to yet another clue).

When the seeker has found all the hiders, assign a new seeker and begin again. (Note: this activity requires parental supervision to be sure children are not led by clues near roads or any dangerous situations).

For a variation, seekers can use oral clues—tweet like a bird, bark like a dog, or, as our son is fond of yelling, "I'm not here!"

High Fly

This baseball game for two people is a perfect way to work on outfielding skills while having fun.

Use four large markers (sticks, rags, etc.) to indicate the boundaries of the fielder's square. Recommended boundaries are thirty feet wide by fifty feet long. Use a fifth marker to indicate the throwing line. Finally, pick out a minimum height that the ball must be thrown (a telephone wire is the ideal height, but no aiming at the wire).

The player "at bat" throws the ball. The ball must go up to the specified height—and then come down within the well-marked fielder's square. If the fielder catches the ball, the "batter" is out. If the batter throws the ball out of the fielder's box, he or she is out. If the ball lands in the fielder's box, the batter scores a run. If the fielder touches the ball but does not catch it, a run is also scored. What happens after three outs? The batter and fielder switch positions.

Play nine, seven, or five innings—then take a lemonade break.

Safety Reminder

Adult Supervision

Required:

- Five boundary markers (sticks, rags, etc.)
- An open yard or park
- A visible tree branch or telephone wire
- Baseball
- Baseball glove

GOT IT!

Hobby Horse

Required:

- Paper bag
- Wrapping paper tube
- Newspapers
- Crayons or markers
- String or tape

Optional:

- Construction paper or felt
- Yarn or cornsilk
- Scissors

Here's a handy idea for putting those wrapping-paper tubes to good use—homemade hobby horses, which are great for backyard races and the like.

The wrapping paper tube makes a perfect body. You can easily convert a paper bag into the head. Draw the eyes, ears, mouth, and nose on the bag with crayons or markers. For a fancier horse, you can make those features on construction paper or felt and then glue them onto the bag. You can attach yarn or cornsilk to the back of the head for a mane. When you're done with your drawing, stuff the bag with newspapers.

Once the head is finished, insert the cardboard tube into the bag opening and tape it or tie it shut with a piece of string. Tie a loop of string or colorful yarn around the tube for the reins. Your child can then mount the steed and be off to the races—around the backyard, around piles of leaves, or even over small twig hurdles.

As a great hobby horse hero once proclaimed, High Ho Brown Bag!

Holiday Wreath

Here's how to make a nature wreath that will be a fine Christmas addition to your house or apartment.

First, take a nature walk and gather natural ornaments such as pine cones, gum balls, sycamore balls, hemlock cones, spruce cones, douglas fir cones, acorns, and interesting-looking seeds. Have your child put them in his or her "collection bag" (a paper or cloth bag that you've elevated to special status for the purpose of this walk).

When you finish the walk and return home, cut out a piece of corrugated cardboard and make a ring about two inches wide and fifteen inches in diameter. It's easiest if you can trace objects that will yield a ring with those dimensions. If not, do the best you can freehand—the cardboard will be covered up. (You can also use the method described in #130 to make a hoola hoop.)

Wrap fine wire around each cone or seed (careful of sharp points), then punch two small holes in the cardboard where each object is to be attached (your job). Feed the wires through and tie knots—the objects will stay snugly in place.

Hang the wreath in front of a regular fir wreath, or use it as a "stand-alone" on your door or wall. Everyone is sure to comment on its splendor.

Safety Reminder

Adult Supervision

Required:

- Yard materials
- Sheet of corrugated cardboard
- Fine wire

Hoola Hoop

Remember the hoola hoops of the 1950s? They're experiencing a great revival in the 1990s.

You can make a perfectly functional hoola hoop from a large sheet of cardboard. Take a piece of string and measure off eighteen inches. Place a pin or tack in the center of the cardboard (watch out for young children), tie a string to the pin, then tie the other end of the string to a pen. Stretch the string and draw, and you'll have a circle about 36 inches across. Now re-tie the string so it's an inch-and-a-half shorter and draw another circle. Cut on both lines (your job), and you'll have a hoola hoop one and a half inches wide.

If you can, show your child how to use a hoola hoop—otherwise, just explain the basic idea. Don't feel bad, we couldn't do it very well either! Once your child gets the hang of it, there are lots of games to be played. For example, how long can the hoop be sustained in motion? Can your child wave his or her arms while doing the hoola? In a group setting, the kids can compare hoola dancing styles or pass the hoop from person to person.

Sound silly? Well get with the times!

Required:

- Large sheet of cardboard
- String
- Pin
- Pen
- Scissors

Horse

No, this has nothing to do with animals. It's actually a delightful variation on an old basketball game.

One player takes the ball and makes a weird shot—say backwards or sideways. If he or she succeeds, other players then try to duplicate the shot. Failure to make the shot earns a player an "H."

When everyone's tried his or her hand at the shot, the first player does another crazy shot, and the others try to make it. If anyone doesn't make the shot on the second round, that person earns an "O." This continues until someone racks up all the letters to spell "HORSE," at which point he or she is out of the game.

You can either play until all but one player and the "originator" are left, at which point the remaining player becomes the "originator," or you might have the game structured so that as soon as one person is out, the game starts again.

Of course, you can use any word you want. And for an extended game, how about "hippopotomonstrosesquipedalian"?

Required:
• Basketball and court

Hot Potato

This game, which goes back many years, can be played with a small group of kids (best with at least four or five) and a variety of common objects.

It's very similar to musical chairs. Everyone sits in a circle except for the "caller." The caller closes his or her eyes, and the rest of the players pass around the "potato." (Traditionally the game is played with an actual potato. You can use a soft rubber ball, a damp sponge, or a homemade beanbag. To make a bean-bag, pour half a cup of dried beans into a plastic bag, squeeze out most of the air, tie the bag with a twistem, place it into an old sock, then tie off the sock with a knot or another twistem.)

When the caller calls "Stop!" whoever has the "potato" leaves the circle—which is why the players toss the "potato" along as fast as they can (it's also why you want to use a soft "potato" that won't hurt anyone if things get wild). The game is over when only one person is left. The sole remaining player becomes the caller in the next game.

OK, let the tossing begin!

Required:
- Soft rubber ball or
- Sponge or
- Bean bag (beans, plastic sandwich bag, 2 twistems, sock)

STOP!

Hot-Weather Fans

They're cheaper than air conditioners, quieter, and are lots more fun. We're talking about summer fans that you and your child can make from paper or leaves.

To make a paper fan, first have your child decorate both sides of a piece of paper with crayons, markers, or tempera paint. Then, fold the paper accordion style, about a half inch at a time. Fasten one end with a paper clip or staple, then unfold the fan. You're ready for cooling action. (You might want to staple on a cardboard handle for more effective wrist action.)

An altogether different approach is to use leaves (preferably ones already on the ground). Children will have fun fanning themselves, each other, or you with a branch that still has some leaves on it.

Finally, if the kids get bored sitting around fanning themselves, suggest a contest to see who can develop zany fanning styles. Ever heard of the chicken strut fanning technique? How about the kangaroo heat buster? In any case, you can always count on the old elephant ear flapper to keep 'em laughing and cool every time.

Required:

- Paper
- Markers, crayons or tempera paint

Optional:

- Stiff cardboard
- Stapler
- Paper clip

House Painting

Required:
- Clean paintbrushes
- Buckets

Optional:
- Clean rollers
- Stirring stick

A ll children are fascinated by the thought of painting a house, but you may not want to let yours loose quite yet with a bucket of semi-gloss stain. So why not let them practice for a few years?

Just fill a bucket with water, give your children clean brushes, and let them "paint" a part of your house. You can provide clean rollers as well. How about a clean stirring stick so the "paint" has the right consistency?

Point out that when water touches wood, brick, or siding it turns the material a darker color. They really can see "progress" as they move along. (This is also a good opportunity to explain how water evaporates—changes from liquid to "air" as it heats up—see activity #84.)

Don't stop with the body of the house, though. Children can paint the foundation, porches, driveway, sidewalk, trees, lawn—anything that won't mind water.

There is an ulterior motive to this, of course. Someday you may want these same children to work with real paint—and give you a hefty family discount on the job.

How Old Is It?

You can figure out the age of a tree by counting its annual rings (see activity #72). But did you know you can also date twigs just by looking at their bark?

Every tree branch ends in a "terminal bud," which contains the growth for the next season. Come spring, the leaves sprout from that bud and the twig lengthens. At the end of the growing season, the leaves fall and a new bud is formed to protect the tip of the growing branch through the winter. Wherever the terminal bud is formed, a band is left around the twig.

By looking at the distance between the bands, you can get an idea of how fast the twig grew and how many seasons it's been growing. The more bands, the more seasons; the longer the distance between bands, the more the twig has grown that year.

After you explain this concept to your child, compare the bands on twigs from various trees in your area. Try to find the twig with the most growing seasons, the twig with the greatest and least growth, and so on.

When it comes to dating twigs, the bands are hard to beat.

Required:
• Your time only

Hummingbird Feeder

Hummingbirds are amazing. The smallest of all birds—3½ inches long—they can fly at up to fifty miles per hour! They can even fly backward or hover in mid-air. Their wings beat so quickly that you can't even see them move.

All this action burns up a lot of calories, and you can help refuel the critters with a hummingbird feeder. Normally, hummingbirds dine on the nectar of certain flowers. But they'll appreciate a good shot of "hummingbird juice" from your very own feeder.

The feeder itself can be made from a small *clear* plastic container. Dissolve one part sugar to three parts hot water. Then add some beet juice—hummingbirds are attracted to the color red. Fill the container half full with the mixture. Wrap a string several times around the middle of the container and tie it securely. Hang the container from a tree branch and wait for your first customer.

If you have hummingbirds in your area, your child is in for a treat as these amazing creatures stop by for a drink.

Required:

- Clear plastic container
- Sugar
- Water
- Beet juice
- String
- Tree branch

Ice Brick Architecture

Here's an idea that will turn cold weather into great fun.

Safety Reminder

Adult Supervision

Collect clean cardboard milk and juice containers and fill them with water. Leave them outside overnight or long enough to freeze. When your children inspect the cartons, they'll have a ready-made set of ice bricks. All they have to do is to peel off the carton. (Make sure that your kids have gloves—you don't want anyone getting "freezer burns.") You might also want to slice off the tops (your job) and pour warm water on the sides—this will make it easier to slide out the ice bricks and reuse the forms.

Required:
- Empty milk and juice containers

Optional:
- Scissors

What can your Arctic architects do with the ice bricks? How about building small-scale castles or houses? Use snow as mortar; add a bit of water, and the ice bricks will stick together. Your kids can also use the bricks to make walls for a camp site. After a hike around the backyard or the North Pole, it's comforting to know that they can return to their safe camp.

How about some ice furniture? Make an ice chair. (Put some snow on the seat—it might be a little more comfortable.)

Finally, consider making ice brick signs for the front lawn—wouldn't your street address look nice in ice?

Ice Cube Sculpture

This is probably the safest and easiest kind of ice sculpture ever invented. Instead of chipping away at blocks of ice with chisels, you and your child build up geometrical forms.

All you really need for this activity is a collection of plastic containers (yogurt containers, cottage cheese containers, etc. filled with water—and temperatures below freezing. Choose a variety of container sizes and types, then set the containers outside. Once the water freezes, remove the ice cubes (or cones, pyramids, etc.).

You should have a good assortment of shapes. Try making various arrangements of the giant ice cubes, including stacking them, placing them side-by-side like a wall, or making geometrical shapes. One technique is to apply a thin film of water between the ice cubes while you stack them; when the film freezes, the ice cubes will remain stuck together.

You might also sponsor an ice-sculpture contest, seeing who can make the tallest sculpture or the sculpture with the most contiguous individual pieces. (Or the most decorative—contestants can add berries, leaves and twigs.)

And when the sun comes out? Watch the sculpture melt and change—that's real living art.

Required:

• Plastic containers

Icicle Art

Here's an activity that will allow you to create fancy crystal artwork with nothing but some water and a few containers.

The basic concept is to punch a very small hole near the bottom edge of a plastic container (definitely an adult job). Now wait for a day when the temperature drops below freezing (the colder the better). Fill up the container with water, and place it on a table, bench, wall, etc., so that the hole is unobstructed and the water can drip. As the water drips, it will build up into an icicle and hang down from the container bottom. (For safety, keep kids from playing directly underneath long stalagtites.)

You can also punch two holes toward the top of the sides, attach a string to each hole, then hang the container from a tree limb. In that case, you might want to punch multiple drip holes to make an icicle "field."

Regardless of how many holes you punch in the container, size is the key factor—if the holes are too small, the water won't drip fast enough; if too large, the water will run out before it freezes. Experiment.

Safety Reminder

Adult Supervision

Required:
- Plastic containers

Optional:
- String

Insect Home Hunt

Safety Reminder

Adult Supervision

Required:
• Your time only

Even if you live in an apartment building surrounded by acres of parking lots, you don't have to walk too far to find insect homes. Here are some homes to look for:

Ant hills. Ants often make homes in cracks within the pavement or concrete—you'll see small volcano-shaped piles of sand at the openings. (Put a small piece of candy or scoop of jam near the entrance if you want to see some real activity.)

Spider webs. Just look around the foundations of buildings, between fence posts, etc. See #293 for a description of web types.

Galls. Ever notice spherical bulges on plants? They're the plant's response to eggs laid by wasps and other insects stems, leaves, flowers, and even roots. When the mature insects are ready to exit, each one cuts a doorway in the gall. Look for these holes.

Cocoons and Gypsy Moth Webs. Look carefully for these fine temporary residences.

Watch your step—you just might be about to squash someone's porch!

Instant Sandbox

Even if you live miles from the beach, your children can still know the pleasure of playing in sand. Just make an instant sandbox, as described below.

You'll be pleased to know that you don't have to build an elaborate structure. You probably already have something that will work fine. A wading pool is perfect. A cardboard box fits the bill, too (line it with a plastic bag or drop cloth. Even an old dish pan can hold some sand, albeit a small amount (good if you're living in an apartment and have to carry it out to play). One purchase is required—sand. You can find play sand at many hardware and garden stores. It has an especially nice texture, and it's often sterilized.

Your kids will probably enjoy helping you fill the container with sand. Once the sandbox is ready for action, give your children buckets, cups, and small shovels. Plastic cars, trucks, and animals are always a hit.

If you leave the box out at night, keep it covered—you don't want to give neighborhood cats the wrong idea.

Required:

- Wading pool, box with plastic liner, or dish pan
- Play sand

Optional:

- Toys (cups, shovels, trucks, etc.)

Invent a Constellation

The ancients might have had a better view of the night sky, but your child is just as good at creating constellations. Pick a nice starry night and ask your child what he or she sees in the way of people, animals, common objects, etc. Make up stories about them as the ancients did. We've included some alternate constellations to get you and your child thinking about what can be found in the heavens above.

Required:
• Your time only

Meatball Minor
Pancake Major
Orion's Coffee Cup
Aunt Jane's Earlobe
The Great Giraffe Neck
The Donut Dazzler
King Kong's Tricycle
Heavenly Hot Dog
The Treehouse Trio
Celestial Spaghetti
Guys from Space

Sound silly? Remember, they actually did name one galaxy the Milky Way.

Invisible Dog

Invisible dogs are everywhere. Some are on the ground—regular invisible dogs. Some are in the air—invisible flying dogs. And some are in buckets of water or wading pools or even (for you coastal folks) in the ocean—invisible swimming dogs.

Your child can have any kind of invisible dog he or she wants, and any size or color, too. All your child has to do is "catch" one and put it on a leash. A piece of string tied to a cardboard handle will do. This accomplished, the idea is to walk around with the invisible dog, talk to it like a real dog, and try to teach it to speak (your child can bark for the dog in an attempt at ventriloquism), sit up, shake hands, roll over, and (this requires extra imagination) fetch. Of course, your child will want to teach the dog to be well-behaved around others.

For a variation, one child or parent can hold the leash while the others guess the dog's name and what trick the dog just performed.

And the best part is you can feed the dog invisible dog food—paid for with invisible money.

Required:
• Rope

Good Doggie

Ironkids

In the world of athletics, the Ironman contests are considered among the most difficult of all endeavors.

These contests combine three Herculean tasks: a 2½ mile swim, a marathon run, and a 100-mile bicycle ride. You don't have to go that berserk, but why not have an Ironkids contest with the children in the neighborhood? The idea is to combine three activities suited for kids—say, shooting baskets into a box, hopping across the driveway, and throwing a ball in the air and catching it. One child chooses the activites for each round.

Required:
- Two round balls
- Box

Optional:
- Softball
- Football
- Soccer ball

Among activities to choose from in an Ironkids contest are running races (down the driveway, around the block), crawling races (on soft grass), distance throwing of a softball or football, distance kicking of a soccer ball, and a running and a standing-still long jump.

When the race is over, the winner gets to choose the next set of Ironkids activities.

You could even do this in your home as an Ironparents contest. Cook the dinner, pick up the toys, and wash the dirty pans. Go!

I See

Here's an activity that you and your child can do any time—walking to the store or school, riding a bus, or just sitting around the back yard. We play it often with our son Noah, and have found it sharpens everyone's observation abilities.

One person picks out an object by saying something like, "I see something blue and white with a round top" (a mail box). The others look around and try to find it. Whoever guesses it gets to select the next object.

You can scale the activity up or down for children of any ages (adults can play this too, at garden parties). For very young children, select something obvious, like a telephone pole, a brightly colored house or car, a person walking across the street, a dog, etc. For older children look for subtle items, such as a squirrel or bird nest, the last red leaf on a tree, a utility plate cover, trim on a roof, curlicue on a railing, a bird feeder in a neighbor's yard, etc.

What wonders will you discover right in your own backyard?

Required:

• Your time only

I Went to the Moon . . .

Required:
• Your time only

Does your family boast any child or adult astronauts-in-training? Then here's your chance to share some of the sights you've seen on your imaginary space-shuttle voyages. This is also a perfect way to pass the time while waiting for a bus, or during long walks when tired kids need distraction.

Players take turns completing the sentence, "I went to the moon and saw . . . ." One way to complete the sentence is with a reversal of reality on Earth. You might say something like, "I saw a dog walking a person," "I saw a baby putting its mommy to bed," or "I saw a person washing his car with dirt." Then, see how much you can find out by asking other questions. For example, "Where were the dog and the person going to go on their walk? What would they do once they got there?" See how much you can learn about what life is really like . . . on the moon.

The possibilities are endless. Our son, Noah, has already made several trips to the moon. Recently, he told us that he spied a purple elephant wearing a straw hat. That wasn't so unusual—compared to the alligator sitting in a lawn chair, sipping pink lemonade and reading a book!

HEEL, BILL!

Jack, You, and the Beanstalk

When Jack scattered his package of enchanted seeds, a legendary beanstalk instantly appeared. As anyone who has ever planted snap beans can tell you, that's not too far from the way it is. One of the simplest and quickest vegetables to grow, beans are perfect for kids to harvest by themselves. When your bean crop is ready this summer, why not celebrate with a family "pick-a-thon?"

Required:
- Bean plants
- Container

Each person gets a container, and then everyone races against the clock to see who can fill his or hers with the most beans. (Adults should first make sure that everyone knows how to pick the beans without hurting the plant.) Alternatively, you can see whether you can fill the pot (or pick enough for everyone to share at the dinner table), or whether the pickers can fill their containers to a predetermined mark. You can also hold contests for the longest bean (but not the smallest—you don't want to pick the beans too young), the curliest, the lumpiest, etc.

Like most vegetables, beans taste best when they're eaten soon after they're picked. You might find that your beans are magic, too, as you watch them disappear!

Journey on the Wind

Question: what's free and can take you anywhere in the world—and beyond? Answer: the wind. Well, at least in your mind. Here's how to harness this wonderful power and become a frequent flyer right in your own backyard, in a meadow, or at the beach.

Required:

• Your time only

Pick a nice windy day and find a soft spot to lie on, or spread blankets or towels. Tell the flyers to lie on their backs, close their eyes, relax their arms and legs, and wait for the wind to whisk them into the air. Ask each person to describe what it feels like to be traveling by wind. What do they see? What does the ground look like?

Now suggest that the wind has taken them to a faraway place. Describe the landscape . . . the plants and animals . . . the people (what do they look like, what do they wear, eat, etc.) . . . the cars and houses.

When everyone has told his or her version, suggest that the return "flight" is about to take off and carry them home. Seat belts buckled and tray tables up for takeoff, please!

Juggling Acts

Juggling is an art form that anyone can learn with a bit of practice. And it's great for backyard entertainment.

You'll need one to three soft balls, oranges, or toilet paper tubes stuffed with bean bags (make a bean bag by pouring half a cup of navy beans into a plastic sandwich bag, closing the bag with a twistem, inserting the bag into an old sock, then tying off the top of the sock.) Start your child out with one object to get used to its feel by passing it back and forth between his or her hands, giving it a light toss. (Small children will delight in "juggling" with one object. In this case, don't worry about moving up to two.)

If your child handles one object well, move up to two. This is a big jump—remind your child to be patient. The idea of this exercise is to get your child used to a rhythmic way of using his or her hands.

Older kids may be able to move up to three balls, which is where the real challenge begins. The child should use the same rhythmic, circular motion he or she used for two balls.

If you want to give your child a hint on how to juggle, simply explain how you make housework, work work, and kid work all work together!

Required:
• Three balls

Optional
• Three plastic bowling pins or oranges

Jump Rope Games

Required:
• Jump rope

The jump rope is one of the oldest childhood games in the world. Yet in our high-tech world, this venerable game has all but become a lost relic. Here's how to revive the jump rope tradition with games your kids are sure to enjoy.

The simplest thing for children who have never jumped rope is to take turns jumping and swinging. Two kids turn a rope ten to twelve feet long, while one jumps (you can jump, too, if you're up for it). Once everyone is comfortable with the jumping action, move on to something a bit more complicated.

For instance, how about "Double Dutch?" This involves turning two ropes in opposite directions toward the middle. Each person has to jump over both ropes—which means a lot of time in the air and good coordination.

Groups of kids can also line up for rapid jumping; as one child jumps twice, he or she moves to the back of the line and the next child continues. If you cut the jumping to one cycle, the line will move pretty quickly and the excitement will run high.

For a series of traditional rhymes that can be chanted while jumping, turn to the next activity.

Jump Rope Rhymes

Here are several rhyming/games that your children can recite as they jump rope:

House for sale
Car within
When I move out
Miss/Mr [ ] moves in.

The jumper calls out the name of another player for the last line. That person then begins jumping.

Policeman policeman do your duty
Here comes so and so
The American cutie
[He/she] can wiggle [he/she] can waggle [he/she] can do the splits
But I bet a million dollars [he/she] can't do this!

The jumper wiggles, waggles, kicks a leg up high, then does a trick. The next person has to come in and do the trick, too.

"A" my name is Albert *[or some other name beginning with "A"]*
And my wife's *[or dog's, son's, daughter's, etc.]* name is
Alice *[or some other name beginning with "A"]*
We grow Artichokes *[or some other food that begins with "A"]*
And we live in Alaska *[or some other place that begins with "A"]*

The next jumper must then repeat the rhyme using the letter "B." Pity the jumper who gets to "X"!

Required:
• Jump rope

Kick the Can

This old game is actually a variation on Hide and Seek—but with an interesting twist.

You'll need four or more kids, one of whom is the "kicker" or "it." "The kicker kicks a can (with smooth edges) or a bucket, and then covers his or her eyes and counts to a hundred—assuming your child can count that high; otherwise, the kicker can recite a favorite song or poem. The idea is to give the others a chance to hide. At the end of the count, the kicker puts the can or bucket upright, then says, "Ready or Not, Here I Come."

When the kicker finds someone, he or she says the hider's name, races the hider back to the can, and tries to be the first to kick it again. If the kicker fails and the hider kicks it, the game starts again. If the kicker succeeds, then that hider must stand near the can while the kicker seeks other children. While this is happening, other hiders can risk their own capture to free a fellow hider by running up to the can and kicking it—before being spotted by the kicker. The captured players then go and hide again. And the game goes on.

Required:
• Can or bucket

98, 99, 100
Ready or not,
here I come!

Kid Olympics

This activity will test your child's stamina, strength, and coordination. More important, it will provide great outdoor fun!

To sponsor a Kid Olympics, select a nice soft grassy area—in your backyard, in a park, or in a field. Now see who can excel at acts like tumbling (check for rocks and twigs on the ground first); the long jump (you might want to have a tape measure or yardstick on hand); and the cross-yard dash.

Parents can measure the results and record them in a family book of records. Or try awarding medals (these can be made out of mud medallions #195, or beach jewelry #19). To keep things from becoming too competitive, you can have the kids try to improve on their previous records, rather than beat the other contestants.

If your kids tire of conventional sports activities, try your own "crazy Olympics," with contests like slowest walking, fastest backward walking, crab crawling, and the short jump. And don't forget the greatest challenge of all: the ten-yard kangaroo hop.

Required:
- Your time only

Optional:
- Tape measure or yardstick
- Mud medallions (#195)
- Beach jewelry (#19)

Kids' Garden (Basic)

Most children are fascinated by gardening activities—digging, planting, watering, and so on. Even if you have a very small plot of dirt, you can grow a surprising amount of food. (Planted wisely, a ten-by-ten-foot plot will provide you with vegetables all summer long.)

Required:
• Seeds

Optional:
• Kids' gardening tools (#329)

This particular activity is geared for young children. The plants are easy to grow, some sprout fairly quickly, and the mature plants are interesting. Try these:

Radishes. Sprout in three to ten days, and reach fruition in three weeks.

Beans. Dramatic when they break the ground.

Zucchini. Prolific when they reach maturity (get the bush variety to conserve garden space).

Carrots. A classic. They prefer sandy soil.

Cherry tomatoes. They're easier to manage than full-sized tomatoes.

Lettuce. It's fun to see leafy rows sprout up.

Follow the directions on the seed packets—every variety is different. Make a map of your garden so your child will know where to water (use twigs as markers). And of course, use the homemade kids' gardening tools described in #329!

Kids' Garden (Advanced #1)

We outlined a starter garden for younger children in the previous activity. If your child is ready for a more challenging garden, try planting these:

Full-sized tomatoes. Seeds or starter plants. As they grow, pinch off shoots that form where each leaf meets the stem. This will keep the plant from growing too many gangly side branches. Once the plants reach a foot, have your child help tie them to stakes with strings or strips of cloth.

Red peppers. Get starter plants. These might need to be staked, too. Kids will need a little patience as the peppers turn from green to red.

Melons. Great fun! If you want to grow watermelons and don't live in a hot climate, buy one of the ice box species—they have a shorter growing period. Remember, with any melon you need *lots* of space.

Squash. Fun to grow—just be aware that they can take over your garden.

Required:
• Seeds/starter plants

Optional:
• Kids' gardening tools (#329)

For more ideas, just turn to Kids' Garden—Advanced 2 #156. Do both advanced gardens and your table will be overflowing all summer long.

Kids' Garden (Advanced #2)

Here's yet another set of plants that take a bit more tending than the plants listed in the basic garden (#154):

Required:
- Seeds/starter plants
- Stakes
- String

Optional:
- Kids' gardening tools (#329)

Pumpkins. Halloween will have special significance if your child has grown his or her own jack-o-lantern since it was a pup. Like melons, these need *lots* of space. Find a seed variety that your garden supply recommends for your area, then get set for garden sprawl.

Cucumbers. Cukes like to climb, so you'll need to drive two stakes into the ground. Have your child help connect cross strings between the stakes. Plant the cucumber seeds in a row in front of the cross strings. By mid-summer you should have a cucumber jungle.

Sunflowers. Some species reach twelve feet in height. But there are smaller varieties, too. Your child will get special satisfaction out of growing something so big (the birds will appreciate the effort, too).

As with all gardening activities, follow the instructions carefully on seeds and starter plants, and your junior gardener will help keep plenty of healthy food on your table.

King of the Mountain

This ancient kids' game tests strength, endurance, and physical creativity.

First you need a hill of soft grass, sand, or snow. One person starts out as king of the hill, and all the other children aspire to the throne. Unfortunately, there can only be one king.

Safety Reminder

Adult Supervision

Those seeking to overthrow the king can devise strategies to get him or her off the hill (parents supervise closely). Rather than charge one at a time, they can all charge up the hill at once, from different directions, and make the king defend his or her kingdom on all flanks.

Of course, this strategy could backfire for some children who may help depose the king only to find themselves looking up at a brand new head of state.

A more civilized game involves play with tails (see #318). Each person wears a tail (a piece of cloth inserted in the back of his or her pants). Whoever pulls out the king's tail becomes the new ruler—and must guard his or her tail.

How's that saying go? So much loyalty in the fief . . . .

Required:
• Your time only

Optional:
• Strips of cloth for tails

Landmark Catalog

Most of us go about our day oblivious to the richness of the world around us. Here's an activity that will open your eyes to all sorts of interesting things.

Required:
• Your time only

Take a walk with your child and count: the number of pavement cracks between your house or apartment and the nearest corner, bus stop, store, etc . . . the number of street trees on your block . . . the number of stop signs, "No Parking" signs, etc . . . the number of fire hydrants . . . the number of parking meters . . . the number of street signs, etc.

As a variation, try guessing ahead of time how many of each item you'll find. Or have everyone try to guess the total number of parking meters along a particular route from home to downtown.

You and your child can also make a "Landmark Catalog" detailing distances between your house and a school, shopping center, etc.

Finally, you might want to keep a notebook of all your hard-to-collect data. Perhaps publish a neighborhood "book of lists"—use it to break the ice at the block party or Neighborhood Fair (#200).

Landscape Calendar

Here's a way to make a nature calendar with scenes from your neighborhood.

First have your child sketch images of the neighborhood or scenes of walks in the park or rides in the country. Your child might want to do all the sketches at once, or during separate walks or rides. Since the artwork will be used on a calendar, you might want to make this a year-long activity and do one sketch per month. Have your child paint sunsets, landscapes, people, street scenes, close-ups of plants and trees, pictures of the sky—everything you would expect to see in a nature calendar.

When you have enough paintings, affix each one to a sheet of posterboard roughly twice the size of the painting paper. On the bottom portion of the posterboard, use a ruler to draw boxes for the appropriate number of days. If you make the calendar in December, you'll be all set for the following year.

Whatever you do, hang the calendar on the wall for everyone to admire it—and to remember their fine walks about the neighborhood.

Required:
- Painting materials
- Posterboard
- Ruler
- Markers

Large-Scale Tic Tac Toe

W ho says you can only play tic tac toe with paper and pencil? Move the game to the big back yard, where you can play it on a large scale.

First you'll need to create a tic tac toe playing board. You can do this with garden hoses or lengths of string or rope. If you're on the beach, dig lines in the sand. You can do the same with a fresh snowfall.

Next you'll need some X's and O's. Try these: flower pots, rocks, leaves, balls, branches, pine cones, sea shells, driftwood, and other natural playing "pieces." During winter, try using snowballs for O's and icicles for X's. You and your child can also make large-scale tic tac toe pieces out of paper plates from picnics or from hard foam food containers from fast food and take-out restaurants (draw X's and O's with markers or crayons.)

For a variation, try "human tic tac toe." With this game, the object is to get three body parts in a row—without moving off the squares!

Required:

- Pine cones, rocks, and other natural elements

- Garden hoses, string, or rope (not necessary for winter/beach)

Optional:

- Flower pots, paper plates, fast-food containers

- Markers or crayons

Lawn Helpers

Young children love to help take care of the lawn (unfortunately, they usually want to push the lawnmower). Here are some ways they can help without getting involved with spinning blades.

Instead of dumping your grass clippings, place them in piles so your child can collect handfuls and use them as mulch in your flower beds and garden. A thin layer of grass clippings will help keep the weeds at bay.

If you don't want to mulch your flower beds, your child can help prepare the clippings for a compost pile (#25). This is done by spreading out the clippings in a section of garden or driveway and letting them sun dry. (Deep layers of moist clippings won't compost as quickly.)

Finally there's the most fun activity of all, when the mower has been put away: grass clipping tag. The person who's "it" tosses a handful of clippings at the people playing the game. The first person to be caught wearing a grass shirt or skirt is "it" for the next round. Let the grass fly!

Required:
• Lawn mower (for your use)

Leaf It on the Plate

Here's an activity that demands the utmost in balance and coordination.

The idea is for two people to put paper plates on their heads, then put a leaf on top of the plate. Then race.

Now, speed alone won't cut it—the object is to finish the race with the leaf still on the plate and the plate still on the racer's head.

Required:
- Paper plates
- Leaves

Optional:
- Milkweed
- Feather
- Dandelion

As an alternative, players can race with a blade of grass on their plates, a milkweed, a feather, or a dandelion.

Players can also have different kinds of races besides running. They could walk backward, crawl, hop, skip, or moonwalk à la Michael Jackson. If it's difficult for players to keep the plates on their heads, they can balance the plates on their fingers like a waiter carrying a tray.

Whatever your kids do, the object of the game is to . . . leaf it on the plate!

Leaf Pile Olympics

Wurk what can you do with a yard full of
leaves (or piles of leaves from leaf
cleanup games)? Sponsor a backyard leaf
Olympics. Here are a few suggestions.

Leaf-pile broad jump. Build up a large
pile of leaves that the children can
jump into from a starting line. Make
sure that the leaf pile contains nothing but soft leaves.

Leaf-pile hurdles. Rake a series of small
leaf piles and arrange them in a line.
The children jump over the piles as
they run, just as they would real hurdles in track. Points are subtracted if
anyone disturbs the leaf piles while
traversing them.

Leaf obstacle course. Create a series of
small leaf piles that can be used as
an obstacle course. Perhaps the idea
is to jump over the first two, then
hop sideways over the next pile, and
so on.

Leaf kicking. Rake some piles of leaves
and see who can kick up the biggest
mess! Which brings us to the last
idea: leaf pile cleanup—see who can
clean up a designated area of the
lawn or driveway the fastest!

Required:
• Leaf rakes

License Plate Math

Believe it or not, license plates are a great way for kids to learn basic math. Here are a few activities.

Required:
• Your time only

Optional:
• Pencil and paper

Read 'em. A young child will see the license plate KD1 533 and read, "1, 5, 3, 3." An older child will read "1533" or "one thousand five hundred thirty-three." Walk along a street and have your child practice reading at his or her skill level.

Add 'em up. For children who can do simple math, see who can add up all the numbers in a license plate. Or subtract a designated number, say "1," from the last digit.

Grand Totaling. Add up all of the digits on all of the license plates on one side of the street—then subtract the total of all the digits on the other side. As a variation, read off or add up the cars as they pass by an intersection, or add up the total digits of cars passing by within a certain time interval. Who knows—the city might even pay you for monitoring traffic. Then have your child count up your cash!

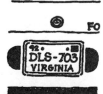

Lichens

Have you ever noticed a tree that seems to be growing right out of a rock? The tree owes something to the lowly lichen, which paved the way for its growth.

Lichens are those gray-green crusty plant forms that grow on rocks. They grow there without dirt, and actually consist of two plants that live together and support each other. One plant is a fungus, the other an alga (the singular of "algae"). As the lichens grow, they break down the surface, forming dirt so that larger plants like mosses can grow, followed by small leafy plants. Eventually trees grow there.

Your child can explore the world while looking for these wonderful path blazers. The three main types to look for (see illustration) are crustose ("a"—these look like crust), foliose ("b"—appear like crumpled paper) and fruticose ("c"—which have the appearance of small plants with stems). How many can you find on one of your walks?

Required:
• Your time only

a.

b.

c.

Life Form Count

Required:
• Pad and pen

Do you think your corner of the world is devoid of interesting life forms? Try this activity.

First pick a spot in your backyard or garden, your front porch, a square of sidewalk, a park bench, etc. Then play naturalist—just observe what walks, crawls, or slithers by. Remember, nothing is too humble to be included on your list: ants, moths, mosquitoes, butterflies, flies, bees, and other insects; worms and caterpillars; squirrels and chipmunks; birds; cats and dogs.

As your child points out various critters (at a healthy distance), jot them down in a notebook or pad. You might also give hints if your child is missing something interesting. ("Look at the lamplight—see those bugs flying around . . . Hmmm, there seems to be something making its way across the pavement.") When you're done, pick a different spot and compare the different forms of life your child spots.

It will be interesting to note whether your child remembers to include one living being that will definitely be in the picture—people!

Litter-Free Zone

Do you cringe every time you walk through your park (or take a stroll on the beach) and see litter? Your child, and his or her friends, can help do something about the problem by taking responsibility for "litter-free zones."

A litter-free zone might consist of the area underneath a park bench, by a certain tree, around a playground entrance, etc. When you visit the zone, take along one bag to collect recyclable items and another for transporting trash to the nearest receptacle. Take the recyclables to your recycling center if you don't have curbside pickup; otherwise, sort them with your own recycling materials. If your state has a bottle bill, cash in the bottles at a redemption center and use the money to purchase materials for making "Litter-Picker-Upper" T-Shirts.

If you have several children involved, try drawing a litter-free zone map. Send the map and a story about your kid's efforts to your community paper. Who knows: maybe they'll print the map as a public service and inspire others to help with the effort.

Required:
- Paper trash bags

Optional:
- Paper and pencils or markers

Living Thermometers

Nature tells us all sorts of things, including the temperature during summer months. If you're within earshot of a cricket, then you're all set for an interesting demonstration of how to compute the temperature based on the number of chirps per minute. Male crickets chirp by rubbing their wings, both to attract females and to ward off competing males. (And some probably do it because they just plain enjoy making music!)

Required:
• Watch or clock with second hand

Optional:
• Thermometer

Use a watch or clock with a second hand, then count the number of times a cricket chirps in a sixty-second span. Now subtract forty from the count, divide the result by four, and add fifty. Voilà! You have the temperature in Fahrenheit degrees.

Older kids will enjoy doing the "cricket math." They can also do cricket quality-control checks by comparing the computed results with a thermometer or the time/temperature recording on the telephone.

As a variation, have your children work backward—guess how many chirps they're going to hear and what the computed temperature will turn out to be.

Oh, by the way, don't try to track down the living thermometers—even the most vocal cricket is hard to find.

Local History

Every city, town, and community has some colorful history. But as the years pass, it gets buried in official archives. Your child will probably enjoy unearthing a bit of the past and visiting the sites where small and great events transpired.

Visit your city hall or the library and learn about your area. When was your city or town founded? What's the significance of the name? What notable events took place? Were any noted scientific or medical discoveries made in your area? Were any noted artists, writers, or national celebrities born there?

Once you've learned about your city or town's local history, make a historical map. Get a city or town map and mark the historic sites. Circle the names of streets named after town founders or celebrities. Then use the map as if you were a visitor from out of town in search of a good historical journey.

Older children might enjoy making a small local history brochure, writing up key facts and dates. Be sure to take photographs during your site visits, as they'll be useful in the brochure.

So what's most interesting about your city or town?

Required:
- Map of your city or town

Optional:
- Paper and pencil
- Camera

Low-Tech Weather Kids

A s Bob Dylan once wrote, "you don't need a weatherman to tell which way the wind's blowing." He was right, and your child can prove it.

On a mildly windy day, have your child pluck a few blades of grass or collect a few fallen petals. Next, have him or her toss the grass or petals into the air. Use a sundial (#312), a compass, or your own sense of orientation, and you'll know which way the wind blows.

Another variation is to have your child guess which way the wind is blowing before tossing the grass. Again, try it yourself—it's harder than it seems.

Just one word of caution: the act of tossing the grass may be more interesting than the "orienteering." Be careful that your lawn isn't turned into a desert!

Required:
• Your time only

Lynn & Richard's Walking Game

Ever been out walking with a child who suddenly wants to ride in the stroller, only the stroller is half a mile away? This activity, suggested by our friends, Lynn and Richard, will perk up your child and get you home quickly.

The game is kind of like a mental version of the carrot and the stick—as your child goes for the carrot, he or she will have moved a "stick's length" ahead.

Let's say you're at a street corner, having just crossed the street, and you spot a mailbox up ahead. Call out, "I see something blue and white." Your child sees the mailbox and runs ahead to touch it. (Keep the distances short so you can watch out for driveways and cars. You can also run with your child to the object ahead.) You might then call out, "I see a green post with a red sign." Your child then heads for the stop sign.

Use fire hydrants, manhole covers, parking meters, trees, gates, hedges, telephone poles and other urban items to move your child along. Before he or she knows it, you'll be home!

Required:
- Your time only

Magic Acts

Would one of your children like to turn a younger brother or sister into a frog? Or would a younger sib like to transform an older one into a statue for a day? Probably so. While we can't make either happen, we do have a suggestion for making magic wands that will be almost as satisfying.

Required:
- Sticks
- Yard materials
- String

Optional:
- Tape or glue

Each child first searches for the perfect stick—in the backyard, on a neighborhood walk, in the park, or on a trek through the country. To complete the wand, attach dried leaves and long grass to the stick with tightly wound string. You can also affix unusual leaves and seeds with tape or glue for "power magicians" (use these with caution—you could inadvertently turn your house or spouse into a kumquat).

Once the wands are done, set your magicians loose to cast and remove spells (encourage good deeds, of course). Your kids will also get a charge out of making up chants using exotic-sounding words like "xenophobia," "demographics," or "macroeconomics." For added fun, create some nature finery to complement the wands (see activity #71).

Please! If your kids do unlock some mysterious transformative powers, send 'em over to our house—we always have a garden full of weeds!

Mailbox Decorations

Through rain, sleet, and dark of night your mail carrier brings your mail. You and your children can show some appreciation by decorating your mailbox.

Winter—you can tape pine needles to the mailbox, or string lights around it (a job requiring your supervision). Or you could make cutout snowflakes (see Snowflake ID #280) and tape them to the box. (For a rural mail box, build a snowman nearby).

Spring—your child can decorate the box with fresh leaves, flowers, dandelions, or even original poems.

Summer—decorate the box with sports clippings from yesterday's ballgame, original drawings of ice cream cones, seashells, or driftwood.

Fall—tape colorful leaves to the box, or decorate it with drawings of pumpkins or footballs.

Other year-round decorations are old stamps or postcards. Maybe your carrier will like the decorations so much that he or she will bring fewer bills!

Suggested:

- Yard or beach materials
- Tape
- Christmas lights
- Old stamps
- Postcards
- Cutout snowflakes
- Sports clippings
- Drawings

Make a Rainbow

Part of the magic of rainbows is their unpredictability. But it probably won't spoil your children's appreciation for them if you demonstrate how to create rainbows right in your own backyard.

To make a rainbow you'll need a garden hose with a nozzle capable of producing a fine mist. You should have your back to the sun when you turn on the water. Hold the hose upward so you get a good arc (you're trying to simulate a gentle rain). Your child, with his or her back to the sun, should see a small rainbow in the spray; the sunlight is split into its component colors as it passes through the water droplets. (Your child might have to move around a bit to find the right spot.)

You and your child can experiment as to what time of day and angle of the sun produces the best rainbow. You can also determine the optimal amount of water pressure for generating a fine spray.

There might not be a pot of gold at the end of these self-made rainbows, but the enjoyment your child experiences will surely be priceless.

Required:
- Garden hose and nozzle

May Day

No one knows for certain how May Day started—various experts trace it back to the Egyptians and, more recently, the druids. But one thing is certain: by the late 1800s it was quite popular.

In its original form, May Day entailed making May Baskets filled with flowers. Children would leave the baskets on people's door steps. They would also decorate a pole with brightly colored ribbons and carry it in a parade, then place the pole in the ground and dance around it.

Your kids can rekindle this beautiful celebration by leaving their own flower May Day baskets on neighbor's doorsteps (see #351 for a description of how to make baskets).

They can also decorate a May Pole (a smooth garden stake or dowel) with six-foot-long streamers or ribbon. After carrying the pole on parade throughout the neighborhood, place it in the ground and divide the kids into pairs. Some of the children run in one direction, some in the other, lifting their streamers as they pass each other. The streamers will become entwined, wrapping the pole in colorful braids.

And if you get all tangled up? Just call out "mayday!"

Required:
- Baskets (see #351)
- Fresh flowers
- Stake or dowel
- Streamers or ribbon

Measuring Snowfall

How much snow really fell in your yard last winter? How much is out there now? This activity will turn your child into an expert on the subject.

At the first snow of the year, take a long, straight stick or yardstick and have your children place it in the snow until its bottom touches the ground. Select a level area that isn't subjected to excessive wind. If you're using a yardstick, your children can read off the snowfall level and jot it down in a notebook. If you have a plain stick, children can tie a string or colored ribbon at the point the snow comes up to on the stick. You can then measure the snowfall with the ruler.

At each subsequent snowfall, children can measure the new snowfall and compare it to the previous spot on the stick. Add a new ribbon to a plain stick. If all the snow melts before the next snowfall, they start measuring at the bottom again.

It will be fun for the older children to keep track of how much they shoveled all winter. For the younger children it will be fun to know how much *you* shoveled.

Required:

- Yardstick or any long, straight stick
- Colored ribbons or string

Optional:

- Logbook

Megaphones

Here's a new and interesting way for people to say what's on their minds.

You can make megaphones from many common objects. The simplest is the toilet paper or paper towel tube. Just have your child hold the tube up and start chattering. His or her voice will be amplified in funny ways.

Another option is to take a milk jug and slice off the bottom just below the handle (a job for Mom or Dad). Your child holds the milk jug by the handle, then talks through the mouth. The jug will definitely do strange things to the speaker's voice. (Try noting the difference between half-gallon and gallon jugs.)

Finally, combine both concepts. Insert the tube—or a long wrapping paper tube—into the mouth of the milk jug (see #182 for this technique). Talk through the tube and watch what happens.

A group of kids can raise quite a cacophony. Megaphones can be used constructively in cheerleading (see #52) or other sporting activities. In any case, get ready for some unusual sounds emanating from the backyard.

Suggested:

- Toilet paper, paper towel, or wrapping-paper tubes
- Milk jugs
- Scissors

Microworld

What goes on in a small patch of ground during the course of a day? Here's a good way for your junior naturalist to find out.

Make a microworld by cutting out a twelve-by-twelve-inch hole in a piece of newspaper. Place it over the ground in the morning, then have your child observe the various goings on. You might want to dig down an inch or two in one portion of the microworld and turn the soil over. First, though, note the natural constituents—moss, plants, etc.

Have your child take a look at the microworld every hour, jotting down who's come and gone. Perhaps a worm started off in the upper right corner and is now gone. Maybe an ant has carried a heavy load of building materials from one side to the other. Or perhaps a bee visited a clover plant and carried off a bundle of nectar.

Of course, your child can investigate several microworlds at once, perhaps comparing the activity in different parts of the yard. Maybe you'll find a real party animal of a grasshopper who hits all the hot spots!

Required:
- Newspaper
- Scissors

Optional:
- Notebook and pencil

Middle of the Pack

This is a good game for four or more children. All they need is a soft rubber ball and an open area of grass. You can use a volleyball or soccer ball if a soft rubber ball isn't handy.

The children form a circle and one person stands in the middle. The children in the circle roll or toss a ball between them. The idea is for the players in the circle to pass the ball so that it touches the player in the middle—without that player's intercepting it.

The player in the middle must stay put, but he or she can rotate to keep an eye on who has the ball. The strategy for the players in the circle is to throw it among themselves so fast that the player in the middle spins in circles and gets confused.

The player who rolls the ball and touches the person in the middle gets to take a turn in the center of the circle. A variation on this rule could be to let every player get a turn in rotation.

Adults can play too. Just think of this as a game for middle-aged kids.

Required:
- Soft rubber ball, soccer ball, or volley ball

Midsummer Tree Decorations

Required:

- Flowers and other yard materials
- String

Optional:

- Popcorn
- Mud Medallions (#195)

For something different this summer, why not decorate a tree with natural and homemade ornaments? Nothing beats nature in its pure form, but this activity shows your kids how to build on the natural beauty growing about them.

Plan a hike to find a recipient for your "arboreal splendor." Of course, you can select a tree or shrub that's growing right in your own yard. For decorations, use string to hang pine cones, gumballs, individual flowers, and garlands made out of clover, dandelions, leaves, etc. (see activity #71).

For decorating fun that takes a little more planning, make your own decorations ahead of time. You can string some popcorn to make garlands (the birds will enjoy it), or make special tree ornaments out of clay (see Mud Medallions, #195).

You can also select several trees and use complementary decorations, or create a "theme arboretum" (flowers on one, medallions on another, and leaf garlands on a third).

Whether you choose one tree or ten, invite your children's friends and others in the neighborhood to help complete the masterpiece. Then stand back and enjoy the view—with cookies and milk or lemonade in hand.

Migrating Bird Watch

If you live in an area where birds migrate, your child can chronicle an event that you've probably seen dozens of times but never really watched carefully.

On a calendar or in a notebook, have your child record the first day that flocks of birds appear to be traveling south for the winter or returning north for the spring. Your child can also note the number of flocks that pass by overhead, the time of day they seem to be traveling, the kinds of sounds they make, and other important data.

Geese are delightful subjects because they fly in a V-formation and often honk as they fly by. You can also count and record the number of geese in formation. Other birds, like robins, are more difficult to count because they tend to bunch up. Even so, your child can keep rough track of the number of flocks that pass overhead.

Use the opportunity to explain how different animals weather the winter; some hibernate, others store up food and poke their heads out for occasional adventures, and still others head for the warm country.

What's *your* winter style?

Required:
- Calendar or piece of paper

Milk-Jug Crosses

Here's how to make an unusual piece of sporting gear.

First you'll need two quart-sized milk jugs. Slice the jugs about six inches from the top (definitely a job for you). Cut four quarter-inch slits into the mouth of the jug—to allow a narrow wrapping paper tube to fit snugly into the container (see illustration). Wrap a few layers of tape around the mouth to ensure that the paper tube doesn't slip.

Required:

- Quart milk jugs
- Wrapping paper tubes
- Tape
- Piece of corrugated cardboard
- Scissors

If the tube fits too loosely, don't slit the mouth of the jug. Instead, build up the tube with layers of paper and tape, then tape the outside of the mouth to ensure that the tube stays put.

Finally, reinforce the inside of the paper tube with a piece of corrugated cardboard the same length. The piece of cardboard should be wide enough that when it is bent into a "V" and inserted into the tube, it will stay firmly in place.

Now turn to the next activity and put your homemade sports gear to work.

Milk-Jug Crosse Games

Here are some exciting things to do with milk-jug crosses (see #182).

First, play some warmup catch with a tennis ball or racquetball (allow throwing only with the crosse). Young children will enjoy simple volleying.

Once you're accustomed to using the crosses, try involving several players. Or try using the crosses to pitch the ball into weighted buckets.

Then there's the game of lacrosse (our own variation, actually). You'll need a group of kids and enough crosses for each one. The object is to toss the ball into the opposing team's goal (a bushel basket or box). Players can throw the ball to fellow teammates or go for the goal themselves.

To start the play, the referee throws the ball into the air and a team member from each side tries to catch it. The one who does gets to run toward the goal (players can intercept throws and pick up fumbles). After each point is scored, the referee tosses the ball into the air again and the play continues.

Practice now—don't wait until this becomes an Olympic sport!

Required:
- Milk jug crosses (see #182)
- Tennis or racquetball

Milkweed Games

The milkweed plant is a natural source of entertainment—when you blow on it or expose it to the wind, its wonderful little seeds disperse in unpredictable patterns. (For a description of milkweed, see Grow a Butterfly, #120.)

Required:

• Milkweed or other feathery, windborn flowers

Optional:

• Timer or stopwatch

One milkweed game involves having children pick a milkweed seed pod and split it open. At the count of three, everyone blows on his or her seed pod or "flower" to see whose seeds disappear first. Or, you can set a time period—the object is to see whose seeds will disappear into the wind first. (You can hold the stopwatch, give the count, and arbitrate disputes about photo finishes and the like.)

A variation on this game entails holding the seed pod or "flower" in the air and waiting to see which seeds disappear when the wind blows.

Finally, you can draw a line on the lawn or driveway, and your children can have milkweed "races." The object of a milkweed race is to see whose seeds can cross a finish line (a chalk line on a driveway or a piece of string or rope on your lawn).

On your mark, get set, blow!

Mime Sports

In these games your child won't need a ball, a bat, a glove, or anything for that matter—just imagination. (Best played with you and one child.)

First decide upon a sport. If it's baseball, one person is the pitcher, the other is the batter. The pitcher throws an invisible ball and the batter swings an invisible bat. You act as announcer and umpire, and call out the action. Sometimes the pitcher throws strikes and celebrates accordingly. But other times the batter crushes the ball and does a home run trot, being sure to touch all the invisible bases. The pitcher can also change roles and become an outfielder, making spectacular catches.

If the game is football, the quarterback throws an invisible ball to a receiver who catches and alludes an onslaught of invisible tacklers.

In basketball, you and your child pass and dribble an invisible ball and then make spectacular dunks and long jump shots—into an invisible basket.

Now, if you enjoy this kind of imagination game, turn to page 590 and read about an unusually exciting activity.

Required:
• Your time only

TWO POINTS!

Miniature Golf Course

Safety Reminder

Adult Supervision

Required:
- Yardsticks
- Sponges
- Rubber bands
- Plastic containers
- Household objects

Optional:
- Baking tin
- Mailing tubes or milk jugs

Why pay the high price of a round of miniature golf when you can have your own course right in your back yard—with common items found around the house?

First make safe golf clubs by attaching a stiff sponge to a yardstick with rubber bands. Next, gather items for the "course" and the individual "greens." Yogurt and cottage cheese containers make excellent "holes" (place them on their sides if you don't want to insert them into the ground). Place obstacles such as outdoor toys, cardboard boxes, flowerpots, etc. between the "tees" (a mark on the ground) and the holes. For more sophisticated courses, add mailing tube or milk jug tunnels (cut off the milk jug bottom and widen the mouth).

Add a few sand traps and water holes (use a baking tin with a small lip), supply a small ball (golf ball or squash ball, or a whiffle-type ball if your kids tend to get overzealous in their putting style), and explain the rules (better yet, let your child invent his or her own) and your family may be ready for the PGA by the end of the summer.

Mini Obstacle Course

This is easy to do, fun to set up, and fascinating to watch.

The idea is simple—you and your child work together to build an obstacle course for a golf or Ping-Pong ball. A course might start on a rock or at the top of a box, or along a board propped up with bricks. Try and see if you can make the ball roll longer and longer despite various additions to the track. Place rocks, pine cones, sticks, etc. in the path and see if the ball gets stopped.

You can also make a tunnel out of a shoebox—or multiple tunnels within the same box. (Make sure the openings in the front of the box align with the openings in the back.)

Once you've got the course perfected, try playing with two people. Race the two golfballs or run one ten times to see if it acts differently each time. Change the course and try again.

For you golfing parents out there, this is the beginning of your child's education on the erratic behavior of golf balls.

Safety Reminder

Adult Supervision

Required:

- Golf balls or Ping-Pong balls
- Board
- Yard materials
- Shoebox
- Scissors

Mirror Games

Safety
Reminder

Supervise Closely

Required:
- Plastic mirrors (one per person)

Optional:
- Garden hose
- Rope

Who needs expensive high-tech outdoor toys when a plain old mirror will provide endless fun? Just give your child a PLASTIC mirror and you're all set for an entertaining afternoon, assuming the sun is out. Be sure no one shines a mirror in anyone else's face.

Here's one of our favorite mirror games. Draw a maze on your driveway or sidewalk with a piece of chalk. Show your child how to create beams of light with the mirror's surface, then see whether you and your child can manipulate your mirrors so as to pass your beams through the maze without touching the "walls" (no simple task).

Another game involves using a reflection from a mirror as a "token" in a ready-made obstacle course. For example, if you live in a clapboard house, see if all the players can move their light beams along the edges of the wood without deviating, moving row by row. Brick patterns also make tortuous tracks to follow.

Finally, try a garden hose or length of rope placed on the ground. The players try to move the light beam along the hose or rope without "falling off."

Lights, mirror, action!

Moon Watch

Our son, Noah, once got quite sad when we were returning from a dinner outing. "The moon isn't following me anymore," he said. We then explained how the moon moves and the idea of the phases of the moon. We also started making "moon calendars." To keep track of the moon's changes and its effects on you, try making a moon chart of your own.

Take a large sheet of construction paper or posterboard and draw in the appropriate number of boxes for each day of several months. In each box draw a large circle. Clouds permitting, observe the moon and draw in the appropriate shading (if any). Continue this process until you've been through an entire cycle. The phases of the moon are as follows: new moon (Fig a), first quarter (b), full moon (c); last quarter (d).

By the way, you might check your child's behavior against the moon calendar—was he or she acting particularly zany on a particular day? Chances are it was on or near the full moon.

Required:

- Construction paper/posterboard
- Markers or crayons

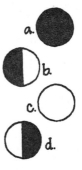

Mostest and Leastest

Four- and five-year-olds love to point out the biggest and the smallest, the "mostest" and the "leastest." They seem to be intrigued and comfortable with absolutes.

So how about taking a tour of your neighborhood to see what they have to say about the mosts and leasts? Virtually everything you encounter can be put into a mostest or leastest category.

Required:
• Your time only

For example, which is the biggest tree on the street? Which house has the fewest windows? The smallest shrubs? The most steps? The longest walk? And which lawn do you think has the most blades of grass? Where's the longest driveway? Who has the biggest garage, or the most red paint? Which neighborhood dog barks the loudest?

Where things can be quantified, try challenging your child's answers with questions like, "Gee, are you sure that one has the most window panes—how about the green house across the street?"

In any case, you and your child can invent categories so that every house or yard wins something—even if it's the yard with the most weeds.

Mother, May I

This traditional game can be played with a group of children just about anywhere.

One child serves as "Mother." The other kids line up and face Mother about twenty feet away. Mother selects one of the children and says something like, "Susan, you may take five giant steps." The child who was addressed then responds with, "Mother, may I?" Mother then says, "Yes you may."

Mother then addresses another child, and the game continues until one of the children reaches Mother. Whoever makes it to Mother first becomes Mom for the next round.

Sound simple? It is. Except that in the excitement of the game, someone is bound to take their steps without asking "Mother, may I." When that happens, Mother reminds the player of his or her manners and the player is sent back to the beginning of the line. Mother can also make the game intriguing by only honoring the silly steps—"twirly" steps, one-foot hops, and so on.

For a variation, try this one: Fourth-Cousin-Once-Removed On My Father's Side, May I . . . ."

Required:
• Your time only

Moths or Butterflies?

Required:
• Your time only

Butterflies and moths are closely re-lated, but they're easy to tell apart if you know what to look for. When they land, butterflies bring their wings to-gether up above their backs. A moth folds its wings flat out to the sides. Their antennae are different too—butterflies have thin antennae with knobs at the end; moths generally have feathery an-tennae. Finally, butterfly bodies are typi-cally long and thin, while moths tend to be fat and fuzzy. The illustrations below show the difference. Can your child find examples of butterflies and moths in your backyard?

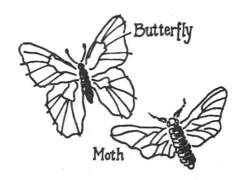

Butterfly

Moth

Mud Flats (Basic)

If you've whipped up a batch of home-made bricks (see #7), try the following suggestions for putting them to good use:

Simple Houses. Stack the bricks one atop the other to make walls. Use longer bricks to span the tops of windows and doors. For roofs, your child can use pieces of cardboard, rows of twigs, etc.

Garages. Make three walls and cover the top with cardboard or twigs. Then park toy cars and trucks inside.

Great Walls. Stack up your bricks and make walls for towns, forts, castles, etc. Your child might also enjoy digging a highway and using the bricks to make tunnels.

Bridges. Dig a bed for a stream, then span it with a sturdy brick bridge. Use a piece of wood as the bottom, then build up the sides with layers of bricks (use cardboard or twigs to make a roof for a covered version).

Adobe Cities. Pile up an embankment of dirt, then use the bricks to build a whole town on the hillside—create lots of windows and doors.

Onward! Even the Great Pyramid at Cheops started with one block.

Required:
- Basic brick-building supplies (see #7)

Mud Flats (Advanced)

Once you and your child have become mud flat experts, consider
these advanced building techniques.

Play mason. Instead of stacking the
bricks dry, use a fresh batch of semi-
liquid mud as mortar in between
each layer. Smooth the excess with a
plastic knife or spoon.

Make a popsicle-stick roof. When the mud
is setting in the baking tin, lay popsicle sticks in the mud. The sticks will
strengthen the roof slabs when the
mud dries.

Create preformed walls. Before you pour
the mud mixture into the baking tin,
insert plastic objects to make holes
in the wall where you want doors
and windows. You can also use plastic to create the angles of a pitched
roof. When the mud sets, remove
the forms. Let it dry. Presto: an instant prefab wall. (Note: you might
have to add straw or grass clippings
for added strength. Start off small.)

Required:

- Brick-making
  supplies (see
  #7)
- Pieces of plastic
- Popsicle sticks

Optional:

- Backyard
  materials

Finally, consider using the bricks for a
little "astro-cosmological" art. Make a
mini-Stonehenge—perhaps your child
will be the first to understand what the
ancient druids really had in mind.

Mud Medallions

Elsewhere we've described how to make mud bricks for use as a building material. But don't stop there—your child will probably also enjoy making mud jewelry.

First mix up a batch of mud as described in #7. Roll out the material onto a piece of wood covered with wax paper, or a cookie sheet.

When the mixture sets, use jar tops, plastic containers, or other common kitchen items to cut out discs. Before the mixture dries, have your child inscribe his or her name or initials or do a drawing using a twig or stick. Be sure to make a hole at the top before the mud dries. Pass a string or ribbon through the hole of the dried medallion and it's ready to be worn. (Smaller medallions can be attached to bracelets.)

Finally, consider writing the family name on a large medallion. Hang it by the door and you'll have art for the whole house.

Required:
- Mud for molding (see #7)
- Baking tin or pan
- Jar tops, plastic containers
- Twigs/sticks
- String or ribbon

Musical Water Buckets

Required:
- Buckets or dishpans

Optional
- Radio or tape player

Sure, we all played musical chairs when we were kids. Here's a twist that will delight your children and cool them off on a hot day.

You'll need a bucket or dish pan for each player, and something to make music. If you're not embarrassed by your voice, sing or hum a favorite tune. Otherwise, bring out a battery-operated radio or cassette player (please use rechargeable batteries). Arrange the buckets in a circular pattern. Have the children walk around the buckets in rhythm with the music. When the music stops, everyone sits down in the buckets or dish pans, one of which is filled with water!

A more traditional version of this game entails filling all the buckets with water but having one less bucket than the number of players. The children walk around the circle, plunking themselves into the nearest bucket when the music stops. The child who is still dry gets to sit out the rest of the game. Remove a bucket and continue the process until only one player remains. The winner gets the honor of a final dunk in the bucket.

Bottoms down!

Naming the Flowers

The common and scientific names assigned to flowers mean little to a child. This activity enables your child to invent appropriate names of his or her own. It also stimulates your child's powers of observation.

Take a walk through your backyard, neighborhood, park, etc, looking for different flowers. Have your child select a name and then explain why. Here are some common names we've dreamed up during walks with our children.

Required:

• Your time only

Trombone flowers: Flowers with long petals held together

Puppy flowers: Pansies with dog-like faces.

Little bells: Flowers with many hanging bell-like petals.

Spaghetti flowers: Flowers with dangling stamens.

Peekaboos: Flowers that hide in their petals, like lilies.

Sponge flowers: Flowers with tight petals, like geraniums.

Tower flowers: Flowers with a tall pistil.

These might not pass muster in Botany 101. But they're sure a useful way for your children to organize the richly diverse world of nature for themselves.

Natural Memory Game

Required:
- Yard materials
- Towel or bucket

This activity will help build your child's memory (it will also test and flex yours), and it's fun to do.

Collect two sets of nearly identical natural objects (e.g., two red maple leaves, two twigs or rocks of approximately the same size and shape, two acorns, two shells or pieces of driftwood, etc.). Have your child close his or her eyes, then make a distinctive arrangement with one set of objects (perhaps draw a "board" out of chalk). Your child then takes a brief look, after which you cover up the arrangement with a towel or bucket. Your child's mission is to make an identical arrangement with the second set of objects.

You can vary the difficulty several ways. For younger children, use fewer objects and allow a longer look before covering up. Use more complex arrangements for older kids, and shorten the viewing time.

Once your child has the hang of it, let him or her do the object selecting and arranging, and you try the duplication.

Oh all right, you can have one more peek. But just one.

Nature's Art Forms

This activity allows you and your child to use various yard materials to "draw" all sorts of objects and animals.

First gather a collection of pine cones, acorns, twigs, and small rocks. Decide what you're going to "draw," then use the yard materials to create outlines. For example, use the twigs and sticks to create outlines (of a house, a car, a dog, a face, etc.) Then use the other objects to create details.

For example, acorns and other nuts can be used for eyes; a pine cone makes a fine nose or a tail. Pine cones can also be used to make feet or chimneys. You get the idea.

You might also take a "Rorschach" approach. Place the yard materials into a bucket, then dump them out on the ground and spread them around. What common images do you and your child see? Make a new pattern, or isolate the objects you've identified and add more details. Remember, there is no "right" and "wrong" with this activity.

You might see anything, from your child's favorite stuffed animal to the entire cast of The Wizard of Oz.

Required:
• Yard materials

Optional:
• Bucket

Neighborhood Fair

Do your neighbors have gardens? Do their kids do any handicrafts? This activity just might get them started on both.

Pick a day to hold a "country fair" in your backyard (or an agreeing neighbor's). Have your kids make up invitations (on scrap paper) announcing the date and place. They can also help set up booths (made out of boxes) or card tables. Here are some starter ideas.

Suggested materials:

- Paper and pencil for invitations
- Boxes/card tables
- Outdoor crafts
- Homemade food treats
- Soft drink cans
- Ball or bean bag
- Prizes

Crafts display. Your kids can show their beach jewelry (#19), summer fans (#133), leaf canvases (#14), or medallions of mud (#195).

Food. Have kids help in preparing cookies, lemonade, or sun tea (#314). They'll also enjoy tending a booth.

Animal Displays. Maybe you don't have cows or goats to display, but a grasshopper collection or a freshly groomed dog might make a fine attraction.

Tossing games. Set up a dozen empty soft drink cans on a box and tape a number to each one. The thrower selects a number, then tries to knock down the can with the same number using a ball, pine cone, or bean bag. The prize—perhaps a corn husk doll (#67).

If any monies are transacted, donate them to a favorite community charity.

Neighborhood Walk Find It

This is a "Find It" game for those who live in a suburban neighborhood or subdivision.

You start with a list of five items that one player makes up. The list can include entries such as: a red door, a gray roof, a picket fence, a paved driveway, a basketball hoop in a driveway, a signpost, a stop sign, a swingset, a dog on a leash, a squirrel, a flagpole, a "Keep Off the Grass" sign, a front porch, a porch swing, a mailman or mailtruck, a mailbox, a lawn sprinkler, a cracked sidewalk, a sewer grate, a ball in a yard, a smoking chimney, a gravel driveway, a two-car garage, a house with aluminum siding, a pile of wood, a puddle, a dog house, an ice cream truck, or a house number whose digits add up to 13.

The first player to discover all the items gets to make up a list of his or her own for the next round. Who knows what you'll find!

Required:
- Your time only

New Orleans Experiment

This activity turns your garden or flower bed into a backyard geology lab.

The goal is to demonstrate how different materials settle in water. Fill a clear plastic container about a third of the way with gravel, sand, and dirt. Add water until the container is nearly full. Put a tight-fitting lid on the container, shake it up and let it sit for a while. Then have your child describe what has happened.

Required:
- Gravel
- Sand
- Dirt
- Plastic container
- Water

Each kind of rock or ground material carried by the water settled at its own rate. The largest pieces—gravel—settled quickly to the bottom. The next-biggest particles, sand, formed a layer on top of and in between pieces of gravel. The very fine mud particles settled on top of the sand.

Explain to your child that this is what happens in the real world when a fast-moving stream or river deposits different kinds of rock to a quieter body of water. As in your child's container, the sediment settles out when the water slows down. New Orleans is built on sediment deposited where the fast-flowing Mississippi River meets the quieter Gulf of Mexico.

How about bringing a little bit of New Orleans into your own backyard?

Night Skies

Ok, let's find out who really knows the difference between the the Big Dipper and a Big Mac. For those of you who need a refresher course, here are some easily recognizable constellations (as you'd see them on a summer night in the Northern Hemisphere). You might also want to head to the library for a book that shows a full range of constellations and describes their mythological connections. In any case, see if your child can find them on a clear summer night. Alternatively, your child may wish to invent his or her own constellations as the ancients did (see #142).

Required:
• Your time only

Optional:
• Book about constellations

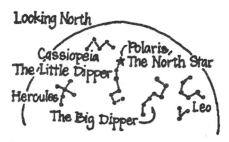

Noisemakers

Birds ravaging your garden? Have your child build noisemakers that will keep critters away.

The easiest way to make a set of noisemakers is to collect used aluminum foil tins, punch a hole in the rim of each (your job), then tie the tins to a string connected to two stakes (space the pans so they touch). As the wind blows the pans, the racket, along with the shiny reflections, should keep the birds at bay.

Another approach is to collect jar lids or frozen juice can lids, punch holes in them (adult job), and string them together. Tie knots to keep them from sliding so they'll dangle like a chain. Hang them from the cross strings between stakes, and they should make quite a racket when the wind blows them into each other.

Yet another technique involves alternating aluminum foil pans and "strikers" made from strings and bolts. Tie two or three bolts to a string every two inches. Make sure when you tie them to the cross strings on the stakes that they're close enough to the aluminum pans to strike a good blow.

Even if these techniques don't save your crops, they'll make for an interesting-sounding summer.

Required:
- Aluminum pans
- String
- Stakes

Optional:
- Frozen juice can lids or jar tops
- Bolts

No-Net Tennis

This is the first step to getting into big-time tennis tournaments.

No-Net tennis is a game for two people. It's designed to be played with a tennis ball but no racquets.

First, find a good flat sidewalk with a crack to serve as a "net." Mark off back boundaries with chalk or twigs. One player serves, which means throwing the ball so it bounces once on his or her side and then once on the other side of the net.

If the receiving player catches the ball, he or she then serves. But if the receiving player misses the ball, the serving player gets a point and also retains the serve.

If the serving player makes a bad serve (the ball bounces twice or not at all on his or her side of the net, or it doesn't land in the marked-off box on the other side of the net), the serving player loses the serve.

Play up to 7, 11, 15, or 21 points.

For a variation, players can catch the ball in a plastic yogurt container or baseball glove.

However you play, this is a game your children will grow to "love."

Required:
- Flat sidewalk
- Chalk or twigs

Optional:
- Plastic yogurt container
- Baseball glove

No-Snow Men

Safety Reminder

Adult Supervision

Required:

- Set of children's clothes
- Newspapers
- Paper bag

or:

- Set of sticks or stakes
- String or rubberbands
- Scrap material

Why wait until winter to have a snowman adorn your front yard—your kids will enjoy making "no-snow people" for the yard all year round. Here are a few suggestions.

Collect a complete ensemble of children's clothes and stuff them with wadded newspaper. You might have to use safety pins to hold the pants and shirt together. Fashion a head out of a paper bag filled with newspaper, using markers to make facial features, eyes, a nose, mouth, etc. Safety-pin the head to the body. Give the "snowman" a hat and scarf and put him out in the yard.

Another technique involves making a stick figure out of stakes or branches. You can lash or rubberband the pieces together. Drape material around the sticks to make clothes, limbs, and a head, and you'll have a ragdoll-style snowman suitable for display.

Your children might want to make a variety of "no-snow people" to accommodate each season. They might also want to name them and conduct an outdoor "no-snow people" sculpture display. Invite the neighbors for a viewing, and you'll be the center of attention on your block.

Old-Fashioned Broom

If you're lucky enough to live in an area where broom sage grows, your children will have a vast supply of broom-making materials. If not, you can make do with stiff grass and other vegetation, or thin, flexible twigs for constructing home-made brooms.

For a long-handled broom, you'll need a sturdy branch or a dowel and a handful of sage grass or twigs with the cut ends tamped and evened.

To make a broom, tie a six-foot piece of twine to something secure, at waist height. Tie the other end to the handle, about two inches from the end. Take about one-third of your broom material and slowly feed the tamped ends between the string and the handle as you turn the handle one full rotation. Continue distributing the remaining broom material around the handle in this fashion until you've used it all. Finish winding the string around the handle and tie a knot to hold it in place.

While the broom might not have quite the sweeping power of a factory-made job, your child will enjoy using his or her homemade version. Who knows—he or she might even volunteer for sidewalk cleanup duty.

Required:

- Dowel or branch
- Broom sage, thick grass, or twigs
- Twine

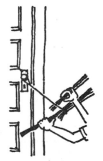

One-Way Timer

Many of the activities in this book involve timing sports activities and games. Here's a way to make timing itself into an activity.

Take a piece of wax paper (unwrinkled), or a piece of coated magazine stock and carefully curl it into a cone. The cone should be large enough to rest on the rim of a clear plastic container. Tape the paper together and snip the very tip off the cone, leaving a tiny hole. You now have a funnel.

Next, measure out a small quantity of sand of a consistent grain size and pour it into the funnel. Time how long it takes for all the sand to fall from the funnel into the container. If the sand rushes out in a few seconds, the hole at the end is too big—refold the funnel. If it doesn't move at all, the hole is too small—enlarge it. By experimenting with the volume of sand (and funnel size), as well as the hole size, you can make funnels for different lengths of time—one minute, three minutes, etc.

Start counting!

Required:

- Wax or coated magazine paper
- Scissors
- Sand
- Clear plastic container
- Measuring cup
- Watch

On the Road

No one wants a highway passing through their backyard. But here's how to make one that's non-polluting and (relatively) quiet. And your child will have a great time "motoring" from A to B.

The backyard roadway consists of a set of street signs made out of cardboard taped to broomhandles, dowels, or garden stakes. Cover the cardboard with construction paper or color it with crayons, markers, or tempera paints. Children with reading skills can write "Stop," "Slow," etc. Pre-readers can make up their own symbols (perhaps a blue swatch means stop, wave your arms, and screech like an owl). Place the signs in the ground, or in a bucket filled with dirt or sand, in a road pattern around the yard.

Your child can then pretend that he or she is a car, bus, or some other vehicle merrily tooling down the highway. And you can be a traffic cop. Be sure to set up a table, chair, or chaise lounge in one of the "rest stops"; AAA recommends that every backyard motorist take a lemonade and cookie break every hundred miles or ten minutes—whichever comes first.

Required:

- Cardboard
- Dowels, broom handles, or four-foot stakes
- Construction paper
- Crayons, markers or tempera paints

Optional:

- Buckets

Open-Air Theater

What summer would be complete without a children's play in the backyard?

You can make a theater by stringing up a clothes line and using sheets for the curtains. Set up some chairs in front, and the world stage is ready for action.

Suggested:

- Costume materials
- Clothesline and sheets
- Book of plays

Your children can write their own scripts and make up costumes from your old clothes or fabrics from the sewing room (you decide what's up for grabs).

Get involved to whatever degree you feel necessary without taking control from your kids. You might suggest a traditional fairy tale or, for an older child, a play such as *A Midsummer Night's Dream*. (Books of plays for children are available at the library and some bookstores.) The older child can serve as director, assigning roles to younger children and telling them their lines.

Make sure the whole family watches the show. Better yet, get other children from the neighborhood involved and make it a community effort. It may be off-off-off-Broadway, but even superstar actors and actresses started somewhere!

Orchestra of the Outdoors

The great outdoors is filled with things that can be used to make music. Here are just a few suggestions for the backyard or beach.

Tap sticks or pieces of driftwood together for a pleasing percussion sound. Or use them to tap recycled aluminum pie tins, buckets, or pots and pans filled with varying amounts of water. (Use water from a wading or swimming pool, then pour it into the garden or around a tree when you're done.)

Fill a plastic container with a few acorns or pebbles, close the lid, and voilà! Instant maracas. On the beach, place shells in the containers. You can also tie strings through holes in shells, then wave the strings so the shells clang into each other.

Children can put on solo concerts, or get together for various ensembles. What!?? You've never heard of Beethoven's Concerto in E Minor for Two Trash Cans?

Required:
- Sticks or driftwood
- Plastic containers with lids
- Acorns or pebbles
- Shells
- Buckets, pots, pans, or aluminum pie tins

Outdoor Checkers

There's no point hanging around indoors playing checkers on a nice summer day. Here's a version made for the great outdoors.

First make a playing "board." Use chalk on the sidewalk or driveway. You can also scratch a board in the soil, or in the sand if you're at the beach. For dark-colored squares, use diagonal lines or "cross hatching," or wet the squares with water.

Collect jar and plastic container lids for use as "checkers." For example, the "red" checkers might be yogurt container tops, while the "black" checkers consist of metal jar lids. Another approach is to have your child tape pieces of black or red construction paper onto the various jar lids to designate their colors.

In winter, try giant "snow checkers." Use a broom stick to carve a checker-board, then use plastic-coated paper plates for checkers. You'll need a water-proof marker to designate red and black "checkers," unless you have enough colored paper plates. (Supervise the use of indelible markers.)

Provide your child with broom handles or long sticks to move the pieces so the board won't get ruined, and you're all set for the world's first winter checker playoffs.

Required:
- Chalk
- Plastic container or jar lids
- Construction paper

Optional:
- Coated paper plates
- Waterproof markers
- Broom handles or long sticks

Paperweight

Here's a fun activity with a practical product—a paperweight.

First have your child pick out a rock roughly the size of an adult fist. After washing and drying it, provide non-toxic paints for your child to use (supervise the use and cleanup).

In addition to abstract designs, your child can paint animal faces using different colors for the eyes, ears, nose, and mouth. Another technique is to search for a rock that actually looks like an animal (say, an oval rock with features like a cat curled up, or a rock that resembles a head.)

Children can also paint pictures on the rocks—perhaps a sailboat in front of a sunset, or a house with a tree in the front yard.

Yet another approach is to customize a rock for someone else. Just paint the recipient's name, and make sure your child autographs and dates his or her work.

Finally, children can make paperweights for their rooms. Perhaps paint a singer or musical notes—then call it . . . "rock concert!"

Required:

- Interesting rocks
- Non-toxic paint and brushes

Pavement Art

The next activity will show you how to turn unsightly pavement cracks into high adventure. This one shows you how to transform them into great works of art.

One way to create pavement art is to use the cracks as elements of pictures or scenes that your child draws on the asphalt or concrete with chalk (you can also purchase boxes of extra wide "driveway" chalk.) For example, a crack may serve as a smile or a frown on a face, a wisp of hair on a head, a stroke of lightning in a landscape scene, the tentacles of a squid or octopus, or the mast of a ship.

Your child can also make masterpieces without the chalk, using sticks, stones, pine cones, leaves, and other natural material to finish the pictures. For instance he or she might use a pavement crack for a mouth, two large stones for the eyes, a pine cone for a nose, two leaves for ears, and blades of grass for hair.

Boy, now wouldn't that make you crack up?

Suggested:

- Chalk
- Natural materials

Pavement Journeys

Is your driveway riddled with cracks? Good! You've got a terrific playing board for a game that will test everyone's sense of balance and dexterity.

The idea is simple—the players try to get from one end of the driveway to the other by traversing the cracks. (This can also be done on sidewalks.) You and your child can walk "tightrope style," keeping each foot on the crack, or you can get to the other side "hopscotch" style, hopping along the cracks. Anyone who places a foot off the crack goes back to the starting point.

Alternately, two players start at opposite ends of the driveway. One player takes a step (or a hop), then stops. The other player then does the same. The real fun comes when two players are nose-to-nose and must get around each other while maintaining a foot on the driveway crack.

Finally, you can embellish the game by asking the players to find the longest path from start to finish. Or players can be required to bounce a large ball along the crack as they wend their way from beginning to end.

On your mark, flex your toes, go!

Required:
- Your time only

Pebble Art

If you're one of those parents who returns from a walk with your child five pounds heavier until you empty your child's rock and pebble treasures from your pockets, this activity will be a natural.

Required:

- Pebbles
- Glue
- Paper plate or lid from shoe box

Optional:

- Sand
- Tempera paints

The first step is to collect small pebbles of various shapes, textures, and colors. You might want to separate your "harvest" into plastic containers (yogurt containers and used Styrofoam coffee cups are good choices).

Next, provide your child with a shallow shoe box lid or paper plate and a bottle of non-toxic glue. Your child can randomly glue an assortment of pebbles to the plate or box to create an abstract design, or you can suggest that your child first make a simple drawing and then glue his or her treasures to make "rock relief" artwork.

An interesting variation involves gluing sand in between the pebbles as a background, or using tempera paint to color the background before applying the glue and pebbles. In any case, let the pebble artwork dry thoroughly before bringing it inside and hanging it in a conspicuous place for all guests to see and marvel at.

Pendulum Art: Model A

The sand art machine will generate fascinating art forms each time you use it. To make one, you'll need a tripod made out of five-foot-long garden stakes (if the soil is soft, you can use dowels). Drive the stakes into the ground and tie the tops together with string.

Next, take a quart-capacity milk jug (keep the cap on) and slice off the bottom (your job). Punch four holes, one near the cut edge at each corner. Also, punch a small hole in the center of the cap (your job—you may have to adjust the hole size to get the desired flow of sand). Attach a four-and-a-half-foot string to each of the holes near the top edge, tie the loose ends of the four strings together, then suspend the combined strings from the top of the stakes so that the milk jug cap is about two inches from the ground.

Place a sheet of posterboard or thick kraft paper on the ground underneath the jug, then fill the jug with *dry* sand (even-grained play sand works better than construction sand.) Hold your finger over the hole as you fill up the jug. Finally, have your child give the jug a gentle push—as it swings and the sand pours out the hole, you'll see intriguing sand patterns.

Required:

- Five-foot garden stakes
- Posterboard or kraft paper
- Quart milk jug
- String
- Dry sand
- Scissors

Pendulum Art: Model B

If you and your child enjoyed the sand art machine described in activity #217, try this one out. As before, you'll need a garden stake tripod lashed at the top. From the center, attach a modified milk jug, as described for Model A.

Required:

- Five-foot garden stakes
- String
- Quart milk jug and cap
- Scissors
- Pencil
- Dry sand
- Posterboard, paper, or old sheet

With this machine, you insert a pencil in the hole in the cap, then fill the milk jug with sand (for weight). The pencil should protrude just far enough for the point to touch a half-inch layer of sand spread on an old sheet, piece of poster-board, or kraft paper underneath the jug.

Spread the layer of dry sand under the jug—make it slightly concave to match the arc of the pencil. (We found an inverted trash can lid to be a perfect mold). Have your child gently swing the jug—the pencil will dig small trenches in the sand, creating interesting patterns.

You can vary the action by trying objects other than a pencil in the milk jug, such as a paint brush or dowel. Also, have your child try "writing" by manipulating the supporting strings, as one would move a marionette. The result will be wild-looking letters—or writing with a flair, depending on your point of view.

People Watching

Few things are as fascinating in a downtown area as the people. Here are some activities that turn people-watching into an art (best done from, say, a park bench).

First, observe a mass of people walking down the street. Guess which buildings they'll go into. Why? If they don't enter any buildings on your street, guess where they're going and why.

Look at people walking down the street in pairs or groups. Which ones are friends? Brothers and sisters? Mothers and fathers, sons and daughters? Husbands and wives? What makes you think so?

Yet another activity entails guessing what people do for work. Why? (This is a good way to get at some of your assumptions, or your child's assumptions about people and work.)

Finally, consider making a people map. Draw the doorways on both sides of a street, then draw a line as people go into and out of various doorways. Try this in the early morning and at the end of the workday. You might also want to try this over the year during various seasons. Notice any interesting patterns?

Required:
• Your time only

Optional:
• Paper and pencil

Pet "Beauty" Contests

Mirror mirror on the wall, which grasshopper is the fairest of them all? Maybe in your backyard it's the one with the longest antennae. There's only one way to find out: sponsor a pet beauty contest.

Required:
• Outdoor pets

Optional:
• Paper and pencil

Have your child or children assemble their outdoor pets—dogs, cats, bugs, frogs, or whatever—for an official contest. (Make sure that all contestants meet your approval and are handled properly!) Before the contest, have the kids make up certificates. (Dogs might enjoy wearing a banner around their collars.)

Once the contestants have been assembled, the judges can then debate the various physical qualities. Perhaps the dog with the widest yawn will take first prize. Maybe your kids will give the banner to the worm with the best slither. Or to the cat with the most crooked whiskers.

Now, what about Number 3? A bit gangly for a bull frog, but he does plan to go to Juilliard and open a free voice clinic when he graduates!

Pick-up Twigs

Here's a way to make your own set of pick-up sticks without spending a dime. Gather as many straight twigs as you can find, and you're ready to roll. Er, pick.

Give your child a handful of the twigs, and instruct him or her to let the twigs fall where they will. As with traditional pick-up sticks, the idea is to try and pick up a twig without disturbing the pile. If you succeed, you get to try and pick up another. You can also use one of your captured twigs as a lever. As soon as you disturb the pile, it's the next person's turn.

You can play with as many twigs as you like. If you're a purist, you might want to trim off some of the bumps or forks (definitely an adult job). But the bumps and forks will actually make the game more interesting and challenging.

All right, keep calm, concentrate, and you may do half as well as your child!

Required:

• Straight twigs

Piece de Resistance

Most kids don't think about air as having any substance. So they're surprised to learn that air really does offer resistance to other objects. (This activity is intended for older kids.)

To demonstrate the air resistance principle, have your child drop two pieces of paper from a porch or top step. Point out how both flutter down at their own leisurely pace. Now have your child crumple up one piece tightly into a wad, then drop the wad and the paper again from the same height. Of course, the paper wad falls much faster.

Your child will no doubt want to try this experiment with other materials. Try doing it with a flat leaf and a crumpled leaf (both the same size), a piece of scrap aluminum foil and a balled piece of foil (also the same size). Yep, they all do it, so there must be a principle. See if your child can articulate the principle in his or her own words.

Finally, ask whether the crumpled and flat leaf weigh the same—it's the ultimate test of understanding.

Required:
- Paper
- Leaves
- Scrap aluminum foil

Piñata

This classic Spanish game has been used to celebrate birthdays and special events for hundreds of years.

Safety Reminder

Adult Supervision

The traditional piñata is a hollow animal or figure containing toys and treats. It's hung from a tree or rafter. The children strike the piñata with a stick while blindfolded, trying to knock a hole in it so the treats cascade out.

You can make a piñata out of paper maché, or more simply, with several cardboard boxes. Find boxes that can be taped together to make an animal figure, decorate them with leaves and glue (for fur or feathers—a good job for your kids) then place unbreakable toys and food treats in the body. You can also include messages about things to do in the backyard—kind of like a Spanish fortune cookie. (Before decorating the box, you might want to score it with a knife in a few areas so it bursts more easily).

The children take turns holding a long stick or baseball bat. Then, blindfolded, they attempt to strike the piñata. (Make sure the other children stand out of harm's way while they wait their turns.)

Eventually the piñata will burst open, at which point the children rush in and enjoy the treats.

Required:
- Cardboard boxes or paper maché
- Treats and toys
- Leaves and glue
- Stick or bat

Optional:
- Knife

Pinball by the Sea

Playing pinball might not exactly seem like the kind of activity you'd want to do at a beach. But here's a low-tech version of the game that was just made for sand. All you need is a scoop or shovel and several plastic balls (approximately the same size).

Required:
• Sand tools
• Plastic balls

The first step is to build up a large mound of sand—youngsters will enjoy helping with this part. As you build up the mound, add water—you want to be able to make tunnels and trenches. Which brings us to the next step. Create a maze of trenches that branch and interconnect, starting from one central trench on top. If the sand will support your digging, make a few tunnels while you're at it. Make the trenches and tunnels slightly wider than your largest ball.

Place a ball in the top tunnel and let it rip—its course will be affected by bumps and irregularities in the floors of the tunnels. Release several balls and see what happens. If the sand dries out, add some water.

On your mark, get set . . . start tunneling!

Pitch Your Tent

Congratulations! You and your troops braved unspeakable dangers—carnivorous plants masquerading as dandelions, a boa constrictor resembling a garden hose, and a quicksand pit that could consume an entire toy VW! Better pitch your tent before nightfall.

Spread a blanket on the ground (optional), then place lawn chairs at the corners. Drape a large blanket or sheet over the chair backs. Use a smooth garden stake or mop handle in the middle to prop the roof up. (Place the bottom of the stick in a flower pot filled with rocks or sand.)

Designate one side of the tent as the door, and weight down the tent blanket/sheet with large stones where it touches the ground on the other side. To keep warm, place a set of toilet paper tube logs in front of the tent—your child can color them red and place small stones in a circle to make a fire pit or hearth.

Pass out some sleeping bags (beach towel rolls), get out a flashlight, and get ready for an evening in the wilds of your own backyard.

Required:
- Lawn chairs
- Blankets

Optional:
- Paper towel tubes
- Flashlights

Plant a Tree

The idea of planting a tree will probably appeal to your child. Just make sure that he or she understands that there won't be any instant gratification—the thrill comes in planting the seed and waiting for the tree to sprout.

Required:
- Tree seed or nut
- Large coffee cup
- Soil
- Water

Collect whatever tree seeds are prevalent in your area. (Be sure to collect ripened seeds that have fallen naturally.) In the northeast and many other parts of the country, maples grow easily. If you have one in your area, just plant some maple seeds (after playing a few rounds of whirligig races). Acorns also sprout well.

Place the seed or nut in a large coffee cup filled with soil (punch a hole in the bottom first) about an inch below the soil surface, and water just enough to moisten the soil. Keep the cup in a protected place outdoors throughout the winter. Tend the seedlings through the summer. Then in the fall, you and your child can plant your tree-to-be.

Plant Cuttings

This activity teaches your junior gardener how to make new plants from bits of old ones. It's very economical, and a great way to feel like you're "recycling" nature, too.

First, select the right kind of plants—not all are suited to making cuttings. Tomatoes, impatiens, azaleas, evergreen euonymus, and geraniums all work well. Cut off the top end of a growing stem about four to five inches long and remove all but the top two or three leaves (plants lose water through evaporation from their leaves, and cuttings don't have roots to soak up enough water.)

Insert about two inches of the cuttings into a container filled with a mixture of sand and peat moss (half and half). The cuttings have the best chance if you place them in a container rather than directly in the ground. Place the containers in a cool location with some light. When you see new leaves, the plants will have rooted. Wait a little longer, then transplant them into potting soil and place them where they will get good light (but not direct sun.) Gradually move the plants to a sunnier location.

Keep the soil moist but not wet, and your child should soon see hardy new plants growing in your garden or flower bed.

Required:
- Plant cuttings
- Container
- Peat moss

Plastic Recyclers

Is your trash filled with non-recyclable plastic bottles, or bottles that can't be recycled in your area? Here are some suggestions for turning them into useful or decorative items.

The first step is to clean the bottles. Then decide which ones can be pressed back into service and which will simply make interesting works of art. Plastic milk and cider jugs make excellent rain catchers. Slice them off underneath the handles (an adult job), and place them out in the garden. By the way, you can use the handle portions as funnels, or for playing milk jug catch with a rubber ball.

Cottage cheese and other plastic containers can be turned into watering cans for delicate seeds. Just punch small pin holes in the bottom (also your job), fill them with water, and hold them up for a fine spray.

Other bottles make fine modern art pieces. Decorate them with scrap aluminum foil, straws, and other waterproof materials. Use twistems to attach the pieces together. Make your art pieces wild-looking enough and they may do double duty as scarecrows!

Required:
- Non-recyclable plastic bottles
- Scissors

Optional:
- Scrap aluminum foil, straws, twistems

Plates in Space

Frisbees are lots of fun. But there's nothing like a homemade flying saucer to stimulate your child.

Every flying saucer needs a saucer—which is sitting in whatever bag or box contains your paper plates. All the better if you can find some recycled ones from a picnic. You might want to tape two together to create a curved top and bottom (double up very thin plates). Your child can use crayons, markers, or tempera paint to add insignias, gas caps, "do not step" signs, etc. before proceeding.

Once the saucer part of the ship is complete, you'll need to fashion the cabin for the crew. A paper bowl is ideal for this purpose. Again, your child may want to use crayons or markers to draw windows, doors, etc. Affix the completed cabin to the center of the saucer with glue and let it dry.

Toss the newly created spacecraft as you would a frisbee (it's all in the wrist). You can play catch, or several players can each fling their flying saucers and try to land them closest to the landing pad.

On your mark, get set, and go for a close encounter of the third kind!

Required:
- Paper plates
- Paper bowl
- Glue

Optional:
- Crayons, markers, or tempera paint

Pom Pom Pull Away

R uth's father, Arch Loetterle, remembers this game from his childhood.
Here's how it works.

You'll need at least five kids (the more
the better), and a playing field roughly
twenty feet square. (Mark off with string,
a sidewalk edge, etc. On the beach, draw
lines in the sand.) One person serves as
the "tagger" and stands in the middle of
the field. Everyone else lines up on one
side of the square, facing the tagger.
When the tagger calls out, "Pom pom
pull away" everybody starts running
and tries to get to the other side without
getting touched by the tagger. Anyone
who does get touched joins the tagger in
the middle. Anyone who runs off the
playing field boundaries becomes a tagger as well.

Now everyone is on the opposite side
of the square. The taggers simultaneously call out "Pom Pom Pull Away,"
and the players run toward the opposite
side, trying to evade the taggers. The last
person remaining untouched becomes
the tagger for the new game.

For more children, or older kids, increase the size of the playing field. This
will boost the challenge—and the fun.

Required:

• Your time only

Pom Pom
Pull Away!

"Poohsticks" #1:
(The Real Thing)

Safety Reminder
Adult Supervision

Required:
- Access to a stream
- Sticks

Optional:
- Recycled foil
- Non-toxic plants
- Ribbons

Remember how Winnie the Pooh and his friends amused themselves with stick races in the local stream? Well, you don't have to be a "silly old bear" to enjoy it yourself.

In the classic story, Pooh and his friends drop sticks off the upstream side of a bridge, then dash over to the downstream side to see whose stick emerges first from under the bridge. You and your children can do the same in a suitable park, conservation site, campground, etc. (Be sure to supervise children closely.)

If you have a stream but not a bridge, your kids can select a "finish line" downstream, perhaps marked off by a rock or a branch, then toss their Poohsticks into the water and run down to the finish line to see which stick crosses first.

Players can enhance the game by decorating their sticks to make them more recognizable. Use leaves, flowers, recycled foil, colored ribbons, etc.

Finally, everyone can be a winner if you make the object of the game to see *which* stick or leaf finishes first, rather than *whose* stick arrives first. That's certainly in keeping with the cooperative spirit of the 100 Aker Wood.

"Poohsticks" #2:
(Urban Version)

Required:
• Rainwater

Optional:
• Sticks
• Chalk

If you've read Poohsticks #1 (#231) and find yourself distraught over the fact that you don't have access to a stream, let alone a stream with a bridge, take heart: you can still play in the true spirit of Pooh.

To play "Poohsticks without sticks," collect rainwater in a bucket or fill the bucket with water from a wading pool. Then find a stretch of sidewalk, driveway, or parking lot with a slight slope. Mark off a finish line with chalk or a stick on the downward side, then have each player pour out a cupful of water along the top of the slope at the same time. The idea is to see which rivulet reaches the finish line first. For a noncompetitive version, players can try to predict which rivulet will get to the finish line first, second, third, etc.

Of course, you can always just wait for a good rainy day, put on your raincoats and galoshes, then look for natural water races in the world about you. We believe Christopher Robin would have found it great fun.

Potato Planting

The potato is the fourth-most-important plant crop in the world (behind wheat, corn, and rice). It is however, the MOST important vegetable in the world. Here's how to plant your own.

Take a couple of potatoes and cut them into one-inch and half-inch pieces, making sure that each piece has at least one good eye on it. Place the pieces four inches deep in the ground, with the cut side down and the eye up. Space them twelve inches apart.

Required:
- 2 potatoes
- Gardening tools

Mulch the soil on top with leaves or grass clippings to keep it cool for the potatoes to grow in. When the potato plants are five to six inches tall, mound the mulch around the plants to ensure that the potatoes are kept out of the sun. (Otherwise they turn green, indicating the development of natural toxins. Never eat green potatoes.) Keep the plants moist; in six to eight weeks you can dig up the whole plant and harvest "new" potatoes. Or, wait until the fall, when the whole plant above the ground dies, and harvest regular-size potatoes.

Wow—look what was growing underground!

Potpourris and Sachets

How would you like to have nature's best aromas wafting through your house? This activity will help you do just that.

These days potpourris and sachets are quite popular. A potpourri consists of an open bowl of fragrant flowers; a sachet is a cloth sack containing the same materials, but ground up. You can make them yourself, and at a fraction of the cost of what you'd pay in a boutique.

Start off making a potpourri—it's easier. You and your child can grow and then harvest, or collect from a field, the following: lilac petals, rose petals, lavender petals, sweet pea petals, mint leaves, rosemary leaves, and thyme leaves.

Place the flower petals and plants on a sheet of paper and allow them to dry (but not in direct sunlight). Herbs can be hung in a dark closet. When they are completely dry, place the materials in a bowl—your house will smell delightful!

To make a sachet, first grind up the petals and plants by hand with a mortar and pestle or with a blender (your job). Then place the plant matter in an old sock (or one orphaned by the dryer). Close with a twistem and place in a drawer—you'll have the best-smelling clothes in town.

Required:
- Fragrant flower petals and plants
- Sock
- Twistem
- Mortar and pestle or blender

Powers of Observation

Here's a variation on the old scavenger hunt—it's ideally suited for neighborhood and urban walks. Rather than providing lists of items to be found and turning your kids loose, you call out items that can be seen from wherever you are on your walk, and wait until one of the children can point them out.

One way to do the activity is first to travel the route yourself, taking note of interesting things for the activity (you might also watch for interesting landmarks when you're driving to and from work, school, errands, etc). Look for items like clocks, ornaments, and different-shaped windows; signs with interesting objects, shapes, people, or animals; and flagpoles, statues, and gargoyles. Gear the level of difficulty to the age of the children (or child) doing the activity.

Another way to play is to select items "on the fly." The first person to spot the item gets to choose the next one. (If you're playing with just one child, simply take turns being the "chooser" and the "spotter."

With a little practice you might get to be half as good as your kids at finding the ice cream store.

Required:
• Your time only

Punch Ball

This set of games hasn't made it into the Olympics yet, but it's still great fun to do. The idea is to keep a large rubber ball or onion bag ball (#300) in the air as long as possible.

The basic punch ball game entails hitting the ball with your palms facing upward. The participants keep volleying until someone drops the ball.

Once everyone has the hang of it, try this variation. One person calls out a hitting style, like hopping on one foot when you bat the ball, twirling before batting the ball, or jumping twice to the side *after* hitting the ball. Take turns calling out the required batting antics. A variation on this variation is for the caller to shout, "Jump!" or "Hop!" at which point everyone jumps or hops at the same time.

For added spice in the backyard, try volleying through an oscillating sprinkler when the lawn needs watering. If you use an onion bag ball, wrap the newspapers in a plastic bag before putting them in the mesh bag.

Heads up!

Required:
- Soft ball or onion bag ball

Optional:
- Oscillating sprinkler
- Plastic bag

Touch your nose!

Putting the Garden to Bed

The last of your harvest is in and it's time to winterize the garden plots. Your kids can have a great time helping you with the various tasks.

First, you'll want to dig out all your exhausted plants—tomatoes, peppers, eggplants, etc.—a task your child will do with relish (no pun). If you haven't made a composting bin, this is a good time to make one (see #25). Put plant matter and any spoiled vegetables into the bin.

Rake the soil smooth—your child can help with a homemade rake (see #329), and you're ready for the final prep: planting winter rye. Winter rye is a hardy variety of grass that will stay green even in the harshest weather (plant it before the ground freezes, of course). You can purchase winter rye seeds at your gardening supply store or nursery. Have your kids help toss the seeds (evenly) onto the garden plots and water them as necessary. In ten days or less your garden will be lush and green.

Come spring, mow your garden "lawn" once and then dig the grass into your soil. The decayed roots will add valuable humus to your garden soil, a treat your rutabagas will be sure to enjoy.

Required:

- Gardening tools (yours and homemade #329)

Optional:

- Composter (#25)

Quick Quicksand

The car sinks slowly into the quick-sand pit, soon to be drawn into oblivion. Onlookers gasp as they wonder about the fate of the inhabitants.

A scene from an Indiana Jones movie? No, the car is a toy, and the quicksand "pit" a plastic container. Here's how to make one yourself.

Required:

- Plastic container
- Scissors
- Duct or plastic tape
- Garden hose
- Small, heavy toys

Take a large yogurt or cottage cheese container or bottom of a quart milk jug and cut a half-inch hole in the side near the bottom. Cut eight half-inch slits radiating from the hole, like the spokes of a bicycle wheel. Push a garden hose into the hole, then seal the edges around the hose as best you can with duct or wide plastic tape. Now fill the container with sand, not quite to the top—do not pack or tamp down. Place a rock or small, heavy toy on top of the sand and turn on the spigot so the water trickles into the container (test beforehand to determine how much of a turn of your faucet handle produces a trickle). The sand will rise slightly as the water seeps between the grains, weakening its ability to support the toy. In other words . . . quicksand!

Rain Dancing & More

For thousands of years, traditional peoples performed dances designed to change the weather. We could do with a few of our own now and then. This activity is an opportunity for your children to capture some of that tradition and have fun too.

The idea is for children to invent their own dances to help bring on the rain (or make it go away), make the sun come out, make the snow start or stop falling, or make the wind pick up or die down.

The dances might be free-form, or the children might try to introduce specific symbolism. For instance, in a rain dance, the participants can shake their hands over their heads to simulate rain. Or they might pretend they're opening and holding umbrellas. You might also ask the children to select certain pieces of music for the dance—nothing like some backyard choreography.

For variety, children can take turns making up dances, steps, and chants. Dances can last as long as the children want, or you could set an egg timer when it is time to try a new dance.

Finally, be aware that the dances do not have to be related to nature—they can be done to help the home baseball team win, too.

Required:
• Your time only

Reading Tree

Reading is such an important activity for children that parents should make every effort to incorporate it into play activities.

Required:
- A good book
- A big tree

One way to do this is to make reading a ritual, an event that a child looks forward to doing. One way to structure the reading ritual, especially in the warm months of summer, is to find a private "reading tree" with thick roots that you can nestle in. A good shade tree will make the session particularly appealing.

The goal of the activity is for you to reserve quiet time when your child can sit in your lap and listen to you read, or read to you. For younger children, you can read a story and see if they can repeat it to you from memory.

For some sessions, let your child pick the stories from his or her bookshelf or the library. Other times you might surprise your child with a book of your own choosing.

Get into a regular reading habit, and your reading tree won't just be a gift for an afternoon or a summer—it's a gift for life.

Recycled Boats

Even with the new environmental con-
sciousness sweeping the nation,
there's still a lot of packaging waste to be
dealt with. This activity will give your
child a chance to help the planet a bit by
putting some non-recyclables to good
use.

Start by collecting Styrofoam containers. While some fast-food chains are
changing to paper, many local take out
places still use "clamshell"-style Styrofoam containers for salads, burgers, and
other moist foods. Turn those tubs into
boats and rafts! After a good cleaning,
you can separate the tops and bottoms,
and your child can give rides to small toy
animals and figures in the wading pool
or a deep puddle.

Alternately, keep the clamshell intact
and punch a hole through the top, near
the middle. Poke an unsharpened pencil,
a dowel, or a stick through the hole. You
now have a mast. Tape a sail made from
construction paper to the mast, and
you're ready for a sailboat race. (You
might want to place a dab of glue on the
bottom of the mast to help anchor it.)

Best wishes for a good gust of wind!

Suggested:

- Fast-food
  Styrofoam
  containers
- Pencil, dowel, or
  stick
- Paper
- Tape

Optional:

- Glue

Red Light Green Light

This old game can be done on a driveway, backyard, beach, or the park. You'll need at least four or five kids to make it exciting.

One person serves as the "stoplight," and the others as "cars." The "cars" line up shoulder to shoulder and face the stoplight from about twenty feet away. The stoplight turns around with his or her back to the cars and says, "Green light," at which time the cars can move forward. But without warning, the stoplight can suddenly shout,"Red Light!" and whip around quickly. Anyone the stoplight sees moving has to return to the starting line.

When someone reaches the stoplight, the game is over and the person who made it all the way gets to be the stoplight for the next game (flip a coin if it's a tie). For a more challenging game, increase the length of the playing field.

The cars have to weigh the advantage of moving quickly toward the stoplight and risking getting caught in motion, or moving a short distance and stopping before the stoplight turns red.

Green light—and they're off!

Required:
• Your time only

Red Light!

Red Rover

This is a traditional game designed for a large group of kids—you'll need ten to twelve or more at a minimum—even classgroups of twenty-five or thirty can enjoy it.

Safety Reminder

Rough and Tumble Play

Required:
• Your time only

Divide the kids into two groups and have them line up, holding hands tightly. The two groups face each other about twenty feet apart. Each side has a "caller." The caller from one side shouts, "Red Rover Red Rover send [*name*] right over." If Sally's name has been called, she runs to the opposite side, aiming for what she thinks will be the weakest connection. Her goal is to break through the line. If she succeeds, one person from the opposing side must return with her and join her ranks. If she fails, she joins the caller's side.

The caller from the opposite side then shouts, "Red Rover . . ." and the process continues. Whichever side has the most players at the end of the playing time wins the round.

Players can devise sneaky running strategies and use psychological tactics to spice up the game. Your job—supervise and make sure Red Rover doesn't take to the air or burrow underground.

Relay Races

This is a great activity for a group of kids. Just go out in the back yard or park, divide the kids into two groups, and off you go.

First, decide on the length of the relay races. You may want to line up one half of each team at either end of the course so each member runs one leg. Or you may want the kids to run from the starting line to a set destination and back again, where they touch the next runner's hand.

Required:
- Open space

Optional:
- Containers for water.

Relay races do not have to involve just running, however. You can have the kids crawl backward like spiders, hop on one leg, skip, walk, balance a block on their noses, or run while singing "Mary Had a Little Lamb."

Another possibility is to have the kids carry various unbreakable containers of water; the first team to finish without spilling any water wins. In this game, older children could carry cups filled almost to the top while younger children could be given containers with more leeway for error.

When the race is over, the winning team gets to choose the next kind of race.

Resident Expert

To children, the world immediately outside the front door is anything but humdrum. This activity will give your child a chance to observe the details of the neighborhood and record them for posterity.

Find a looseleaf notebook and insert section dividers with categories like plants, animals, geology, architecture, etc. With the "Book of Local Knowledge" in tow, take a neighborhood walk. Now, you might not get very far the first trip; perhaps your driveway or front walk is inhabited by two different kinds of ants, a variety of worms, and, in the spring, certain types of caterpillars. Older kids should jot down descriptions; play scribe for younger kids.

Maybe on the next trip you've started noting the common trees on your street. Is a certain kind of architecture or roof line common to the area? Describe or sketch it.

Use a rain gauge (#50) or snow gauge (#176) to compute average precipitation in the area. Note the first snowfall, when leaves begin turning, and when buds first appear.

Over the months, you and your child will create a unique archive—compare it year to year and feel a new connection with your immediate environment.

Required:
- Looseleaf notebook
- Paper and pencil

Retake-Out

Take-out packaging is one of the greatest challenges to the environmentally-minded consumer. If you can't get your local bistro to use non-foam packaging, work at the other end—press the foam containers back into service. The same goes with plasticware.

Required:

• Packaging from fast food and take-outs

Ask your child to think of as many things to do with the packaging as he or she can after the containers are cleaned. You might give some suggestions, like, "How could we use these in the garden? (good seed starter cups); During nature walks? (great for holding objects you've found)."

You can also ask for ideas for using the containers as toys and games. For instance, use them as "targets" for maple seedling races, or as bins for acorn or pine cone tosses (see activity #1).

Finally, don't forget the plastic flatware. See if your child can suggest creative uses for spoons and knives—like building a dirt city (#75) or shaping a sand castle fort #255).

Most important, don't forget the simplest thing of all—reuse the take-out materials on a picnic!

Ricochet Ball

Do you have a small rubber ball with good bounce handy? If so, all you need is a set of steps and you're ready for action. (Racquetballs are excellent for this game.)

The basic idea for two-person ricochet ball is this. One person bounces the ball off a step and hopes that the other person can't catch it. If the other person fails to catch the ball, the thrower gets the point (more on that in a moment) and he or she continues "pitching." If the other person catches the ball, he or she becomes the thrower.

As for scoring, make different steps worth different points. You can also decide that certain steps are worth a bonus—in addition to a certain number of points for hitting the step, you can double or triple your total, add ten points, etc. Conversely, you might agree that hitting certain steps costs you a penalty—you must subtract points, or divide your existing score in half, etc. You can also make the points contingent on whether the ball is caught on the fly or a subsequent bounce.

Now, follow the bouncing ball . . .

Required:
• Rubber ball

Ring Glider

Is it a bird? Is it a plane? No, it's a ring glider.

This unusual glider is sure to attract attention if your child plays with it in the park. To make one, you'll need two strips of paper about an inch wide. One strip should be 7 inches long, the other 10 inches. Tape the two strips into loops. Then tape the loops to a straw, one on the front and one on the back (see illustration). Hold the straw with the small loop in front and launch the glider—it will sail effortlessly through the air.

For added fun you can make a glider fleet and invite a group of kids to fill the air with them. The kids can have glider races, or designate landing pads in the dirt—see who can get their glider to hit the targets. A variation entails creating tunnels out of large cardboard boxes—cut off the ends and try to fly the gliders through the openings. Finally, think about contests based on duration, speed, height, or acrobatics.

Don't be surprised if you see two guys in trench coats watching with binoculars—they might be wondering how you came across a classified aircraft design!

Required:
- Paper
- Scissors
- Tape
- Straws

Optional:
- Cardboard boxes

Rites of Spring

The changing of the seasons is one of the oldest reasons for celebration—there's something fundamentally reassuring about the predictable cycles of nature. Here's a few celebration ideas that children can do each season.

Spring. The first spring-like day, collect broken branches with buds on them and put them in a vase of water. What better way to bring a little springtime into your house (and maybe trigger a spring cleaning)?

Summer. Collect flowers and other signs of the summer. Make flower chains and bracelets that your children can wear during the ritual that welcomes the warm days ahead. Perhaps have everyone take a ceremonial walk through the sprinkler the first day the lawn needs watering.

Autumn. Have your children collect the first leaves of autumn and take them inside for pressing in a large book. Rites of autumn can include any of the leaf pile activities described in #163.

Winter. Have the children line up and take a walk during the first snowfall—with their mouths open to taste the first signs of winter!

The best thing, of course, is that the seasons always change, so its never too long before your kids can celebrate a new time of the year.

Required:
• Your time only

Road Games

Here's a traveling game that makes use of the changing scenery as well as your children's imaginations.

The idea of this activity is for everyone in the car to work together telling a story based on what they see out the window. One person is assigned to be "Director." The job of the director is to call out one direction for the players to look in and then start developing the story.

For instance, the director can say, "Once upon a time, there was a *right*!" The player with the first turn says, "brown cow" because the first thing that player saw when he or she looked right was a brown cow. The first player continues. "The cow likes to play on the ..." The second player then says "slides" (the first thing in his or her view to the right), and the story continues with the next player. At the end of the round the director calls out another direction.

Just pay attention to what's FORWARD if you're driving.

Required:
• Your time only

Rock Gardens

Even if you only have a postage stamp-sized backyard, your child can make an interesting rock garden. In fact, by following the instructions for the underwater rock garden (see below), you don't need a backyard at all.

First collect rocks of interesting shapes, sizes, and textures. Don't restrict yourself to the backyard. Take a walk around the neighborhood or the park—if you see something interesting, put it in a backpack or sack. Don't forget the beach—it's a wonderful source of interesting rocks.

Back at home, have your child place the rocks in whatever patterns he or she likes. Suggest stacks of rocks, rocks in circles, squares, and other geometrical shapes, or simple random patterns.

If you don't have a backyard, wash off your specimens and have your child arrange them in a strong clear plastic container. Fill the container with water to enhance the rocks' color and beauty. (Change the water periodically to keep it from growing algae). You might also add pebbles to the bottom for extra effect. At night, try shining a flashlight on the rocks—it will make for an interesting light show!

Required:
- Rocks from the yard or neighborhood

Optional:
- Clear plastic container

Rolling Stones

Here's a game that can be played with a handful of pebbles and a dozen flower pots or buckets.

Place the flower pots in a circle roughly twelve feet in diameter, designating twelve stations of the "game board." Also designate one as a starting station. The idea is for children to move as human game pieces clockwise around the circle from station to station until they reach the twelfth station, using rocks as "dice."

Here's how it works. One player is the "roller" and stays in the center of the circle. The roller puts three different-colored pebbles in a cup and then throws them on the ground. Each pebble represents a different number from one to three. Whichever pebble lands the farthest away from the roller represents the number of stations the player whose turn it is must move. It is then the next player's turn. The first player to reach the twelfth station is the winner. And the winner becomes the first roller of the next game.

Required:
- Three small pebbles
- Flower pots

Rorschach Frost

The frost on panes of glass and car windshields can be a delightful opportunity for you and your child to exercise your imaginations and creativity.

Frost forms when the cold air on the outside causes the warm air on the inside to freeze on the glass. (You can leave a storm window open a crack to generate frost on your own panes.) It also tends to form around irregular surfaces in the glass and move outward.

On a cold day, walk around the neighborhood and observe the frost on houses and cars. What do you see? Animal faces? Geometrical patterns? Leaves? Have each person state what he or she sees, then compare notes. (Sometimes just getting another person to see the pattern you've identified is a task in itself!)

Finally, do some frost drawings on your own glass—use your gloved hand to add facial features, arms, legs, tails, etc. to naturally occurring patterns. Kids might also enjoy writing their names in the frost.

Who knows . . . maybe this is how Jack Frost got his name . . . .

Required:
• Your time only

Running Bases

This is a game for young players who want to develop their baseball skills. Important! The game is meant to be played with a tennis ball or rubber ball—*not a hardball!*

Set up two bases, (old rags, cardboard) sixty feet apart. Two players serve as fielders and one as a base runner. The two fielders play catch, always aware of the runner. The runner starts out on one of the bases. While the two fielders play catch, the runner takes a lead and then dashes back to the bag when the throw comes to the fielder at the runner's base. When the runner thinks he or she has a chance, the idea is to attempt to steal a base.

Hint for runners: Take a lead immediately after your fielder throws the ball. Then, as soon as the other fielder throws it to yours, take off running for the other base. The ball has to reach your fielder and then go back to the other to tag you before you reach his or her base.

When a runner is caught three times, it's time to switch places.

Play ball!

Required:
- Bases (cardboard or old rags)
- Two baseball gloves
- Rubber ball or tennis ball

Sand Castle Tools

You can spend a small fortune on castle-making forms the next time you go to the beach or playground sandbox, or you can make your own for free.

To make a good castle, you'll need some turrets. Any tall plastic container or coffee can will do. Pack the containers with moist sand and turn them over in the four corners of the castle-to-be. You should have a turret fit for a king! Use a small raisin box to cut spaces on top (archer's lookouts).

Now you'll need some interconnecting walls. Take a quart-sized cardboard milk or orange juice container, cut off one side, and seal the top. Pack the container with moist sand, then turn it over—instant wall.

Use plastic spoons, knives, and popsicle sticks to create detail and cut holes and doorways. After digging a moat around the walls and filling it with water, use some popsicle sticks for a drawbridge.

Supply some popsicle stick figures or toy people, and you're all set for a medieval day at the beach or sandbox.

Required:

- Tall plastic container or coffee can

- Quart milk or orange juice container

Scarecrow

A homemade scarecrow will give your garden a dramatic touch. It might even keep the birds away. And it will definitely be fun for your child to help construct.

First drive a five or six-foot wooden stake in ground (your job). Use twine to lash a three-foot cross piece about six inches from the top. Lash another twelve-inch cross piece about halfway up from the ground.

Now you and your child can dress the scarecrow. Hang an old adult-sized shirt on the top cross piece; use the lower cross piece for an old pair of pants. Fill up the clothes with straw, hay, or leaves. Make a head out of an onion bag or nylon stocking and find an appropriate hat. (Some scarecrow makers skip the head altogether and just put a hat on top.)

Your child might want to add some other touches, like a dandelion necklace (see #71) or a corsage or boutonniere. He or she might want to give it a name, too. If so, fine—wish Bartholomew good morning each time you go out.

Required:

- 1 5-foot stake
- 1 3-foot stake
- 1 12-inch stake
- Old shirt
- Old pants
- Straw, hay, or leaves

Optional:

- Bag
- Hat

Scenic Landscapes

Here's an activity that will bring out your child's artistic talent—and test his or her visual memory at the same time.

Take a walk through the neighborhood, park, or countryside at different times and ask your child to pay particular attention to the lighting, architecture, scenic areas, and so on. You might also suggest to your child to remember things such as the reflection of the sunlight on a pond . . . the lighting on a building . . . an unusual tree (which might be described as a certain animal) . . . a building that resembles an animal or has unique curves or lines.

Have your child paint on the spot (bring paper and crayons or markers) or, when you get home, suggest that he or she try to recall the details of the various scenes and recreate or interpret them with crayons, markers, or tempera paint. The next day, try to repeat the walk, bringing the artwork along for comparison.

Don't judge your child's art by its accuracy—the idea is to coax your child into observing things more closely. What better way for you to see the world through the eyes of your child?

Required:
• Painting materials

258

Safety
Reminder

Adult Supervision

Required:

- Large rubber ball or beachball
- Plastic jug with the top cut off

Scoop 'n Dodge

This game has its roots in Africa, but a variation of it can be played in your backyard, at the park, or the beach.

Cut off the top portion of a plastic milk jug (adult job). Draw a line about an inch from the top. All players except one stand shoulder to shoulder ("fillers"). Place the jug in front of the centermost child, and a pile of loose dirt next to the jug.

One player (the "hitter"), holds a soft rubber ball or beach ball and stands about ten feet in front of the others. When the game starts, the fillers rush to the jug and try to scoop dirt up to the line with their hands. Meanwhile, the hitter throws the ball at the fillers; anyone hit is eliminated.

If the hitter eliminates all the fillers, the game is over and the hitter holds his or her position for the next game. If the kids dodge the ball and fill the jug, the "hitter" becomes a filler for the next game, and the child who got in the last scoop becomes the new hitter.

Didn't you always dream that your child would play for the Dodgers?

Search for Animal Homes

Even in the city the everyday world is filled with all sorts of animal homes we normally don't even see. If you can take a nature hike into a wooded area, all the better. In any case, if you and your child keep your eyes open, you might find one or more of the following domiciles:

Required:
• Your time only

Birds' nests. Look among the branches and leaves—they're often hard to see, and for a good reason. Look for holes in trees too—they're the residence of choice for woodpeckers. Remember, though, never to touch or disturb a nest in the springtime.

Squirrel nests. These consist of leaves packed into a fork in a large branch. Squirrels generally build them very high off the ground, so you'll have to look carefully if the leaves haven't fallen yet.

Snakes, groundhogs, gophers, and moles. Look for holes in the ground (and keep fingers away).

Muskrats and beavers (Around fresh water bodies). Muskrat nests consist of piles of dirt and leaves; beaver homes look like helter-skelter piles of wood.

Finally, don't forget to look for cat doors, dog houses, and ant hills as you walk the neighborhood. They count too!

Seashore Wind Chimes

We're all familiar with the sound of the sea in a large conch. Here's another way to use shells to get pleasing sounds out of seashells: the seashore wind chime.

Find a piece of driftwood roughly an inch in diameter and a foot long. You'll also want to find some smaller pieces, to make different tiers for the chime. Next, collect shells of various sizes and shapes. Look for ones that have holes in them.

Now you can assemble the entire wind chime. Cut lengths of string about twelve inches long and tie them to shells of various sizes. Then tie the other ends to the driftwood, adjusting the lengths so the shells will bump into each other. You can also tie more than one shell to a string for enhanced sound effects.

If you've collected very small shells, make "minichimes" with small pieces of driftwood and assemble in a multi-story fashion (see illustration).

Finally, attach a string in the middle (or wherever to balance the driftwood) and hang the chime from a branch or porch beam for a pleasant natural symphony.

Required:
- Shells
- String
- Driftwood

Seaside Obstacle Course

The beach is a natural place to create an obstacle course that will challenge your child's dexterity and skill. Bring some shovels, buckets, and scoops and other beach implements, then get to work making the following.

Required:
- Buckets, scoops and beach implements

Trenches. Any good obstacle course will have a tortuous trench that your child must traverse single-footed.

Hurdles. Build up a series of small mountains for your kids to hop over.

Seaweed tightrope. Create a maze of seaweed that your child must walk along without falling off.

Footprint hop. Make a series of footprints of your own in the sand. The object is for your child to hop in them without missing a step. The more the footprints curve, the more difficult the exercise.

You can connect all of these obstacles, or use them as separate courses. And let your children invent their own rules. For example, whoever misses a hurdle might have to stand with their feet buried in the sand for sixty seconds while singing a song. So unless you're up for a little beach crooning, better do some warmups and practice those jumps!

The Secret Lives of Animals

Required:
• Your time only.

Sssss..

Kids generally ascribe human qualities to animals. You can harness that tendency and, at the same time, find out what animals really do when people aren't looking.

First, have your child observe the surroundings and pick an animal, bird, or insect. Let's say that your child spots a squirrel. He or she would describe the squirrel's family, what the squirrel does during the day, what the squirrel does for fun, and so on. For variety, your child can also demonstrate what the squirrel does when it's happy, sad, or afraid.

Groups of kids can do the activity by selecting animals for each other, or pooling their ideas. For example, one child might start off describing life in the beehive or ant colony. Another might recall some of the great birthday parties given on behalf of the queen. And another might demonstrate the fine art of extracting nectar from a flower. Perhaps the group might fly in formation around the hive or line up for a foray away from the colony.

Haven't you always wondered what skunks do for entertainment?

Shadow Games

One of the great things about playing with shadows is that you can usually count on them to be there when you need them. Just orient yourselves properly with respect to the sun, and you're all set for the following games.

Shadow Hiding. Line up—can your child hide his or her shadow behind you so that your shadow is the only one showing? Alternately, can you align yourselves so that your child's body is behind yours, but his or her arm shadows add an extra pair of limbs to your shadow? (Makes a great "shadow creature.")

Shadow Tag. Play a game of tag, but instead of touching the other person, whoever is designated "it" tries to "touch" the others' shadows with his or her own.

Shadow Mimes. Shadows make the perfect mime figurines—after all, they're mute and can be highly animated. Put on solo or group mimes. Also, you can either decide ahead of time what everyone will be doing, or simply do a spontaneous act.

Shadow Charades. See if your child can guess what kind of animal or activity you're portraying with your shadow. Then switch places and let your child do the acting.

Pick your timing carefully—the games can be called on account of sundown.

Required:

• Your shadow

Shell Faces

The beach is an infinite source of art materials; here's just one way to take advantage of it. Collect shells of various sizes. You might want to make a collection kit that consists of yogurt containers or coffee cups placed in a shoe box. Sort the shells by size, shape, and color.

Once you have a good stock of shells, your child can assemble shell faces. Use the largest shells as the heads and smaller shells as facial features, eyes, etc. Use any holes or interesting features of the shell itself for a mouth.

Your child can also embellish the faces by decorating them with paint or markers.

When the faces are completed, you can attach them to popsicle sticks and make puppets, put them on a string to make a pendant or necklace, or use them to decorate boxes, special presents, or pictures. You can also make a shell face collage by gluing a number of shells together in a box lid, on a paper plate, or on a piece of posterboard.

Just think, you can have great original art without shelling out a fortune!

Required:
- Shells
- Paint or markers
- Glue
- Popsicle

Optional:
- Box lid
- Paper plate
- Posterboard

Shipwrecked Smarts

The notion of being shipwrecked on a tropical island has sparked some of the world's best adventure stories. (It also sparked one of the most inane programs in the history of television.) How would *your* family make do if it were marooned on an island? Find out in your own backyard. (Or on the beach.)

First, define the boundaries of the island. Then send everyone on a search for survival tools and "food." You might suggest digging a pretend fire pit—add some logs and you're all set to cook dinner and ward off unwelcome critters.

How about shelter? With luck, you were able to grab a blanket before your ship went down. Drape it over some chairs and you have a hut. For a more authentic feel, drive some stakes into the ground and make a lean-to.

Of course, you'll want to build a raft for your eventual return to civilization—or at least to paddle around the island. A blanket with milk jugs tied to the corners to keep it "afloat" will do just fine.

Hey, what was that sound coming from the volcano?

Required:
- Backyard/beach materials
- Blanket
- Milk jugs

Sidewalk Game Boards

What's so interesting about a piece of sidewalk? Nothing, if you just assume it's a way of getting from "A" to "B." But with a little imagination, it can become great entertainment for your child.

First, select a sidewalk square. Look for interesting patterns formed by cracks, coloration, or imprints of leaves and footprints. If you can't find a pattern, simply use chalk to draw your own game board (with pathways, squares, targets, etc.) or create a board with twigs, pebbles, etc. Then try the following:

Required:
• Your time only

Optional:
• Chalk
• Yard materials

Let your fingers do the walking. Agree on a "path" consisting of cracks or other features in the sidewalk surface, then have each player close his or her eyes and see if they can "walk" their fingers along the route.

Maple seedling or leaf landings. See whose maple seedlings can twirl onto a designated "target." You do the same with leaf flutter races.

Acorn or pebble toss. The idea is to toss a small object onto a certain spot, a crack, etc. Different portions of the "board" can be worth positive or negative points or direct you to do certain tricks or feats.

Now, who needs TV when you can play your own version of "The Block is Right," "Walk of Fortune," or "The Sidewalk's Wild?"

Sidewalk Globe Trotters

Even young children are attracted to basketball, but some kids are just too small to shoot jump shots. This activity solves the problem.

To play, you'll need a court (a stretch of sidewalk or driveway will do fine). At each end of the court, draw a line with chalk, or create one with twigs. Next, place a sand bucket or large container in the middle of each boundary line. Fill the buckets halfway with sand, dirt, or smooth rocks to keep them from toppling. Supply a tennis or small rubber ball and let the games begin.

The idea is to bounce the ball so that it lands in the bucket on the opposite side of the court while standing or kneeling behind your bucket. Players try to intercept the ball before it reaches the bucket on their side, then bounce it themselves into the bucket across the court for a point.

Encourage your kids to invent their own scoring schemes and rules. Perhaps players gain extra points if the ball bounces more than once before going into the bucket. You can also give extra points for spectacular "dribbling."

Who says young kids can't jump?

Required:

- Sand bucket or large plastic container
- Tennis ball or small rubber ball
- Sand, dirt, or rocks

Signal Flags

Here's how to breathe new life into old rags—signal flags. The simplest flag consists of a piece of cloth tied to a ruler, stick, or dowel. If you want to get fancy, you can tie-dye the flags or use fabric paints to create designs and insignias.

Once the flags are made, you and your child can use them in various games, such as red light/green light (in which case you'll need a red and green flag). The "traffic light" stands in the center of the yard. When he or she holds out the green flag, everyone can walk, hop, crawl, or "motor" around (see #209). When the red flag is displayed, everyone freezes.

Older kids can use the flags to send secret messages to each other by assigning words to flags of specific colors and different waving positions.

You can put the flags to good use, too: wave a red flag when it's five minutes before cleanup time, and a green flag when it's actually time to head inside. On your mark, get set, go!

Required:
- Rags/T-Shirts
- Rulers, sticks, or dowels

Optional:
- Tye dye materials
- Fabric paints

Simon Says

Remember the old game, Simon Says? Whatever "Simon" does, everyone else must do, too—but with a few catches, as you'll see in a moment. Simon Says can be played in the backyard, on the beach, in a driveway, or in a park. All you need is six or more kids. The game works as follows:

One person plays "Simon," and the others stand facing him. Simon instructs the others to perform an action by saying, "SIMON SAYS, do this," then demonstrates what is to be done. The other children must imitate Simon. If Simon only says "Do this" while showing the action, the other players are NOT supposed to imitate their leader. Anyone who does so then steps out of the game. Players must also step out if they fail to imitate a certain action when they're supposed to.

Simon's strategy is to get the game moving so quickly that the players fail to notice when he just says "Do this" before demonstrating an action.

Now then, "Simon says, turn off the television . . . ."

Required:

• Your time only

Simple Croquet

Croquet, anyone? You won't need a fancy set to play this version. In fact, you don't even need much of a yard or playing field.

First, you'll need to make some croquet mallets. These can be made by rubber-banding a dry sponge to a yardstick (same as the miniature golf clubs described in #186). You can also rubber band two sponges to the yardstick, with a piece of corrugated cardboard in between for additional rigidity.

Next you'll need to set up a hoop system. You can make hoops out of corrugated cardboard (about one inch wide) and tape the ends to popsicle sticks. Insert the popsicle sticks into the ground to keep the hoop in place. Two garden stakes with a string bridging the tops work well, too.

Finally, you'll need a foam or soft rubber ball that will fit through the hoops. The object is to hit your ball through all the hoops within a specified period of time. Who knows—this could become a big hit in high social circles.

Required:

- Corrugated carboard
- Popsicle sticks or garden stakes and string
- Yardstick
- Dry sponges
- Rubber band
- Small foam or soft rubber ball

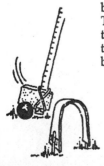

Siphon

Would you like a quick way to drain your wading pool? Try making a siphon, and educate your older child about the principle of air pressure at the same time.

To make a siphon, all you need is a garden hose and a funnel. Have your child hold both ends together upward and insert the funnel into one end. Next, have your child pour water into the funnel until a steady stream pours out the other end. Cover the ends with your thumbs and quickly immerse one end in your wading pool—don't let any air in. When you or your child places the funnel end on the ground (remove the funnel) and at a slightly lower level than the pool, all the water will drain out.

What's going on here? Air presses on the surface of the water in the wading pool. With the hose full of water, there's no counter air pressure in the hose, and the water flows out the path of least resistance—up the hose and out the other end.

Amazing what a little air will do, eh?

Required:
- Garden hose
- Wading pool filled with water
- Funnel

Skipping Stones

This classic activity is as old as the hills (or the lakes and the oceans). But it's still fun for anyone who does it. All you need is a stream or pond and a good selection of rocks.

The first step is to pick out the right kind of stones for skipping. Some stones skip much more easily than others. The thin, flat ones are best, not only because they spin but because they "hydroplane" when they hit the water, bouncing on and off the surface.

Required:
- Body of water
- Flat rocks

Next, perfect your technique—you can't just toss it any old way. Hold your throwing hand in front of you so that your thumb and forefinger form the letter "C." The rock should fit lengthwise into your grip, with the flat side parallel to the ground. Throwing should be done with a sidearm motion, much like a "submarine" pitcher in baseball. And then, at the last instant before release, the thrower should flick his or her wrist so that the rock takes off spinning.

How many times can you make the stone bounce?

Skylines

How many buildings dot the skyline of your city? Only one way to find out—go into town and count 'em.

First, look at a picture of your city, or, if geography permits, find a place where you and your child can see the entire skyline. Each of you should guess how many buildings the city contains.

Once you've seen the city from afar, locating the individual buildings can be a challenge from the street level. Depending on the height of the building, the distinguishing features that made the structure stand out on the skyline may have vanished!

Take a systematic bus ride or walk downtown and catalog each of the buildings, noting the names on the doorways or directories. This will also give your child a firsthand look at the lay of the city.

Have your child sketch the skyline from memory. It will be interesting to see which buildings impress your child the most.

What is the tallest building in your city's skyline?

Required:
• Photo or map of city

Slopes and Angles

Amazing fact: if you slowly pour a cup of sand on one point ten different times, the resulting piles will always have the same shape.

Why is this? It has to do with the fact that every material has a specific "angle of repose." Engineers define this as the limiting steepness beyond which particles will slip downhill. In other words, a pile of sand cannot get any steeper than a certain angle, no matter how carefully you pour it. The angle is steeper for larger and irregular or wet particles. So gravel has a steeper angle of repose than sand, and sand has a steeper angle of repose than dry clay (which has finer particles).

See for yourself with gravel, sand, and dirt in your garden or at the beach. Now then, what's *your* angle?

Required:
- Sand
- Gravel
- Dirt/clay
- Cup

Small-Time Composter

E ven if you live in a garden apartment, your child can still get an appreciation for the way nature works—especially with regards to biodegradation. This activity involves making a miniature compost pile that can be put to work right on a window ledge.

The compost bin itself consists of a jumbo yogurt container or a milk jug (with the top cut off). Cover the outside of the container with a piece of dark trash bag (you can also paint the container black), then cut holes to ensure air flow.

Have your child add grass clippings, leaves, and vegetable scraps. It's important to add some dirt, too—it contains the bacteria you need to get the degradation process going. (Don't use potting soil—it's been sterilized and doesn't contain the necessary critters.)

Place the "mini-compost bin" in the sun, and make sure your child stirs it up every couple of days using a small shovel or spoon. If it's warm enough, in a couple of weeks the bottom of the bin should contain highly enriched soil—a treat for house plants and cuttings!

Required:

- Plastic container
- Trash bag or paint
- Dirt
- Plant matter
- Small shovel or spoon

Smoots and More

Safety
Reminder
Adult Supervision

Required:
• Your time only

Optional:
• Notebook

If you cross the "Mass. Ave." Bridge in Boston, you'll notice that the pavement is marked in "smoots," so named for Oliver Reed Smoot, an MIT student who graduated in 1962.

Why not continue this great tradition and create units of measure for each of your children—the "Rachel," "Susan," "Timothy," or "David." First define the unit of measure—your child's body length, index finger length, arm length, or stride.

Now take your "human yardsticks" out to get some measurements, such as: the dimensions of your property, the length of your driveway, or the distance between parking meters or city trees (keep close tabs on everyone while you're doing your measuring.)

In addition to recording the various measurements you make (for comparison in later years), you can create a guessing game in which your child or group of kids tries to figure out ahead of time the number of "Thomases" from one point to another. The person with the closest guess gets to select the next object for measurement.

By the way, the Mass. Ave. Bridge, according to a bronze plaque at the entrance, is exactly 364.4 smoots—plus an ear.

0 Timothy   1 Timothy

Snowball Targets

This activity is designed to keep your kids throwing snowballs at targets rather than at each other.

Make a target on the ground by tramping down the snow in three or four concentric circles, each about two feet apart. Then have your kids designate the value of each ring. Use a stick to draw a throwing line in the snow, and let your kids take turns racking up points.

An alternative is to set up a collection of yogurt or cottage cheese containers in the snow, either standing in a clear patch or pressed down so the tops are flush with the top layer of snow. If you stand them up, place a rock in each one to keep it from toppling over. You can also push the containers into a snow bank so they're angled slightly upward.

Different containers can be worth different points. To increase the challenge, make the largest containers worth the least points (or even negative points) and the smallest containers worth the most. You can vary the difficulty by placing the containers closer or further apart, so that while aiming for a small, high-point container, the thrower is more likely to lob his or her snowball into the large, negative-point container.

OK folks, let 'em fly!

Required:
• Snow

Optional:
• Plastic containers

Snow Bouquet

You and your child can enjoy floral arrangements even in the dead of winter. Just follow these instructions.

In the middle of winter, look for winter weeds tall enough to stand above the snowfall. Look for dried grasses, weeds with interesting seed pods, or branches with winter berries. Collect these from around your house, or make a special nature walk in the neighborhood or nearby park or woods.

Required:
• Winter plants

Optional:
• Yard materials

For a "vase," simply make a mound of snow. Have your child experiment with different arrangements, featuring various plants and using others as backgrounds.

To make a fancier vase, sculpt the snow into a curved form and decorate it with acorns, nuts, berries, and pebbles. (If the snow is the right condition, you can even make handles—but don't try to lift it!)

Snow bouquets will bring a smile to anyone's face. Make a new one each month and the winter might be all that more enjoyable.

Snowdrift Patterns

During the summer it's easy to look up and describe cloud shapes. Winter provides another opportunity to view interesting shapes—snowdrifts.

Bundle up and take a walk after a substantial snowfall. Look at the drifts and at the piles of snow people have created after shoveling out, and describe what you see (after a very heavy snowfall, parked cars on the street often take on funny shapes).

Here's a list of things we look for in our neck of the woods: Graceful snow whales; lumbering snow elephants; sleeping snow turtles; slithery snow dragons and snakes; giant snow rabbits; snow hippos; snow giraffes; dormant snow volcanoes; snow cars, buses, and trains; and snow spacecraft (complete with aliens in the windows).

Jot down everyone's ideas and note the locations of the drifts—as the temperature warms up and the winds blow, the snowdrifts will change. You can repeat the same walks and note how the drifts have transformed into other creatures and objects.

How about that—the snow rabbit is now a snow pancake!

Required:

- Pencil and paper

Snowflake ID

There must be an infinite variety of snowflakes, right? True, every snow flake is different. A man named "Snowflake" Bentley spent most of his life looking at and photographing them, and never found two alike. Scientists explain this by saying that snowflakes are made up of million of parts. Just as each person is a unique compilation of many parts, so is each snowflake. There are, however, seven basic snow flake shapes, as shown below. Each snowflake is a variation on one of the shapes. Some are quite different from the pinwheel shape that we usually associate with the "traditional" snowflake. See for yourself—take a sheet of dark paper outside, allowing it to cool to air temperature. Then place it on the ground and collect snowflakes. Have your child examine the flakes before they melt. See how long it takes your child to find all seven types. And, for a snowflake game that will test your child's memory, turn to the next activity.

Required
• Dark paper

Snowflake Observation

No two snowflakes are identical, even though there are only seven basic shapes (see #280). Let your child see for him- or herself.

Take a sheet of black construction paper and a magnifying glass into the yard when it's snowing. This is easiest during a warm snowfall (near 32 degrees Fahrenheit) when the flakes are particularly big and fluffy. If the snowflakes are big enough, you may not even need a magnifying glass.

Allow the snowflakes to land on the paper once the paper is cold. Then have your child look at the flakes through the magnifying glass. Remind the child to look fast—snow does melt! For a young child who has never seen the makeup of a snowflake before, this is a fascinating experience. Explain how, despite their size, snowflakes are the building blocks of snowmen and snow forts and snowballs. Let him or her look at snowflake after snowflake in an effort to find two that are alike. Seeing is believing!

Later, in the warmth of your home, children can draw the snowflakes they've seen. Or show them how to cut out snowflakes by folding paper four or six times and then cutting designs in it (with safety scissors). When it opens, it's a permanent snowflake.

Required:

- Black construction paper

Optional:

- Magnifying glass
- Paper for cutting and drawing
- Crayons
- Safety scissors

Snow Forts and Castles

Required:

- Snow
- Snow-shoveling gear

Optional:

- Large pieces of plywood
- Buckets

Snow forts and the like are some of the most redeeming things about winter. Here are a few suggestions for making snow forts that will delight your child.

A classic snow fort needs four sturdy corners—large snowmen bottoms will work well. In between, you'll need some walls for protection. Pile up snow, make more large snowballs or even snow bricks (if the snow is nice and wet), or, if you want to get *really* fancy, make a form with two sheets of plywood, filling up the space in between with snow (make the space about six inches across). Don't forget to leave a door!

For a more castle-like appearance, build up the corners by adding a second tier, like the belly portion of a snowman. Cut archer's ridges in the top with a bucket.

Finally, consider adding a moat around the fort—dig a trench in the snow—your kids might want to slide a sturdy piece of wood over the trench as a drawbridge.

Other than basic safety precautions, just one rule: a session in the fort should be complemented with a hot chocolate and cookie session in the kitchen. Sage advice for any king or queen.

Snow Maze

You don't need a three-foot snowfall to do this activity—although it would certainly boost the fun!

To make a snow maze on a lawn, simply walk through a fresh snowfall and make a pattern for your kids to follow. You can actually plan out a maze, or you can make a random pattern by taking numerous left and right turns as the spirit moves. Then have your children walk the maze and see if they can find the shortest way to get from start to finish.

Kids can also play tag in the maze, the only rule being that they have to stick within the "roadways." They can also pretend that they're cars or trucks moving along a road system, in which case you might want to designate some of the paths as one way (lay sticks in the snow in the shape of arrows to indicate the "proper" directions).

Another approach is to use shovels and carve a maze on your driveway or sidewalk. This has two advantages: cleaner mazes, and a head start on your shoveling!

Required:
• Your time only

Optional:
• Snow shovels
• Sticks

Snow Pies

Who says making mud pies is just for summer? Our children, Noah and Audrey, regard winter as prime time for mud pies. Except that we call them snow pies.

Required:
• Sandbox/beach digging toys and buckets

To make snow pies, break out the summer sandbox and beach gear—plastic buckets, shovels, scoops, and related equipment. You'll also want to supply some (recycled) aluminum pie plates. You'll find that moist snow works better than powdery snow, as it clings together better. Suggest to your child that he or she make the following kinds of snow pies:

— The basic pie—excellent with a dash of sleet
— Icicle-topped snow pies
— Pebble meringue snow pies
— Snow pie à la mode (two scoops of snow on the side)
— Dirt crust supreme

Accomplished snow pie chefs might want to prove their mettle by making sumptuous triple-decker creations, complete with fillings of leaves—our son's record is a five-layer "cake" that lasted for three weeks.

Finally, consider making snow pies with birdseed frosting or stale bread crumb toppings—your fine-feathered visitors may be your child's most ardent admirers.

Snow Shoveling Fun

Young kids seem to enjoy shoveling snow but often aren't much help. Older kids can be very helpful but are often hard to round up for the task. Here are a few activities that will turn snow shoveling into a game—and get your driveway and walkways cleaned in the process.

One activity involves marking off certain portions of the area to be shoveled, then setting a timer and seeing if your child can clear it out before the bell goes off. For groups of children, try assigning each kid to a particular part of the drive or walkway. Make sure they're size-appropriate for the children involved (give heftier kids bigger portions and see who can finish theirs within the allotted time frame).

Another concept is the shoveling race. Start both kids off at the top of the driveway, then see who can clear a path to the end of the driveway the quickest, or before the timer goes off (notice that the use of the timer is one way to make the games non-competitive).

There's only one tough part left—finding something for *you* to do!

Required:
• Snow shovels

Snow Topiary

Who says that snowmen have to look like the venerable old "Frosty?" Why not make them in the shape of animals? Then you can have a whole yard full of snow creatures (including Frosty—we have nothing against him). Roll up huge snowballs as you would to create a basic snowman, then try these:

Suggested

- Snow and yard materials

Snow Elephant. Use branches for a trunk and tusks.

Snow turtle. Use a trash can top for the back.

Reindeer. Find a nice multi-tiered branch that has already fallen from a tree. Use as antlers.

Octopus. Use a rock for an eye and sculpt the eight legs out of snow, using more rocks for the suction cups.

Seal. Make a nice tapered body. Perhaps balance a snowball on his nose.

Decorate your front yard with these critters and you'll be the talk of the town.

Soda Can Bowling

In our first book, toilet paper tube bowling turned out to be one of the most popular activities. Here's a rugged outdoor version sure to bring the same delight.

Collect ten empty soda cans and rinse them out. Place them in a "V" formation on your sidewalk, driveway, walkway, or some other smooth surface. Now give your child a rubber ball, say four to six inches in diameter. You should use a tennis ball, just to "level the playing field." Now, just bowl!

Let your children invent various game rules or scoring options. Perhaps the object is to knock down a special can—or knock down everything BUT that can. (Your child might not tell you the rules until you've bowled, but that's OK.) Older kids might want to practice their math skills by serving as scorekeepers.

You can vary the difficulty by adjusting the distance from the cans to the bowlers, and the distance between the cans. The most important point (as with all activities in this book), is to be flexible. If your child wants to arrange the cans in a circle, then so be it—let the circle be broken!

Safety Reminder

Adult Supervision

Required:

- 10 soft drink cans
- Rubber ball (4 to 6 inches)
- One tennis ball

STRIKE!

Soil Sifter

Do you have a junior archaeologist in your midst? If so, here's a way to find all sorts of fascinating "artifacts" and treasures.

First, you'll need to make a sifter. Cut the metal clips off of an onion bag, then cut the bag so you have a flat piece of mesh (your job). Next, cut out a square or rectangle in the middle of two or three pieces of corrugated cardboard. Make the holes at least two inches smaller than the overall dimensions of the mesh. Stretch the mesh over the hole and staple it, then cover the staple prongs with the other piece(s). (You can make an extra-fine strainer by laying down two or three layers of mesh—good for the beach.) Tape the pieces together at an outside edge with wide package tape.

Now have your child use the strainer in the backyard, garden, flower bed, or on the beach. He or she will find all kinds of interesting twigs, rocks, seeds, bulbs, shells, and even insects (perhaps invite them for a stay at a "Bug Zoo" made of cardboard and screen cages). Of course, supervise and watch closely for sharp objects or other undesirables.

Who knows, maybe your child will find the world's smallest dinosaur!

Required:
- Onion bag
- Cardboard
- Stapler
- Tape
- Scissors

"Nate-a-saurus"

Solar Lab

Has your child ever insisted on wearing dark clothing on a particularly scorching day? This could cure him or her of any such notions in the future.

On a warm day with strong sunshine, place sheets of different-colored paper on your driveway or sidewalk. Make sure one of the sheets of paper is white and another black. Let the sheets cook in the sun for a while, then ask your child to feel them. Naturally, the black paper will be the warmest and the white paper the coolest. Explain that dark-colored things absorb the heat from the sun, while light colored things reflect it.

Try it with pieces of different colored clothing or fabric, too. If you have a black and a white t-shirt handy, lay them out in the sun, then ask, which would you rather be wearing on a hot day?

This is a good opportunity to explain why dark-colored car seats are no fun in the summer. And why people who live in desert regions tend to wear white.

It may also answer the age-old questions of why zebras are black and white— they want to be comfortable all year long!

Required:
- Pieces of light and dark paper or clothing

Sounds of Silence
(With apologies to Simon & Garfunkel)

Required:
• Your time only

It's a good thing that we become accustomed to many of the noises in our daily lives—otherwise we'd be too preoccupied with listening to focus on the task at hand. This activity helps us gain an appreciation for the rich world of sound around us. And it's fun, too.

Select a place for your "sound laboratory." This can be your front or back lawn, a bench by a street corner, a park bench, a subway stop, or even a peaceful meadow. Ask your child to list all of the various sounds he or she can detect. You might give him or her some things to listen for, like the hum of machinery, cars and trucks, the sound of the wind, dogs, cats, birds, music, etc. Then try the same thing in another location—your child will enjoy pointing out unique sounds.

A variation, which can also be done with a group of kids, is to see who can recall from memory all of the sounds at a given location, or even duplicate the sounds he or she heard.

Now, without looking, what's that on your street that goes ta-ta-ta-ta-doo-rum-doodle?

Souped-up Engines

There's an old tradition among young cyclists—the high-revving bicycle engine. The way to turn a bicycle into a roaring motorcycle is simple—use a playing card (or baseball card) and a clothespin.

Attach the clothespin onto a crossbar near the outer rim of the front wheel. Insert the playing card in the clothespin, positioning it so that it interferes slightly with the turning of the wheel by touching the spokes as the wheel turns. If the bike is moving fast, the "thwat" of the cards will be fast and furious and create sounds like an engine.

Have your child experiment with multiple cards—two on each wheel. A group of kids can see who can make the loudest or most unusual sounds. What does it sound like with two, three, or four bikes cruising around the driveway?

Finally, there's a fringe benefit to souping up your child's bike with a playing card engine. If it sounds like a motorcycle, the rider may be more inclined to wear a helmet.

Required:
- Clothespins
- Playing or baseball cards

VROOM!

Spaghetti Garden

Required:

- Seeds:
  tomatoes,
  carrots, green
  peppers,
  carrots,
  oregano, basil
- Onion setts
- Garlic cloves

Optional:

- Starters
  (tomatoes,
  green peppers,
  herbs)

Sorry, this isn't about growing noodles in your garden. But your child will enjoy growing all the ingredients for spaghetti sauce. Here's a gardener's shopping list and recipe (if you don't have a favorite of your own).

In the early spring, buy seeds for tomatoes, green peppers, carrots, oregano, and basil; setts for the onions; and a garlic clove. You might want to get plants for the tomatoes, green peppers, and herbs. Set aside a corner of your garden and have your child plant the seeds according to the directions on the seed packets. Your garden supplier will give you the instructions for the onions, garlic, and the starter plants. Water and tend as needed. At the end of the summer, you and your child can harvest the spaghetti fixings.

Here's a sauce recipe: Immerse one dozen tomatoes in boiling water and then in cold water to ease peeling. Peel and chop them coarsely. Cook 1 chopped green pepper, 5 minced cloves of garlic, 2 chopped onions, and 3 chopped carrots in ¼ cup oil over medium heat until the onions are translucent. Add the tomatoes, ⅛ cup chopped basil and oregano, and salt and pepper. Bring to a boil and then simmer one to two hours. Stir occasionally until the desired thickness is reached. Serve over noodles.

Eat!

Spider Web Detectives

Spider webs may look like random nature works, and indeed each one is unique. But in fact there are several different broad categories (see illustration).

Required:
• Your time only

a) Some spiders spin indistinct webs that resemble sheets of silk, usually hung horizontally.

b) The orb weaver creates a web that looks like the spokes of a wheel.

c) Others create webs that resemble a funnel leading down to the spider's hiding place.

Can your child find examples of each type (keeping fingers away from live critters)?

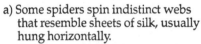

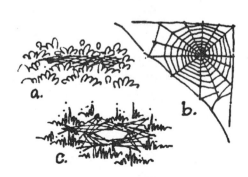

a.

b.

c.

Spot That State #1

This is a game that parents have long used to occupy kids on car trips. But it's also great for just hanging around a street corner or observing cars in a city.

The idea is simple: see how many states you and your child can find. You might want to keep a small notebook handy for the occasion. There are numerous ways to play the game, the easiest being to pick a comfortable spot (best by a stoplight or stop sign) and observe the license plates. You can also walk up and down city streets and take note of the plates.

As a variation on seeing how many states you and your child can find, see who can be the first to find a particular state. Whoever spots it first gets to pick out the next state for people to find.

Yet another variation, designed to work with groups, is to assign different states to different kids, then see who can spot his or her state within a certain period of time.

Now what would someone from Alaska be doing all the way down here . . . .

Required:

• Your time only

NEBRASKA!

Spot That State #2

In this variation of an old travel game, children observe cars and try to spot as many license plates from around the United States as they can.

While children wait to see more plates, they can discuss what they know about the states whose license plates they have already seen. Where is California? What is the capitol of Iowa? What grows there? Does that state have mountains, an ocean, a lake, or plains? Is there a professional sports team in that state, and if so, what star plays for that team? Have any presidents come from that state?

You can also vary the game by assigning points to the states by region. If you live in New England, for example, you're likely to see lots of Massachusetts, Rhode Island, Vermont, New Hampshire, and New York plates. Give those the lowest points, and award the most points to faraway places. And a super-duper bonus to Hawaii!

Required:
• Your time only

Spring Garden Clean-out

Required:
- Gardening tools
- Kid's gardening tools

Optional:
- Composter (see #25)
- Milk jugs

Whether you're just starting a garden or getting a garden in shape for the new planting season, your child can help, using his or her homemade gardening tools (see #329).

The first step is to rake out the leaves and dead plants. You'll probably need to use a regular rake for the first pass—something your child can do too. Once the soil is clear of leaves and plant matter, turn it over with a shovel or fork—your job.

When the tilling is done, your child can help look for rocks. Your child can also use a soil sifter (see #288) to clear out rocks. (He or she might find some interesting artifacts that have made their way to the surface, too.) Finally, smooth out the soil—your child can certainly help with a milk-jug rake.

What to do with the plant matter you cleared from the garden? Make a compost pile (#25). The cycle is now complete, and you're ready for another growing season.

Sprinkler Games

If you're going to water your lawn, you might as well put the precious resource to something really worthwhile—cooling off and entertaining your kids. Here are some suggestions for sprinkler games sure to delight your kids and keep them really cool.

Required:
• Sprinkler

Optional:
• Balls and outdoor toys
• Kitchen pans and utensils

Car Wash. Each child pretends that he or she is an automobile getting its wheels and fenders cleaned. (You can use this in conjunction with On the Road, #209.) One child can collect tokens (pebbles, twigs, etc) or cash (leaves). For extremely dirty vehicles, the attendant might want to hose down the cars before they enter.

Water Olympics. (Supervise closely). These games involve the sprinkler hop, limbo, baton relays, hurdles, and volleyball (use the water stream as a net).

Freeze Game. All the participants walk or dance about the yard until you call out "freeze." (You can spice up this game with an oscillating sprinkler.)

Fountain Art. Try deflecting the spray with cups, strainers, cookie sheets, and other waterproof implements. You'll create interesting displays and probably get soaked while helping to create masterpieces. But that just makes it all the more fun.

Stacking Game

This is a good way to put your Styrofoam cup collection to good use.

Find a flat surface like a driveway, sidewalk, or picnic table. Give an equal number of cups to each participant. At the count of three, everyone can start stacking them top to top, bottom to bottom. The goal is to make the highest possible stack that won't fall over. When one person's stack falls, he or she must start over.

Required:

• Styrofoam cups

Another contest is to stack the cups one inside another, but then fill the top cup with water. Each player takes a stack of cups to a starting line and "runs" to the finish.

The contest might involve a walking race, a running race, a hopping race, a skipping race, or even a walking-backward race. The key stipulation, of course, is that the water cannot spill out of the cup; if that happens, the racer must go back to the starting line and refill the top cup.

No doubt about it: these races will allow you to see how everyone stacks up.

State Knowledge

Do you know your state's official plant or animal? This activity will turn your child into a walking expert on high-level matters of state. Write a letter (or have your child write one) to your state's Chamber of Commerce requesting basic information. Here are some things to learn.

Required:
• Your time only

Optional:
• Paper and pencil

State flora and fauna—find examples of the state flower or bird in your neighborhood. Record sightings in a notebook.

State history—who founded the state and when? Any notables (inventors, political figures, etc.)? Look for examples of the founder's name in street signs, commercial signs, buildings, and so on.

State flag. What does it look like? What's the significance? When was it designed? Look for one in your neighborhood.

What other official symbols does your state have? Look for examples in your own area. And don't forget to ask your child for suggestions of his or her own. Perhaps your state will adopt an official dinosaur yet!

Stationary Volleyball

If you don't have a net or you don't feel like chasing a volleyball all the time, try this activity.

First you'll need to make a pouch for the ball. An onion bag is perfect for the job. Cut the metal clip off of a mesh bag (an adult job). Then insert the largest ball that will fit inside the bag. Close the end by threading a string through the mesh holes at the opening.

Required:
- Onion bag
- Rubber ball
- String or rope

Next, attach a cord or rope to the string you used to close the opening. Tie the other end to a sturdy overhead tree limb (or a hook in a porch rafter). Adjust the height so the ball hangs down low enough for children to hit it.

Now you're ready to play. Break up into teams of two or more players. The teams line up opposite each other and hit the ball back and forth, making sure that it is hit on the forward swing before making a return swing—otherwise, you lose the point. Alternately, forget scoring—just enjoy the simple pleasure of keeping the ball moving.

Statue Stories

Hey—who's that guy on the horse? Or that dignified old gent holding his bowler cap in his hand? You can read the plaques on statues, or better yet, let your child make up a story about the statue's significance. (Older kids can write up their tales.) Here are some suggestions for statue stories.

First, find some statues. If you don't know of any, go on a statue hunt—you've probably walked right by many without paying a lot of attention to them. You might also want to contact your city's chamber of commerce to make sure you don't miss anything especially noteworthy or tucked away in some corner.

Once you've found a statue, ask your child what the person is doing? ("His hat is off because he wants to scratch his head" . . . "His horse is rearing because it was just stung by a bee"). Why was he or she memorialized ("She was the first person to ride a turtle around the common." . . . "He discovered a new recipe for acorn stew").

And of course, ask the person's name. As we learned, one statue in our park is none other than Ebenezer Flapmork, first governor of the Commonwealth of Massachusetts!

Required:

• Your time only

Stick Letters (Easy)

That pile of sticks and twigs on your lawn or in your garden is an "alphabet in waiting." Before using the twigs and sticks to create letters, have your child help you organize them into piles by size (an activity in itself).

For pre-readers, assemble alphabet letters, then ask if anyone knows the letter's name. For children with reading skills, you can assemble complete words for them to pronounce. The reverse of this game is to say a letter or word, and have your child fashion the letters out of the twigs and sticks.

Finally, consider making twig and stick signs with glue and a piece of cardboard or wood. Kids will enjoy making signs with their names on them, or making mailbox signs (for covered porches). And there's a fringe benefit too; you may make your letter carrier's job just a bit more fun to do.

Required:
• Twigs and small sticks

Optional:
• Glue
• Cardboard or wood

Stick Letters (Advanced)

This is a more sophisticated version of the previous activity. It is designed for kids with reading ability.

Gather a collection of twigs roughly the same size. Think of a word, then write it with the twigs. But leave parts of each letter incomplete. Ask your child if he or she can determine the word. When your child guesses the word, let him or her try it with you—don't be surprised if the letters only contain one twig!

A variation involves giving contextual hints about the word. If, for example, you've written the word "BIRD" in partial letters, you can drop hints or make an imitation (eventually flapping your arms). Alternately, your child might be allowed to ask questions, like, "Is it a thing or an animal?" "How many feet does it have?" "Does it have fur?" "What does it eat?" "Does it live it in the water?" And so on. Again, switch sides once your child has gotten the word.

Be prepared—your child will probably come up with a stumper or two!

Required:
• Yard materials

Street Math (Easy)

Street addresses provide a great opportunity for children of all ages to practice their number skills. Here are a few activities.

Required:
• Your time only

Counting/Number Recognition. (For young children.) Have your child recite addresses as you walk up and down the street (great for children who are just learning to recognize double-digit numbers).

Odd/Even. If your child is just learning the idea of odd and even, take an "even-side walk" and then an "odd-side walk." Have your child recite the last digits of the address to reinforce the concept.

Basic Math Operations. Use whatever math process your child is learning to disguise addresses. For example, 4 minus 1, 3 plus 6 Main Street would be 39 Main Street. Another variation involves adding all of the numbers in the address to find out whose house number equals, say 18. The address 6408 would do so ($6 + 4 + 0 + 8 = 18$).

Quick—what's your house number times your child's age plus your own age?

Street Math (Advanced)

Here's a variation on an old mathematical game called "crypto." It will challenge your older child's (and your) ability to do mathematical computations on the fly. The object is to try and reduce a two- or three-digit number to a single digit (you can't do that with every number—but part of the game is discovering when a number won't work.)

To play the game, take a neighborhood or urban walk with your child and call out a number, say six. Let's say you pass a house or a sign with the number "167." Your child would reduce the number by first noting that "6 x 7 equals 42." Then he or she would say, "4 + 2 (from the '42') equals 6." Now you're down to two digits—"1" and "6." Your child then says that "1 times 6 equals 6." Which is the number you called out.

You can also play the game with a group of kids. Perhaps you (or the walk leader) call out "5." The child who goes first (establish the order ahead of time) spots the house or sign with the number 167. His or her answer would go like this: 6 x 7 = 42. 42 - 1 (the first digit in 167) = 41. Add 4 + 1 (from the 41), and presto—you have the desired number!

Your turn—how fast can *you* reduce 324 to 1?

Required:
• Your time only

Street Name Tales

Required:
• Your time only

Optional:
• Pencil and paper

If you don't know the origins of your street names, don't worry—your child can come up with something that's probably more exciting (and can memorize his or her address in the process).

Take a neighborhood walk and note the street names. Ask your child to make up a little story about each one. For example, Royal Avenue might be so named because a king and queen used to come play there, while Forest Street is so named because it used to pass through a dense wood and was inhabited by mischievous elves.

A variation is to connect the street name tales. As you walk from street to street, incorporate the street names into an ongoing story. For example, one day the king and queen of Royal Avenue took a stroll through the Forest (Avenue), where they met six elves who took them up the Hill (Street).

Jot down the stories and their street association. Later, you can recite the story and see if your child can lead you along a route that mentions all the names. Don't be surprised where you wind up!

Street Sign Word Game

This is the old automobile travel game with one important exception—it's not done in a car. Rather, you play it on foot in your own neighborhood or in a shopping district.

Required:
• Your time only

The idea is to walk with your child in an area that has lots of signs and attempt to find specific letters to spell pre-chosen words. Any kind of sign will do—a business sign, a real estate sign, even the sign on a moving truck.

For starters, have all the "sign sleuths" find the letters in their own name. For instance, if the child's name is Jim, he could find a "J" and an "M" in a "Jones Plumbers" sign and an "I" in a sign for the Fire Department.

Another sign game is to have everyone look for the same word. For example, one person calls out a word, say, "Pillow," and everybody tries to find all the letters. The first person to do so gets to pick the next word. In the beginning, you can share letters; but as the players get more observant, the rules can tighten so that a letter in a sign can only be used by one player.

How about trying to find the word "sign"?

Summer Forts

It's easy to make snow forts—just line up large snowballs or make snow blocks. But it's just as easy in the summer—all you need is a collection of lawn furniture, some sheets or blankets, and a large box or two.

Required:
- Lawn furniture
- Sheets

Optional:
- Large cardboard boxes
- Paper towel or toilet paper tubes and tape
- Scissors

Arrange the lawn chairs in a square, with intermediate chairs between the corners. Drape the sheets or blankets over the backs to create "walls" the width of the chairs. Your child or children can peer out over the walls or crawl between the legs (which now constitute a series of tunnels).

For added fun, place a large box at one or more corners. Cut a door at the side so that your child can climb in through the inside walls of the fort. You might want to cut some observation holes in the box or cut out squares at the top, creating a classic castle tower appearance.

The inhabitants of the fort will enjoy using telescopes made from paper towel tubes or binoculars made from toilet paper tubes (tape two together).

Aha! Looks like the cookie delivery person approacheth. Open the gates!

Summer Sled

Your backyard can become an Olympic-style sled trail even in summer—if you have the right kind of "sled."

This kind of sled consists of a heavy-duty cardboard box pulled by a ten-foot-long rope. Punch two holes (adult job) at one end, near the top corners. Then take two plastic lids and punch a hole in the middle of each (also an adult job). Now hold the lids against the inside of the box with the holes aligned to the holes in the box. Feed the ends of the rope through the holes from the outside and tie a large knot on the inside of each.

When you pull on the rope, the knots will pull the lids tightly against the inside of the box. (Without the lids the knots might pull through the holes.)

Now it's time for the rider to get in the sled. An adult or older child grabs the front of the rope and pulls while the child in the back yells, "Mush!" and directs the puller where to go. Get several sled pullers and drivers together and you'll be ready for a backyard "dogsled" contest.

Required:

- Sturdy cardboard box
- A 10-foot length of rope
- Two yogurt-container tops

Sum the Points

Here's a great basketball game for three people. It develops dribbling, shooting, and rebounding skills. And most important, it's fun.

The basic idea is that everyone shoots five foul shots; the player who makes the most baskets gets the ball first. The player who has the ball moves to a preset backcourt line and tries to score while the other two guard him or her. If the shot is missed, everyone tries for the rebound and can immediately shoot again.

Required:
- Basketball
- Basketball court

Once a shot is made, it counts for two points, and the shooter then goes to the foul line. The shooter shoots foul shots (one point each) until he or she misses. When a foul shot is missed, the ball is back in play. Everyone goes for the rebound and can immediately shoot again for two points and a chance to go to the foul line. When someone reaches thirty-three points, the game starts again.

Sound too fast-paced? Don't worry—this game is almost as fun to watch as it is to play.

Sun Cards

Solar energy is not only good for heating homes, it's also great for making interesting pieces of artwork and greeting cards. All you need is a bright sunny day.

First take some heavy colored cardstock and fold it into a greeting card. (If you just want to make an interesting print to hang on the wall, don't worry about folding the paper.) Next, place a number of objects on top of the paper, such as keys, small toys, or a small household gadget with a distinctive shape. You can also cut out shapes or letters from another sheet of paper and arrange them atop the construction paper.

Place the construction paper directly in the sun; by the end of the day, the paper will be faded—except in the areas protected by the objects or pieces of black paper.

FAX paper also works well for this purpose—it quickly turns yellow or brown when exposed to strong sunlight. (This is an excellent way to recycle the stuff, too).

Whatever you do, your child is sure to get a kick out of making genuine solar-powered artwork.

Required:
- Construction paper
- Small objects

Optional:
- FAX paper

Sundial

Before Timex watches, people used the sun to tell time. Here's how you can continue the ancient tradition in your own backyard.

Take an eighteen-inch-square piece of heavy cardboard. Find an area in your yard where you can put it in the same position and orientation each day (you'll want to move it during rain showers or snowstorms). Next, make the upward part (the "gnomon"—see illustration for the shape and folding lines). Tape the two flaps at the bottom of the gnomon to the flat piece of cardboard halfway along one side, as shown.

To calibrate the dial, you and your child will need to orient the upward point of the gnomon to the South (use a compass or go out precisely at noon and orient the sundial so that the gnomon casts no shadow to either side). Next, observe the sundial every hour and mark a line on the cardboard at the edge of the shadow cast by the gnomon. Write down the hour next to the line. The next sunny day, you can use the sundial instead of your watch—and you never have to worry about winding it!

Required:
- Corrugated cardboard sheet
- Scissors

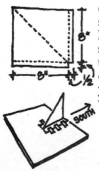

Sunset Watching

One of the most beautiful things about a sunset is the way it changes. Every moment it's different, until it's gone. Here's an activity that turns the changes into a game.

Get the whole family out for a sunset viewing (a picnic dinner is a great way to get ready). As the sky turns colors, have everyone take turns closing their eyes, counting to thirty (ten, for young ones), then describing what's different when they open their eyes again.

Alternately, have everyone close their eyes while you count to thirty; then instruct everyone to open their eyes and describe the changes. It will be interesting to see how each family recalls the shapes and colors.

Another sunset-watching game involves asking people to *predict* what will happen next—the color changes, the changes in the cloud shapes, etc.

But you might also find that the most satisfying game of all is for everyone to sit quietly and watch the sun go down, then describe how good it made them feel.

Required:
• Your time only

Sun Tea

If your children have a lemonade stand (#325) or have opened a Four Seasons Cafe (#104), here's a welcome addition to the menu—for parents.

First you need a solar-powered "tea brewer." Take a large plastic jar with a lid (an institutional-sized one would be ideal). If you don't have a lid, try sealing the container with a plastic bag and rubber band.

Required:
- Tea bags
- Large container with lid (or plastic bag with rubber band lid)

Optional:
- Lemon slices

Next, place the tea brewer on a dark surface that will absorb the sun. Fill the jar with water (let your child measure with a cup—a good way to reinforce measuring skills), and add enough tea bags to make a good strong brew (this might take a little experimenting). If the sun is strong, the water will heat up and the tea will "cook." Allow the tea to steep for a few hours, then serve it up.

As you brew different batches, you might want to keep a log book so you'll know the best amount of water and the right number of tea bags for whatever type of tea you're using.

A twist of lemon for ours, please.

Surprise Map Games

Children are fascinated by the concepts of maps—and delighted when they can actually follow one. This activity turns map reading into a fun and challenging game.

No matter where you live, you can devise a simple map that will take your child on an interesting journey (actually, your child is the navigator—you're there at every step). For example, draw a simple map that takes your child to a shopping area (by foot or by car). Your child reads the map and says, "left," "right," or "straight." The goal is to reach an area marked with an "X." Which could be the ice cream store or bakery.

You can play an interesting variation on the beach involving "buried treasure." Hide an air-tight plastic container filled with treats (also wrapped up) about a foot under the sand. Make a treasure map based on your child's paces, for instance, "From the beach blanket, go twenty paces toward the life guard tower, then turn right and go five paces. Stop at the large piece of driftwood. Turn right and go ten paces."

Just don't forget where you buried the treasure!

Required:
• Pencil and paper

Tadpoles to Frogs

Do you have a pond or stream nearby? If so, try collecting tadpoles in mid-spring. Your children will enjoy watching them grow.

First, prepare an "observation tank." A plastic dishpan or large plastic jar will be fine. You'll want to outfit it with a screen top when the critters get too big.

Required:
- Tadpoles
- Plastic container
- Rocks
- Screen

Now collect some tadpoles from your local pond or stream. (You might want to use a version of the strainers used in Gone Fishin', #118.) Put them into a plastic transfer jar along with the pond water. Provide rocks that project above the surface, so the tadpoles can climb out of the water once they develop legs—remember, they're becoming air breathers. Also be sure to add fresh (not tap) water weekly.

Point out to your child how their legs emerge and their tails disappear as they grow. When the tadpoles become mature frogs take them back to their pond or stream. Visit the pond a year later and thank them for serving as guest lecturers in your home biology class.

Tag Games

Oh sure, we all played the basic game of tag—one person is "It," and It tries to tag anyone else and rid himself or herself of the thankless role. Here are a few variations on the traditional game that your children are sure to enjoy.

For starts, try "squat" tag. With this game, whoever is about to be tagged can simply drop to a squatting position. This makes them off limits to It. When they stand up again, though, they're fair game.

"Zone" tag. This is a good game for the beach or when there's snow on the ground, since you need to mark off areas on the ground. In a backyard or park, you can designate zones by placing certain objects as markers. The idea is that certain areas are "safety" zones—no one can be tagged when standing in one of them.

"Weird movement tag." With this game, It calls out a movement style—walking backward, hopping, masquerading as a frog, etc. Everyone, including It, must move with the style until a new one is called.

How about "tell-a-joke tag"?

Required:
• Your time only

Tail Games

Here's an activity that allows your child to join the animal world—by growing a tail.

Not a real tail, of course, but a tail made of cloth. First, each child makes the tail out of a cloth approximately two inches by eighteen inches long. About five inches from the top of each tail, tie a bulky knot and then have each child insert that end down the back of his or her pants so that the rest of the cloth hangs down like a tail.

Once everyone has a tail in place, the games can begin. The games can take many forms. For example, play football, but instead of tackling or doing two-handed touch, the player is "down" when his or her tail is plucked.

You can also play "tail tag"—the person designated It tries to remove tail feathers rather than tagging the other players. A variation is to have players with different-colored tails. "It" must catch all those with red tails within, say, two minutes, and then grab all the blue tails within another two minutes.

Watch your tail feathers!

Required:
- Strips of cloth

Talking Heads

Have you ever been to a carnival or fair that has a wood animal form with a hole at the face for your child to peer through? You can recreate these entertaining displays in your own backyard.

You'll need some large pieces of cardboard, which you can get by splicing together sections of large boxes. You can also purchase sheets of posterboard for the occasion. Have your child draw a simple animal (you can help, too) with crayons or markers. Add whatever level of detail he or she wishes. But leave the face blank—cut a hole instead (slightly larger than your child's head—cutting is your job).

Now prop up the cardboard against a chair, or make a stand out of more cardboard. Have your child put his or her head through the hole and make authentic animal sounds.

In addition to animals, you can make forms for trees and flowers, common objects like fire hydrants, etc. Make up several forms, recruit a group of kids, and you'll have a human sculpture garden. Use face paints if you really want to get fancy.

Most important, don't forget film for your camera.

Required:
- Large sheets of cardboard or posterboard
- Markers or crayons
- Scissors

Optional:
- Face paints

Target Throw

Here's a way to boost your child's throwing and pitching accuracy.

All you need is an old tire and some rope. And even if you don't have a tire, you can make a similar target with a big piece of cardboard (the side of an appliance box) and some scissors. Just cut a two-foot-diameter hole in the center of cardboard. Another possible target is a length of hose shaped into an "O" and taped together.

Tie the rope around the target with a large, secure knot. Throw the other end of the rope over a tree limb. Tie the rope over the tree limb so that the top of the tire hangs at shoulder level. Use a ladder, if necessary, to tie the rope to the tree (your job).

Once the target is hung, your children can throw footballs, baseballs, tennis ball, or Frisbees through it. They can see how many hits they can get out of ten or fifty or a hundred throws. Or, when they improve, they can try to see how many they can get in a row.

From there, it's on to the major leagues!

Required:
- Tire
- Rope
- Ball

Optional:
- Cardboard
- Scissors
- Short length of hose
- Tape
- Appliance box
- Crayons or markers

Teepees

C hildren are fascinated by the idea that people in other cultures have lived in houses very different from their own. Teepees are particularly interesting and are easy to replicate in your backyard.

Safety Reminder

Adult Supervision

You'll need three to four garden stakes at least five feet long. (If the ground is soft, the stakes don't necessarily need a sharp end; wooden dowels or tomato stakes will do. Make sure there are no rough edges—sand them first if in doubt.)

Pitch the stakes at an angle, then tie the tops together with string or twine. Now take a sheet and fold it so it's slightly taller than the teepee frame. Wrap the sheet around the frame, using clothespins or Bulldog clips to hold it together at the top. Fold one edge around one of the stakes for a doorway, securing it inside. Leave the other end as the flap. Your child might want to decorate the sides with washable markers or fabric paint—perhaps add sun or moon symbols.

Presto! A teepee sure to delight your child.

Required:

- Five-foot garden stakes or dowels
- Bed sheet
- String or twine
- Clothespin or Bulldog clips

Optional

- Fabric paints
- Washable markers

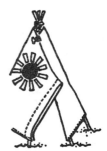

Terrarium

A terrarium is a world in miniature. If you have a large clear plastic container or jug, you can make one in your backyard.

First, have your child add a layer of pebbles—this will promote drainage. Cover the pebbles with a layer of topsoil about two inches thick. Place a few rocks in the terrarium—these will add natural beauty and will hold heat during cold nights.

Next, your child can add branches and moss, as well as small plants dug up from your garden or flower bed. Select plants growing in conditions that will be similar to those in the terrarium. For instance, if the terrarium is going to be in the shade, select shade plants; if it's going to be partly in the sun, have your child plant semi sun-lovers. Water the terrarium so that it's moist inside (not too much!), then cover the opening with a sheet of plastic.

The terrarium will also make a nice temporary home for worms and other critters—make a screen to allow air flow (or use a stocking) and make sure it's not in the full sun.

Your child will enjoy checking the terrarium and maintaining this world in miniature.

Required:

- Plastic container
- Gravel
- Small plants
- Rocks, branches, moss
- Plastic wrap
- Screen or stocking

Theories of the Universe

Where does fire go when it goes out? Where does the sun go when it sets? And why is it hotter in summer than in winter?

These are big questions, and your child probably has some insights that scientists have never considered. This activity will enable your child to describe his or her own unique theories of the universe (of course, gear the following for your child's age and base of knowledge).

Required:
• Your time only

Sit with your child and toss a pebble into the air. Ask why the pebble falls down and not up. Look up in the sky and ask why clouds don't fall to earth. Watch a bird soar through the air. Why can birds fly and people can't, even though people can flap their arms?

Wait for the moon to rise and ask where the moon has been all day. Ask the same question about where the sun spends the night. What is light? What is heat? What is cold?

In autumn, pick up a leaf and ask why it changed color. Why are some leaves yellow and others red? And why do some people lose the foliage on their head?

Big questions, big answers.

Thermometer Kids

If you have an outdoor thermometer, this activity will help your child appreciate seasonal changes in temperature. If you don't have one, purchase an inexpensive model for this activity and future use as well (choose a dial version rather than a glass/mercury model).

Required:
- Dial-type thermometer
- Paper and pencil

You'll also need a log book or a calendar so your child can write down the information. Each day, have your child measure and record the temperature in the morning around breakfast and in the evening around dinner time.

Other thermometer activities include taking readings in the sun and recording the difference (explain why the shade is cooler); computing the average temperature for the day, week, and month (have older children help with the math); and comparing your thermometer with the weather service.

Best of all, if you make an Outdoor Zany Television (#365), your child is all set to do weather forecasts—and speak with authority!

Thirst Busters

What would summer be like without a neighborhood lemonade stand? Besides, it's a great way to give a budding entrepreneur a sense of real life in the business world.

First you'll need a stand. Use a card table if you have one handy, or place a (smooth) board over some bricks or cinder blocks. Have your kids help make a tablecloth (decorated kraft paper works well). Now it's time to make a sign. Supply a piece of cardboard and markers, crayons, or tempera paint. Older kids can do the wording and lettering themselves; read off the letters for younger children. Affix the sign to the table, prop it up on top, or attach it to a garden stake.

Now for the lemonade. Buy a mix, or better yet, make your own. Add 1½ cups of sugar to 2 quarts of water and bring to a boil. Chill, and add ¾ cup lemon juice (the juice from 6 lemons) and one tablespoon of salt. (You can also mix the lemonade with other juice to create exotic offerings.)

Supply paper cups, a pitcher, napkins, and a box for coins, and your kids are ready to go into business.

Today a lemonade stand. Tomorrow ... look out, IBM!

Required:

- Card table or board and bricks
- Kraft paper
- Piece of heavy cardboard
- Markers, crayons, or paint
- Paper cups
- Pitcher
- Lemonade (mix or homemade)
- Money box

Tiddlywinks

Safety Reminder

Adult Supervision

Required:
- Backyard materials

Here's a game that kids have played for generations in the cities and countryside alike. It's simple and fun and builds hand-eye coordination as well.

First, find a twig about four to six inches long (a popsicle stick also works well.) Rest the twig on a fulcrum (a thicker stick, driftwood, rock, etc), so that only about an inch extends beyond the fulcrum's edge. Hit the twig so that it flies in the air, and try to whack it again before it hits the ground. (Of course, parents should make sure no one is in the flight path of the twig.)

Now try your skill with the following tiddlywink games: see how far a player can bat the twig; how many times a player can hit a twig before it hits the ground; how close a player can hit a twig to a target drawn on the ground, and so on.

If you want to have a non-competitive tournament, have the players try to beat their previous scores, rather than each other's scores.

Tightrope Feats

This is a balancing game performed at an imaginary terrifying height.

All you do is lay an ordinary garden hose on the ground so it is straight like a tightrope. The children line up and take turns walking over it as if it were strung between two tall buildings or were a circus act.

The tightrope walkers can hold a broomstick as a balance stick, and another child can announce them as "The Great Suzy," or "The Great Bobby."

For variation, children can walk across the tightrope carrying cups of water filled to various levels, or stacks of blocks, or with a doll or stuffed animal perched on each shoulder.

When the straight tightrope wears out its welcome, you can always lay out the garden hose in oddball curved shapes like the letter "S" or even a continually shrinking spiral.

Relax. Take a deep breath. Concentrate. Maybe you can walk the tightrope, too.

Required:
• Garden hose

Optional:
• Broomstick

Time Capsule

F uture archaeologists or maybe even visitors from another planet may someday wonder what life was like in the area around your backyard. Why not leave some clues?

A time capsule is a fun and easy activity to help children get a better understanding of themselves, their family, their neighborhood, and the time period in which they live.

All they have to do is fill a large yogurt container with artifacts from their lives and their time, and then, with an adult's help, bury it in the backyard or garden.

The best part is scrounging up or making the artifacts. The idea is to select items that describe your children's life and times. Small toys, like a car or doll would work; so would original art, photos of the family, an original story, a newspaper story, a baseball card, or a listing of movies currently playing at the theater.

As a variation, have your kids bury *two* identical time capsules and open one a year later—they'll be amazed at how much can change in just twelve months.

Required:

- Large yogurt container
- Shovel
- Artifacts of your choice

Tools of the Trade

If your child likes gardening, you can invest in some small gardening tools. Or, you can make a few of your own—here are some suggestions.

Scoops. Cut a half-gallon milk jug just below the handle at an angle (a job for you—see illustration), then wad up a piece of newspaper and wedge it from the inside into the opening.

Scratchers and rakes. For a scratcher, cut off the top of a half-gallon milk jug at an angle, then cut serrated "teeth" along the longer cut edge (adult jobs—see illustration) opposite the handle. For a rake, first make a scratcher from a gallon jug. Then cut four quarter-inch-long slits into the jug mouth (your job) to allow a wrapping paper tube to be wedged into the mouth, for use as a handle. Wrap a few layers of tape around the mouth. (See #182 for a technique that can be used to reinforce the handle.)

Buckets. Use the bottoms from the milk jugs from which you made scoops. One-gallon jugs would provide nice-sized containers.

Turn your child loose for some digging, raking, and good old gardening fun.

Suggested materials:

- Milk jugs
- Wrapping paper tube
- Scissors
- Tape
- Corrugated cardboard

Tour Guide

Even if you've taken many neighborhood, nature, or urban walks with your child, this activity can still be great fun.

Required:
• Your time only

Your child, serving as guide, points out key sights for the "untrained eye" to look at, just as an expert guide would direct a group of "city dwellers" on their first foray into the wild. For urban walks, your child assumes the reverse—that he or she is leading country folk on their first tour of the big city.

During the tour, ask your child to point out hidden details—in the woods, interesting seeds on the ground, flowers tucked away in unexpected places, interesting leaves (watch for poison ivy), land formations, bird or squirrel nests, and natural elements.

In the city, your tour guide can point out unique architecture, statues, the tallest building, interesting iron gates and manhole covers. And in the neighborhood, your tour guide will want to point out unique roofs, building materials, flower beds, store signs, and other features. You'll probably be surprised at how much your child knows about the fine details of his or her environment.

Town Planners

I s your child a budding city planner or architect? Find out with this activity. The idea is to create a city or neighborhood in which the buildings and houses are designated by rocks and other natural objects.

First map out the town "site"—roadways, sidewalks, pathways, building foundations, waterways, etc. You and your child can do this by making lines in the dirt with a stick, or by using chalk on the sidewalk or driveway.

Next, place various natural objects on the site to create the details. Let your child decide on the rules. For instance, pine cones might be used as house walls or houses, while stones represent bricks or whole buildings. Your child might decide that acorns represent buses, while certain seeds are people. Other possibilities include the use of pebbles, perhaps for cars or pieces of walls; upright twigs for trees, people, etc.; and leaves for the town "baseball diamond," flags, and so on. In any case, this part of activity is a good way to stimulate your child's imagination.

Oh, by the way, here's a great use for seeds—parking tickets!

Safety Reminder

Small Objects

Required:
• Natural outdoor materials

Optional:
• Chalk

Trash Can Basketball

You say you don't have enough room for a basketball court? Think again. With this activity you'll be ready to host the next NBA playoffs even if you only have a postage-stamp-sized backyard. Or no backyard at all.

All you need is a clean trash can to serve as a hoop, and a large rubber ball. Since trash cans are too deep for most kids (and for many back-conscious parents as well) to retrieve the ball, place a large cardboard box (closed) at the bottom. As an alternative, use a bushel basket or an equivalent-sized box and place it on a chair to give it height.

Give your child a ball with good bounce and let the games begin! You can play traditional basketball or let your child invent his or her own rules. Or perhaps your child will want to line the "court" with multiple "hoops" arranged like an obstacle course.

Oops—time out called on account of trash pickup!

Required:
- Clean trash can
- Large cardboard box
- Large rubber ball

Optional:
- Bushel basket
- Lawn chair

Trash Swap

One family's trash may well be another's treasure—except that we rarely get a chance to find out who's looking for what. Your child can help organize a neighborhood swap and press new life into old discards.

The first step is to pick a site (presumably your backyard—if the swap is big enough, consider organizing a block party). Once the site is selected, have your child help with the announcements. Older children can write up the description of the swap; younger kids can help hand-deliver the announcements to your various neighbors.

Your child can also help label your contributions to the swap, perhaps writing a story (or telling one to you) about the special history or recommended use of a toy, kitchen appliance, or article of clothing.

Here's your chance, finally, to unload that combination can opener, coffee maker, and shoe polisher you received as a wedding present—someone with a cramped kitchen and closet probably can't wait to get their hands on it!

Required:
- Paper and markers
- Stuff you don't need

Travelin' Games

As you tool along the highway or take a jaunt downtown, to the airport, or whatever, you can play an interesting identification game (one that can be modified so you and your kids can play it while walking around town, too).

Make up a list of common—and not-so-common—objects that you're likely to see while traveling the highways and biways. A typical list might include:

Required:
• Pencil and paper

> Barn
> Cow
> Silo
> Tractor-trailer truck
> Police car
> A sign with the letter "X"
> A sign with the number 6
> Something orange
> A motorcycle

You say the first item on the list, and the child who spots that item first calls it out. Then call out the second item. Whoever saw the most items first gets to make up the next list. Every so often, throw in a zinger, just to keep everyone on their toes. (Adjust the level of difficulty to your children's ages and abilities.)

All right, now just where was that purple sign with the three letter X's?

Treasure Map

Map reading can be enjoyed by children of all ages, even the very young. This activity turns map reading into high adventure—and a means to the cookie jar.

First, survey your backyard, local park, or wherever you want to have your child look for treasure. Keep it simple. For a young child, you might select a tree and tie a red ribbon around it. Place a cookie or some other treat in a bag at the foot of the tree, or nestled in the roots, and cover it up with leaves, twigs, or grass. Now make your map. Draw a tree and the ribbon (don't worry about your artistic skills—your child will get the idea).

For older children you can make the map appropriately complex, adding arrows showing which way to turn and the number of steps to walk. (Supervise closely to make sure that the treasure seekers don't take a detour into the street.)

For a good chuckle, have your child draw the map and see if you can get to the treasure. Which, sorry to say, might only consist of the bag, at this point!

Safety Reminder

Adult Supervision

Required:

- Paper and pen/crayons/marker
- Treat
- Bag

Tree Seed Art

Wherever you go you're bound to find interesting tree seeds. With this activity you can turn a seed collection into high art.

First, go on a seed collection hunt. Take along a bag, and keep on the lookout for various kinds of seeds that have fallen on the ground. Some seeds will contain interesting casings or pods, as do honey locust seeds; some, like maple, elm, or milkweed seeds, will be equipped with a flying apparatus; others, like oak or horse chestnut trees, may be in protective shells.

Bring your haul back to the house and set up a worktable in the backyard. Clean off any dirt, then attach the seeds to posterboard using white glue. Your child can paste up the seeds freestyle and create random patterns, faces, outlines, animals, etc.; or he or she can sketch a scene with a pencil, then glue the seeds along the outline.

To preserve the seeds, you might want to cover the board with plastic wrap (Keep the roll of wrap and scraps away from young children.)

Set the posters on a chair when dried, and display it for the family to admire.

Required:
- Tree seeds
- Glue
- Posterboard

Optional:
- Plastic wrap

Tree Swing

This is a good, old-fashioned (and inexpensive way) to go for a swing.

Find a piece of wood (swing bottom) strong enough to hold the weight of an adult and wide enough to support two legs and a rope.

Use a yardstick and a pencil to locate the center of the board. Drill a hole big enough to pass a piece of nylon rope through. Sand down the wood until there are no splinters. Your child can paint or stain the swing bottom if you intend to keep it out during rainy weather. Push one end of a heavy-gauge rope through the hole, then tie a large knot.

Throw the other end over a large tree branch (parents choose the branch). Use a ladder to reach the branch and tie the rope around it. Presto! You now have a swing.

Here are a few rules to observe:
1) Only one person allowed on the swing at a time; 2) those not swinging must stay a safe distance away from the swing; and 3) take turns.

Safety Reminder

Adult Supervision

Required:
- Thick piece of wood
- Yardstick
- Pencil
- Drill
- Sandpaper
- Paint or stain
- Ladder
- Rope

Tug of War

Safety Reminder

Adult Supervision

Required:
• Rope

Optional:
• Wading pool or oscillating sprinkler

What better way for a group of kids to blow off steam than a tug of war?

If you have a group of kids (at least six to eight), organize them into two sides of equal strength and heft. Supply a rope (don't use twine, as that might irritate the skin), check the area for any rocks or hard or sharp objects, then let the two sides tough it out.

For additional fun, put a wading pool in between the two teams with a small amount of water in it (monitor closely for safety). An oscillating sprinkler aimed at the space between the two sides can provide a thrill, too. If it's too cold for a dip, let the childrens' imagination do the dirty work. For example, ask them to imagine that the empty pool or the area in between is: a volcano . . . an alligator pit . . . a shark pit . . . a quicksand pit . . . a vat of oatmeal, honey, or jelly . . . a giant bees' nest . . . or most dreadful of all: the bathtub!

Twig Architecture

Chances are, your backyard or park is filled with enough twigs to make a small city, and then some. Your child will enjoy foraging for natural building materials and then making houses and other structures.

First, have your child collect and inventory small sticks and twigs in the area. Have him or her organize building materials by size. Be sure to look for leaves and dead plant matter that can be used for roofs.

The simplest way to make twig houses is to insert two upright twigs into the ground diagonally at each corner, then lay horizontal twigs, log-cabin style (see illustration). Leaves and plant stalks can be placed across the tops of the twig structures to make thatched roofs. Your child can also make a twig frame, then cover the walls with leaves.

Once you and your child perfect your techniques, try building multi-story structures, or a whole village. If you go for the village, build a stockade fence with upright twigs, leaving a gate for toy cars or horses.

Just be sure not to open the door if anyone with a long snout and sharp teeth shows up.

Required:
- Sticks and twigs
- Leaves and stalks

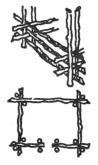

Urban Naturalist

Most of us are pretty oblivious to wildlife in the cities—except when a flock of pigeons leaves its mark on our cars.

With your child to guide you, you'll probably find a surprising diversity of critters roaming your city streets. Take a notebook and pencil and jot down the following:

Required:
• Your time only

Optional:
• Pencil and paper

Cats. How many did you see on your walk? Where are their hideouts? Where do cats feel safe sleeping or resting? Are there any special "cat-walks" that allow them to go from structure to structure?

Squirrels. Urban squirrels are great climbers and jumpers. Can you find them darting around restaurants and bakeries looking for food?

Birds. A city offers a wealth of roosts—lamplights, statues, telephone and power lines, road signs, stop lights, gargoyles, etc. Can you count all the different spots that appeal to the birds?

Insects. Check the cracks in buildings and pavements and the spaces around windows. You'll find everything from flies to spiders.

Finally, recreate your walk during different seasons—you might just find some old friends in new habitats.

Vegetable Garden Signs

It's no problem separating the peas from the potatoes when they're fully grown. But in the early part of the spring, your garden can be a mystery. Here's a way to label your coming harvest and have some fun at the same time.

Cut out three- to four-inch squares of thin styrofoam (a great way to recycle fast-food containers), and have your child paint pictures or symbols on them of the plants you're growing in your garden. Older kids can write out the names. Supervise closely, since you'll want to use indelible markers or paints. Glue the squares to popsicle sticks or smooth stakes.

Alternately, you can have your child paint on cardboard squares sized to fit snugly inside a sandwich bag, and use water-based markers or paints. Tape a popsicle stick to each one. Then slip the squares into sandwich bags with the bottom of the bag at the top of the squares. Use tape to seal all edges that could leak. Eventually condensation inside the plastic will spoil the cardboard, but you'll probably make it through the growing season.

Have your child place the vegetable markers in the proper places. You'll never worry about mixing up your vegetables again.

Required:

- Styrofoam sheets or cardboard
- Paints, markers, crayons
- Plastic wrap or sandwich bags (if you use water-based pigments)
- Tape (if you use water-based pigments)

Vicky and David's Game

Required:

• Common yard materials

Our friend Vicky and her five-year-old son David invented a great activity that can be done indoors or outdoors (just use appropriate materials when doing it indoors).

In a nutshell, one person collects and arranges on the ground readily available objects . . . say a nutshell with a leaf on top. The next person might add a stick underneath. Now you have a head with a hat, and a stick body. The first person can add stick arms, and so on.

You can play "freeform"—just let the object evolve, or you can take turns initiating the game with two objects and having the other person complete it. The whole family or group of kids can play, too, simply taking turns at adding features. A variation is to divide the group into "sculptors" and "guessers." The sculptors agree ahead of time what they're going to make, and the guessers try to figure out as quickly as possible what the sculptors are up to.

However you play the game, let your imagination roam . . . that nutshell and leaf could just as easily have become a fire truck with a flashing red light.

Wagon Games

A wagon is probably the most versatile of all outdoor toys—kids can use it for everything from an all-purpose people mover to a play delivery vehicle. Here are some basic ideas for wagon fun.

Safety Reminder

Adult Supervision

Suggested:

- Wagon
- Two small boxes
- Two chopsticks or twigs
- Two rubber bands
- Empty soda cans or plastic bottles
- Cardboard box
- Towel
- Scissors

Garden Supply Delivery. If you're doing some yardwork, leave certain items by your garage or shed and let your child deliver them (seeds, non-pointed tools, pots, etc). Either call out what you need or make some "walkie talkies" (take two small boxes—animal cracker boxes work well—and attach a chopstick or fairly straight twig to the side of each one with a rubber band.)

Milkperson. Give your child a collection of clean soda cans or plastic bottles. Your child can then fill these with water (preferably from the pool or a rain barrel), and deliver them to various stops on his or her route.

Covered Wagon. Take a large corrugated cardboard box about the width of the wagon, cut off one end, then place the box in the wagon. You may want to drape the box with a towel or piece of fabric. Either way, your child is ready to hit the frontier.

Westward ho!

Watch A Fly

Required:
• Your time only

Flies normally buzz about too fast to see what they really look like. But they are, in fact, fascinating critters. In the fall you can often find flies that look as if they're in the middle of a nap, oblivious to your presence. Actually, their metabolism is slowing down as a response to the changing season. You can collect them on a sheet of paper and watch them move in slow motion. If you have a magnifying glass, you'll see the parts shown below. Who knows—you might also think more highly of these insects as they buzz around your next picnic.

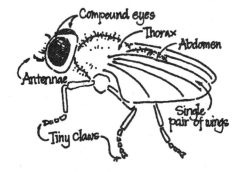

Compound eyes
Thorax
Abdomen
Antennae
Single pair of wings
Tiny claws

Water Slide

This kind of slide is a thrill for children in the summer. It's also a great way to avoid spending money at the toy store.

Use an old shower curtain, or purchase a thick plastic drop cloth from a hardware or paint store. Lay it down on a soft stretch of grass in the back yard and wet it down, first checking that there are no rocks underneath. To keep the curtain or drop cloth continually wet, set up a sprinkler near by. (The sprinkler should be positioned so the sliding children have no chance of running into it.)

To play, the children get in their bathing suits and line up. One at a time, they run on the grass and then slide on their bottoms on the curtain or drop cloth. When the first slider gets off the curtain and clears out of the way, the second slider can go, and so on.

For variety, children can try to walk across the slippery surface while trying to perform acrobatics such as hopping on one foot or walking backwards, or balancing a set of objects in each hand, as in activity #13. (Monitor closely for safety.)

There will be giggles galore as they go slip slidin' away.

Safety Reminder

Adult Supervision

Required:

- Old shower curtain or plastic drop cloth
- Sprinkler

Water Tunnels

Everyone knows how to make sand castles, but children may love taking the concept a step further and building a series of canals on the beach.

The first step is to make a big mountain of sand. The consistency is important. It cannot be too wet or too dry or it will not work. From the top of the mountain, using a cup, scoop or shovel, dig out a canal running through the mountain down to the bottom. At the bottom, dig a hole so the water can come to a rest in a lake. Children can make more than one mountain, or more than one canal in each mountain.

Once the canals are dug, slowly pour water onto the top of the mountain and watch as the water runs through the canals into the lake. Your kids can put toy boats into the lake, or use the water in the lake to moisten nearby sand for a new series of mountains and canals.

In any case, encourage them to take their time. The Roman aqueducts weren't built in a day.

Required:

- A beach
- Scoops, plastic cups, or shovels
- Toy boats
- A bucket to transport water

Water Waste Detective

It's easy for kids to assume that we have an unlimited supply of water—just turn on the tap and the water gushes out. Explain that water is actually a precious resource, then turn your child loose to find opportunities for cutting water waste in your backyard.

First check the spigots. Are they dripping? Place a bowl or pot underneath the culprit and measure how much water you lose over a span of several hours. Calculate how much you'd waste in a week, a month, etc (make analogies, like "enough to fill our car"). Call in a plumber if you can't fix it yourself.

How about hose connections? Let your child watch them in action and determine whether you're watering the driveway and sidewalk as well as your lawn. Replace the parts or hose if necessary.

Ask your child to check for other instances of water waste. Are you emptying your wading pool in your garden or using it to water shrubs? And what about rainwater—are you letting it run down the drain?

Listen to your water detective—he or she just might come up with a planet-saving idea.

Required:
• Your time only

Safety Reminder

Adult Supervision

Required:
• Forked stick

Optional:
• Blindfold

Water Witching

Some people swear by it, others pooh-pooh it as just so much nonsense. We're talking about water witching, water divining, or dowsing—all names for an ancient technique of finding water.

The oldest form of water witching involves finding a forked branch, resting the forks loosely in your hands, then walking carefully about the yard. When the long end of the stick begins to bob up and down, that's supposed to be an indication of water.

If you live in a rural area and know the whereabouts of a water pipe and well, see if the stick does indeed bob about when your child walks in its vicinity. In a city, you can get information about water mains and sewer pipes from your city hall. You can also look for water caps and manhole covers. Try dowsing in various directions from the caps and covers and see whether the stick does anything unusual. As a variation, see if your child can locate water while wearing a blindfold (supervise closely).

You might or might not be convinced when you're done, but one thing is certain—your child will have a great time playing at an ancient avocation.

Water Writing

You have the ultimate disappearing ink right in your spigot—water! Just write or draw with it on your sidewalk, driveway, or patio, and watch it fade from sight. Here are a few "disappearing ink" games you can play with your child. (Please use "waste water" from a wading pool or rainwater collected in a bucket.)

First, you'll need a bucket or pan filled with water. To write, you'll need a paint brush, a paint roller, or a broom. Gauge the activity to your child's age. For pre-readers, paint letters, numbers, shapes, outlines of animals, etc. For kids with reading skills, write words or messages.

On a hot sunny day, the object is for your child to guess the picture or message before the water evaporates. On a sloped surface, the object is to make the correct guess before the image runs off and becomes unrecognizable.

Take turns, of course, and let your child write his or her own water messages. Encourage freehand drawing as well—a waterscape, perhaps.

Now, which end of the brush is more fun?

Required:
- Bucket or pan of water
- Paint brush, roller, or broom

350

Weather Vane

Safety Reminder

Sharp Object

Required:

- Yogurt container with top
- Straw
- Thin cardboard or Styrofoam
- Pin
- Brad
- Sheet of cardboard
- Glue
- Compass

Here's an easy way for you and your child to make a weather vane. First punch a hole through a yogurt container and push in a pencil with the eraser side up (your job). This is the axle of the weather vane. Next you'll need to make the vane itself. You and your child can make one out of a straw and two pieces of styrofoam or cardboard cut into triangular shapes (one small, one large). Slit the ends of the straw so the Styrofoam or cardboard fit snugly. Use glue, if necessary, to secure the pieces (see illustration). Your child can decorate the pieces with crayons or markers before you insert them into the straw.

Put a pin through the middle of the straw (also your job) and into the eraser so that the vane spins freely. Finally, anchor the lid of the container to a piece of heavy cardboard with glue or a brad. Rejoin the container with its top and then put this precision instrument to work.

Use a compass to mark the directions on the cardboard, and your child will always be able to tell you whence came the wind.

Weave a Basket

Basket weaving is a high art in many cultures. It's also fun, as this activity demonstrates (refer to the illustration for the following description).

Your child will need to find long, blade-like leaves—Day Lilies work well. Collect five leaves, one longer than the rest. Lay out the leaves on the ground or a table so the longest is in the middle and centered with respect to the rest.

First weave the bottom by overlapping five more leaves as shown in the illustration. You should have loose ends on all four edges. Fold the loose ends up to make the four sides. Then take another leaf and weave it in and out of the loose pieces to join them together. Add four more rows of leaves in this fashion, and you'll have four complete sides. At the top row, bend the ends over and tuck them in between the woven sides (trim if necessary). For a handle, take the long leaf in the middle and weave the ends back down to make a double handle.

Your child's basket won't be strong enough to cart a full picnic lunch. But it will look pretty filled with dandelions and buttercups (ideal for a May Day basket—see #175).

Required:
• Plant stalks

Weird Yoga

The idea of yoga is to fuse your body and your being, and then free it as one. This is the way of children.

Weird yoga isn't as disciplined as real yoga, but it is more fun, and probably does just as good a job at limbering stiff bodies. The positions in weird yoga are invented on the spot by the participants in a yoga "class."

The teacher stands in front of the class and makes up a yoga pose that everyone must do. The teacher does it himself or herself first, then everyone else assumes the pose (take turns being teacher). For instance: the Double Cheeseburger Pose—bend over forward across legs, stretch out hands; Fire Hydrant Pose—stand on one leg; the Hot Dog Pose—straight in the air; or the Couch Potato Pose—sit and stare like a zombie, as if glued to a television.

Another way to do Weird Yoga is to call out a posture, like the Peanut Better & Jelly pose, and let everyone imagine his or her own rendition. The teacher can then judge the students' interpretations.

The mantra for this game is "fun." Spread the word.

Required:
• Your time only

What's in the Bag

This activity can be done with nothing but a sack or paper shopping bag and some common yard items. It will sharpen your child's appreciation for the power of the sense of touch.

Hunt around the yard for things that can be identified by their feel. Look for unique items, such as pine cones and acorns, as well as common items such as leaves, branches, twigs, rocks etc. A flower petal is interesting and often hard to identify by touch alone. If you have a garden, be sure to put in a cucumber, a tomato, a zucchini, or samples of whatever else you've grown.

When you've finished filling up the bag, have your child reach in and identify the items one by one (without looking) and retrieve them. For added fun, you can throw in a few "ringers"—a sponge, a piece of cardboard, and other manufactured items. A small piece of steel wool might evoke a shriek or two as it's confused with a creepy crawler.

Of course, let your child try the game with you. And brace yourself for anything. Uh oh—what is *that*?!

Required:
- Yard items
- Bag or sack

354

Wheelbarrow

Here's how you can make a wheelbarrow. Refer to the illustration below.

Take two large identical metal jar tops and place them back to back. Punch a hole in their centers (adult job) so that a half-inch dowel will fit through them snugly. Cut a slot about an inch wide in the bottom of a sturdy cardboard box, centered and half an inch from one end (the back-to-back jar tops must fit in the slot; see "a"). Cut two small holes on either side of the box one half-inch from the bottom ("b" and "c"). The holes should be aligned with the center of the slot. Feed the dowel through hole "b," align the two tops in the slot, pass the dowel through the tops, then feed the dowel out hole "c." Wrap tape around the dowel where it passes through the jar tops—this will hold the tops in place. Trim off the excess dowel and smooth rough metal and wooden edges. Now you have a wheel.

Finally, punch four more holes in the box, "d," "e," "f," and "g." Insert two dowels as shown, taping them in front and in back of the holes to avoid slipping. The wheelbarrow is now ready for gardening action.

Required:

- Sturdy cardboard box
- Two identical metal jar lids
- Three half-inch dowels
- Tape
- Scissors

Where's Bigfoot

Even if you have small feet, they're big in your child's eyes. In this game you become a backyard sasquatch, with your children following your tracks through the snow in an attempt to find you.

The game begins the same as Hide and Seek, with your child or children counting while you hide. The difference is that you leave tracks because of the snow. The idea is to use these tracks to your advantage, trying to fool the children (don your biggest boots for the occasion).

One way is to walk backward through the snow, stopping at trees or fences, and then walking forward in an effort to confuse the seekers of Bigfoot. Hop to the left or right to create loops, too.

Try to make your path a maze that wanders to the far corners of your yard. If you're quiet, you can keep moving while your children follow earlier tracks. When you are finally caught, be sure to roar like Bigfoot and pound your chest in glee.

Required:
• Your time only

356

Required:

• Your time only

Which Way?

Is your child developing a good sense of direction? Find out by letting him or her navigate the next time you go for an outing in your neighborhood.

This works best when you're taking a familiar walk—to the park, the library, the grocery store—or any place you often go with your child. Be sure to stay together, but let your child set your course by choosing the direction to follow at each intersection or decision point. It's a good opportunity to teach, or to practice, the differences between "right turn," "left turn," and "straight ahead." It's fun for a child to be "the boss" for a change. It's also nice to know that everyone knows the way home—and how to get there safely.

Remember, there are no "wrong" turns (anything goes as long as the adult says it's okay). Beginners might "take the scenic route," while the more enterprising might discover a new shortcut or even a secret path.

Who knows the discoveries you might make along the way?

Wind Sock

Want to find out how hard the wind is blowing? Just look outside at your homemade windsock.

One of the easiest ways to make a windsock is to cut off the sleeve from a lightweight long-sleeved shirt ready for the rag bag. A section of pant leg will work, too, but only if the material is very light. Insert a collar made from a two-inch-wide strip of cardboard fashioned into a ring. The ring should fit snugly inside the shoulder end of the sleeve. Staple it in place. This will keep the wind sock from collapsing. (Or thread in a ring made from a coat hanger—an adult job.) Poke a hole through the sleeve at the ring. Feed a piece of string through the hole and knot it. Then tie the other end of the string to a tree limb or clothes line.

The stronger the wind blows, the more the wind sock will billow out. You might want to place a small weight at the bottom of the collar to keep the sock pointed at the wind.

Older children can use a compass to determine the wind direction, and keep a notebook of the wind speed based on the appearance of the windsock. As the keepers of the wind data, they might want to issue a small people's advisory before school when the skies are choppy!

Safety Reminder

Adult Supervision

Required:

- Old shirt sleeve or pant leg
- String
- Cardboard or coat hanger
- Stapler

Winter Olympics

Skiing, tobogganing, and ice-boating may be great for the official Olympics, but there are plenty of things you can do right in your own front yard, backyard, or driveway. For example:

Required:
• Your time only

Tunneling. The goal is to see who can dig a tunnel from point A to point B the quickest. (If you want to play a non-competitive version, have the young Olympians compete against themselves, trying to break their previous records, or compete against a timer.)

Snow Hurdles. The idea is to jump over a set of progressively taller snowballs without knocking them over.

Snow Jump. A fluffy version of the standard broad jump. Provide a nice big snow bank for the jumpers.

Snow Discus. See how far the players can heave a snowball discus (as opposed to throwing it).

Finally, consider footprint hopping. Make a sequence of your paired footprints in the snow. Each participant then tries to hop in your footprints without stopping or missing. This is the ultimate test of rubber boot skill and dexterity. Try it yourself!

Words on the Go

This is an activity that can be done just by walking along a street of parked cars (it can also be done while your child is riding *in* a car—an excellent travel game).

The basic idea is to make up the shortest word from license plate letters. For example, let's say the first car you and your child encounter has the license plate, "123 FRG." "Frog" would the shortest word. (Since there are no vowels, the players would have to supply one.) Similarly, FRH could be "froth," and "FRI" could be "frill."

A variation on this game is to "collect" letters by going from car to car and jotting down the license plates. The players would then have to come up with specific word categories, such as animals, foods, etc., and make up words to fit the categories. Or see who can collect enough letters to spell their own name.

Yet another way to play both games is to sit on a street corner that has a stop light or stop sign. Try to make the shortest word from every third car. Or collect letters as the cars stop and go—a tough act in cities like Boston where stop signs are too often all but ignored.

Required:
• Your time only

Optional:
• Pencil and paper

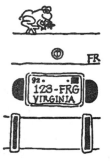

World Under a Rock

Safety Reminder

Adult Supervision

Required:

- Your time only

Here's an activity sure to delight your child. It will probably give you a few surprises, too.

Simply turn over a good-sized rock or brick and observe the fauna living underneath it. Note what kinds of critters live in the cool darkness. Any plant growth?

How many different kinds of creatures did you find? What kinds were they? Older kids can jot down their observations or make drawings of the inhabitants of the under-rock world. (Younger kids should be restrained so as not to turn the under-rock world topsy turvy.)

Next, in one small area, dig down an inch or so, gently moving the dirt. What did you find? Again, describe the inhabitants of this under-rock world. How about the soil itself—what is the texture like?

Important: In places with poisonous spiders, rocks should be turned over with caution and spiders observed with healthy respect for their "space."

In any case, when you're done, put the soil back the way it was, and gently move the rock back to its original position. Now the soil life is again out of sight, but not out of mind.

Worm Condo

W ith this activity, your child can collect wiggly specimens in the yard or garden and observe them for a few days in a luxury "worm condominium"—even the most squeamish child will feel safely separated from the condo's inhabitants.

First you'll need a clear plastic container. Place another container, an inch or so in diameter, inside the larger container; the idea is to create a narrow enough space between the two containers that you'll be able to see the worms tunnel.

Put a piece of screen or stocking on top so you have good air flow (use a rubber band to secure it). Place fresh soil in the condo so your guests will have a supply of food (don't use potting soil—it's been zapped). Make sure that the soil is moist but not drenched—the worms will appreciate it. Watch how the worms move and tunnel, and explain how they aerate the dirt in your garden and lawn, enabling plant roots to grow.

Once your child has observed the worms for a few days, return them to their native habitat, where they can do our gardens a good turn.

Required:

- Plastic container
- Screen or piece of stocking
- Rubber band
- Dirt
- Worms

Yard Signs

With this activity, your family can make playful and creative signs sure to delight young and old passersby alike.

Favorites in our household include, "Beware of Tyrannosaurus Rex" . . . "Please Keep off the Roof" (directed at squirrels) . . . "Great White Shark in Wading Pool" . . . and "Ants at Work."

Write down everyone's suggestions on scraps of paper. Place the scraps into a hat or bucket, then have a child reach in and select one. That will be the sign of the day.

Once you've decided on the message, take a piece of cardboard the desired size and staple two U-shaped straps on the back, one atop the other and separated by about three inches. Slide a garden stake or dowel into straps and tape it to the cardboard. Make your sign out of brightly colored construction paper (use crayons, markers, or tempera paint), and tape it to the front. Place the sign wherever it belongs, and you're all set to impress the neighbors.

Hey, how about this one: "Caution: TV-Free Zone. Bring Your Own Imagination."

Required:
- Cardboard
- Garden stake or dowel
- Crayons, markers, or tempera paint
- Colored paper
- Tape
- Scissors
- Stapler

Yard-Waste Bag Statues

These days giant plastic bag pumpkins are popular in the northeastern part of the country. Just fill them with leaves and they balloon out.

Here's a more environmentally-sound approach to the same idea. First, purchase paper yard-waste bags, now common in hardware stores and supermarkets. (If you can't find them, order them through the Seventh Generation catalog in Colchester, VT, 800-456-1177). Before filling the base with yard waste, have your child decorate the bags with water-based markers or crayons. For example, try: animal faces, funny human faces, abstract designs, statue faces, and anything else that will look good on a four-foot-high bag.

Once the bags are filled with leaves, tie the top shut and then tape on branches for arms. Add a hat made out of an old sack (or use an actual old hat), and you'll have the snazziest looking leaf bag statues on the block!

A bonus—if you leave the bags in a protected place all winter, in the spring you might have some rich compost at the bottom, ready for your garden.

Required:
- Paper leaf bags
- Leaves
- Water-based markers or crayons

Optional:
- Branches
- Sack or old hat

Year-Round Easter Egg Hunt

Suggested:
- Colored eggs

Optional:
- Toy cars
- Dolls
- Plastic balls
- Yogurt containers

You don't have to wait for Easter to have an Easter Egg hunt. In fact, you don't even have to hunt for eggs.

First, pick out the objects of the hunt. Colored eggs, of course, will do, although your children will have just as much fun hunting for toy cars, dolls, old yogurt containers, or plastic balls, etc..

When the children are inside or have turned their backs, hide the eggs or whatever in spots all around your yard. Hide them next to tree stumps, in the grass, at the edge of the house, in bushes, under plants, in the crooks of low tree limbs, on window sills, underneath fences, on top of gates, and hanging from signs.

Once the children have gone out and found all the eggs (be sure and count them in advance so you know when they are all found), start over. You can either have a declared winner, who then may get to be your helper, or simply see how many objects each child can find in a certain time period.

For a twist, reverse the roles and have your children hide the objects from you. Our kids have become quite skilled at this—we're still looking for our cordless telephone.

Zany Television II

In our first book, Zany Television turned out to be one of the most popular activities. You cut out a large rectangle or square in an appliance box, check for staples, cut a door in the back, climb in, and get your revenge on the networks by putting on your own family programming (young kids can do cartoon acts, older children can do interviews, and you can do editorials.) Here's how to extend Zany Television to the great outdoors.

Required:
- Large box
- Yard materials
- Scissors

Spring TV Season: Gather an assortment of (fallen) branches with fresh buds and use them to decorate your cardboard television set. Programming: tips for garden preparation.

Summer TV Season: Decorate your cardboard television set with flowers and fresh leaves. Programming theme: summer mud pie recipes.

Fall TV Season: Decorate your giant television with leaves. Programming theme: five ways to jump in a leaf pile.

Winter TV Season: Make a snow television set by building a snow wall, then cutting out a rectangular shape. Programming theme: unusual ways to keep warm.

Get the whole family out to watch the TV specials. And enjoy the lack of commercial breaks.

Create Your Own Activity

Required:

_____

_____

_____

_____

_____

_____

_____

_____

_____

_____

_____

_____

_____

_____

_____

_____

_____

_____

Create Your Own Activity

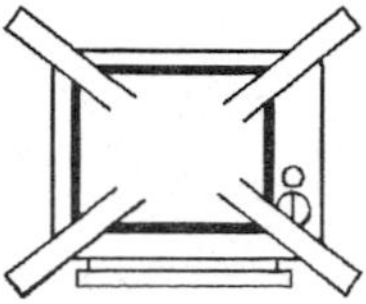

_____

_____

_____   **Required:**

_____

_____

_____

_____

_____

_____

_____

_____

_____

_____

_____

Index

Use the following categories to choose the activites that most interest you and your child.

Backyard Laboratory

Backyard Laboratory (continued)

Backyard Fun

Backyard Fun (continued)

Backyard Fun (continued)

Backyard Fun (continued)

Backyard Fun (continued)

Backyard Fun (continued)

Beach Activities

Celebrations

Community Activities

Easy Games

Easy Games (continued)

Easy Games (continued)

Easy Games (continued)

Environmental Activities

Fall Activities

Gardening Activities

Gardening Activities (continued)

Group Play

Group Play (continued)

Hikes and Walks

Hikes and Walks (continued)

Imagination Games

Imagination Games (continued)

Natural Science

Natural Science (continued)

Natural Science (continued)

Neighborhood Games

Neighborhood Games (continued)

Old-Fashioned Games

Outdoor Arts and Crafts

Outdoor Arts and Crafts (continued)

Outdoor Arts and Crafts (continued)

Readin', 'ritin, 'rithmetic

Recycled/Reused Household Materials

Recycled/Reused Household Materials (continued)

Sports

Springtime Activities

Summertime Activities

Summertime Activities
(continued)

Toys and Gadgets

Toys and Gadgets (continued)

Urban Activities

Wintertime Activities

Your Time Only

Your Time Only (continued)

Your Time Only (continued)

Your Time Only (continued)

OUTDOOR ACTIVITY LOG

#	ACTIVITY	DATE	COMMENT

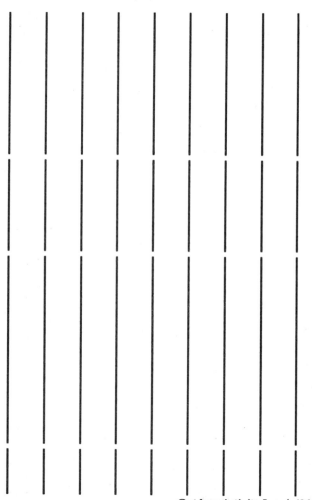

OUTDOOR ACTIVITY LOG

#	ACTIVITY	DATE	COMMENT

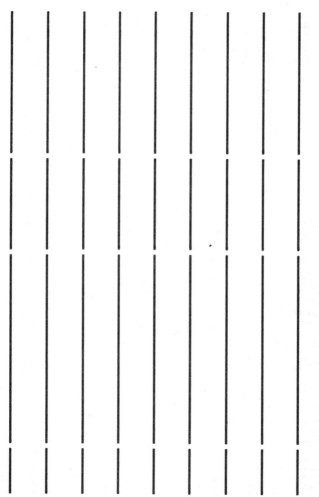

OUTDOOR ACTIVITY LOG

#	ACTIVITY	DATE	COMMENT

OUTDOOR ACTIVITY LOG

#	ACTIVITY	DATE	COMMENT

OUTDOOR ACTIVITY LOG

#	ACTIVITY	DATE	COMMENT

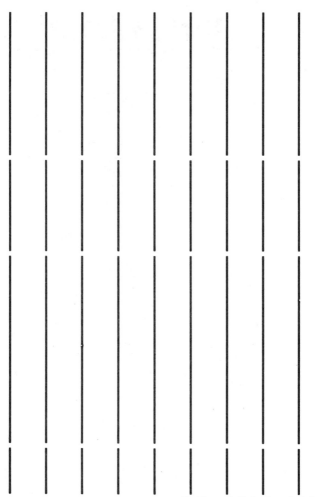

About the Authors

Steve and Ruth Bennett's *365 TV-Free Activities You Can Do With Your Child* (Bob Adams, 1991) instantly became a national hit and a best-selling parenting book. The couple also compiled *Kids' Answers to Life's Big Questions* (Bob Adams, 1992), which consists of responses to a survey given to four-, five-, and six-year-olds across the country, along with original color artwork submitted by the children.

STEVE BENNETT is a full-time author who has written more than 35 books on business and the environment, entrepreneurship, management, and business computing. Steve holds a master's degree in Regional Studies from Harvard University, where he studied the ancient Chinese art of house and tomb placement.

RUTH LOETTERLE BENNETT is a land-scape architect and illustrator. She holds a master's degree from the University of Virginia. Ruth has designed parks, play-grounds, and other public places in a number of cities in the United States.

Ruth and Steve live with their two children, Audrey and Noah, and two cats, Emily and Charlotte, in Cambridge,

Massachusetts. Their television set still lives in the closet, and has gathered much dust since the publication of their original activity book.

Help for taming television in your community, school, or household!

Interested in a school or community TV "turn-off"? Write to us at The Center for Television-Free Parenting, P.O. Box 381646, Cambridge, MA 02238, and we'll give you some ideas for structuring a program and helping your children to use their newfound time creatively.

We also strongly recommend that you look into TV Busters, a national program started by fifth-grade teacher Pat Marker. TV Busters has successfully shown hundreds of thousands of students from Anchorage, Alaska to Coral Springs, Florida how rich life can be with little or no television.

Here's how TV Busters works. Children who participate in the program agree to refrain from television viewing for 20 nights. (News or educational programs watched with parents, however, don't count.) Students fill out "Buster Slips" that record their TV-free activities; they give these slips to their teachers. Classes then compete for the greatest number of slips. Some schools collect prizes donated by local businesses. Others offer special prizes or field trips as rewards. In any case, the TV Busters program can be tailored to the unique needs of your child's school. Mr. Marker even offers special materials for families that want to conduct their own "in-house" turn-off.

For more information about the TV Busters program, contact Pat Marker at Box 600, Excelsior, Minnesota 55331.